Goodbye Russia

FIONA MADDOCKS

GOODBYE RUSSIA

Rachmaninoff in Exile

faber

First published in 2023
by Faber & Faber Limited
The Bindery,
51 Hatton Garden
London EC1N 8HN

Typeset by Typo•glyphix, Burton-on-Trent, DE14 3HE
Printed and bound by CPI Group (UK) Ltd, Croydon, CR0 4YY

A CIP record for this book
is available from the British Library

ISBN 978–0–571–37113–6

Printed and bound in the UK on FSC® certified paper in line with our continuing
commitment to ethical business practices, sustainability and the environment.
For further information see faber.co.uk/environmental-policy

2 4 6 8 10 9 7 5 3 1

For Christina Hardyment

'I am a Russian composer, and the land of my birth
has influenced my temperament and outlook. My music is the
product of my temperament, and so it is Russian music.'

'Music Should Speak from the Heart',
Etude, December 1941

Contents

People, Names, Dates and Sources   XI

Preface   XIX

1915–1918: Revolution, Departure, Arrival   1

Rewind: Life before Exile   35

1918–1930: America, the Glory Years   49

1930–1939: France, Switzerland, Second Exile   145

1939–1943: Gathering In   221

Last Rites   285

Wild Strawberries: Remembering Ivanovka   303

Epilogue   311

The 'Exile' Works: compositions written after 1917   317

Select Bibliography   321

Acknowledgements   325

Notes   327

Image Credits   347

Index   351

People, Names, Dates and Sources

Family

Rachmaninoff, Natalia Alexandrovna (1877–1951)
Rachmaninoff's wife and first cousin, whom he married in 1902.
Born Natalia Satina, Tambov, Russia; died New York.

Irina (1903–69)
Daughter; after marriage to Prince Pyotr Volkonsky, became
Princess Irina Sergeyevna Rachmaninoff Volkonsky. Her family
nickname was Boolya. Born Moscow; died New York.

Tatiana (1907–61)
Daughter; after marriage to Boris Conus, became Tatiana
Sergeyevna Rachmaninoff Conus. Born Tambov, Russia; died
Hertenstein, Switzerland.

Volkonsky [Wanamaker], Sophie (1925–68)
Granddaughter.

Conus [Rachmaninoff], Alexander (1933–2012)
Grandson.

Satina, Sofia (1897–1975)
First cousin and sister-in-law of Rachmaninoff. Sister of Natalia.
Research botanist and pioneer of women's education, working at

the Women's University in Moscow until her emigration in 1921. She later worked at Smith College, Massachusetts, USA.

Satin, Sophia (1915–96)
Sergei and Natalia Rachmaninoff's niece; god-daughter of Natalia, and niece, too, of Sofia Satina. Later in life lived in London. We have followed her chosen spelling of her name, which may help the reader distinguish her from her (more frequently mentioned) aunt.

Siloti, Alexander Ilyich (1863–1945)
First cousin, friend, pianist, pupil of Franz Liszt, teacher of Rachmaninoff.

Secretaries

After leaving Russia, Rachmaninoff had three private secretaries, important figures in his life who dealt with concert schedules, travel, agents and correspondence.

Rybner, Dagmar (1890–1965)
Born in Switzerland of Danish heritage, she studied piano and composition in Germany and New York. Her father was Head of the Department of Music at Columbia University, where she later taught singing. She offered her services to Rachmaninoff when he arrived in New York in 1918, and stopped working for him after her first marriage (to a lawyer, J. Whitla Stinson) in 1922.

Somov, Yevgeny Ivanovich (1891–1962)
Rachmaninoff's secretary from 1922 to 1938, and, with his wife, Yelena, a close family friend. They had first met in Russia. Somov

later worked with Michael Chekhov at his Theatre Studio, Ridge-field, Connecticut (his name anglicised to Eugene Somoff).

Mandrovsky, Nikolai B. (1890–1966?)
Took over from Somov as secretary in 1939 until the composer's death in 1943.

Friends and Colleagues

Balmont, Konstantin Dmitrievich (1867–1942)
Russian symbolist poet. Emigrated 1918, died in France. He made a free Russian translation of Edgar Allan Poe's poem *The Bells*, used by Rachmaninoff in his 1913 choral symphony of that name.

Chaliapin, Fyodor Ivanovich (1873–1938)
Russian bass. From 1895 sang in the Mariinsky, and from 1896, at the Bolshoi, Moscow, living abroad from 1922; close friend of Rachmaninoff.

Chaliapin, Boris Fyodorovich (1904–79)
Son of Fyodor Ivanovich, painter.

Chaliapin, Fyodor Fyodorovich (1905–92)
Son of Fyodor Ivanovich, Hollywood film actor.

Chekhov, Michael (Mikhail Alexandrovich) (1891–1955)
Russian-American actor, director, author. A nephew of Anton Chekhov and a student of Konstantin Stanislavsky, he established the Chekhov Theatre School at Dartington Hall, Devon, UK and then in the USA.

Damrosch, Walter (1862–1950)
German-born American conductor/composer who conducted the first performance of Rachmaninoff's Third Piano Concerto (1909) with the composer as soloist.

Koshetz, Nina Pavlovna (1891–1965)
Kyiv-born soprano and actress, who later lived in America. She was the dedicatee of Rachmaninoff's op. 38 songs.

Koussevitzky, Sergei Alexandrovich (Serge) (1874–1951)
Russian-born double-bass player turned conductor, champion of contemporary music, publisher. Music director of the Boston Symphony Orchestra, 1924–49.

Kreisler, Fritz (1875–1962)
Austrian-born American violinist and composer, friend.

Ormandy, Eugene (1899–1985)
Hungarian-born American conductor. Music director of the Philadelphia Orchestra 1936–80, initially sharing the role with Leopold Stokowski. Conducted the premiere of Rachmaninoff's *Symphonic Dances*, dedicated to the orchestra.

Scriabin, Alexander Nikolayevich (1872–1915)
Russian composer; fellow student, with Rachmaninoff, of Zverev.

Shaginian, Marietta Sergeyevna (1888–1982)
Russian symbolist poet who corresponded with, and met, Rachmaninoff between 1912 and 1917, dedicating her first published set of poems to him. After the Revolution she abandoned poetry and

became a Stalin loyalist and high-profile Soviet activist, historian and novelist.

Slonov, Mikhail Akimovich (1868–1930)
Fellow student at Moscow Conservatory.

Stokowski, Leopold (1882–1977)
British-born conductor of Polish origin, who was music director of the Philadelphia Orchestra from 1912 to 1938. He collaborated frequently with Rachmaninoff, conducting premieres (including *Rhapsody on a Theme of Paganini*) and making an historic acoustic recording (with Victor, in 1923–4) of the Piano Concerto no. 2 with the composer as soloist. He was the dedicatee of the *Three Russian Songs*.

Struve, Nikolai Alexandrovich von (1875–1920)
Musician; business manager and board member of the Russischer Musikverlag, making him a colleague of Koussevitzky and Stravinsky among others. He dedicated a song cycle to Rachmaninoff, with whom he became close friends in Dresden.

Swan, Alfred (1890–1970)
Russian-born, English-educated composer, writer and musicologist, who with his first wife, Katherine, became a friend of the Rachmaninoffs in America, living in California in the 1940s. They recorded their friendship with the composer in an intimate memoir.

Taneyev, Sergei (1856–1915)
Pupil of Tchaikovsky who was director of the Moscow Conservatory from 1885 to 1889.

Vilshau, Vladimir Robertovich (1868–1957)
Pianist and professor at the Moscow Conservatory, 1909–24. He remained a lifelong correspondent and confidant to Rachmaninoff, and a helpful source of information about life in post-Revolutionary Russia.

Zverev, Nikolai Alexandrovich (1833–93)
Pianist and teacher at Moscow Conservatory, whose pupils included Alexander Siloti and Alexander Scriabin as well as Rachmaninoff.

Note on Names

Russian transliteration has no universal standard for names. I have chosen the spelling of Rachmaninoff that he himself used. In general I have used masculine endings except when a feminine form occurs frequently, or to distinguish it from other names (so Rachmaninoff's sister-in-law is referred to as Sofia Satina and his niece as Sophia Satin). In quotations I have left diminutives, often longer rather than shorter, as used by the speaker. In press reports, spellings vary widely. I have 'corrected' in keeping with the spellings chosen elsewhere (so Sergei, often referred to as Serge, or Sergy, is always Sergei). For Russian speakers, the use of the patronymic (the middle name taken from the father's first full name, with -ovich, -evich, or if feminine, -ovna or -evna added) comes easily. So Rachmaninoff is addressed as Sergei Vasilievich. With exceptions, according to context, in general I have stuck to first name and surname.

Dates

Until February 1918 Russia used the Julian (Old Style) calendar – in the twentieth century, this was thirteen days behind the Gregorian (New Style) calendar used in the West. The Gregorian calendar was adopted by the Bolsheviks on 31 January 1918: the next day, accordingly, became 14 February 1918. For simplicity, I have in this book kept dates before February 1918 to a minimum. They are vital for a history of the Russian Revolution, but less important here except as chronological guidelines. Any which do occur are in Old Style, which at least means that the October Revolution occurs in October, not in November.

Note on St Petersburg

The city changed its name to Petrograd in 1914, after the outbreak of World War I (to remove German associations). In 1924, after Lenin's death, it was renamed Leningrad. In 1991, after a public vote, the name reverted to St Petersburg.

Sources

On leaving Russia in 1917, Rachmaninoff left behind his autograph scores and music library (with the exception of the Third Concerto, some songs and the unfinished opera *Monna Vanna*). Until she, too, left Russia, Sofia Satina had the key to his desk, containing the First Symphony. Maria Ivanova, housekeeper, cook and nanny, then took care of it. After her death in 1925, the desk, and the First Symphony score, were lost. Russian materials relating to Rachmaninoff are held in the Glinka State Central Museum of Musical Culture. After a bequest in 1950 from Rachmaninoff's widow, Natalia, the

Music Division of the National Library of Congress, Washington, established an archive of materials from 1918 to 1943, with subsequent help from Sofia Satina and the Rachmaninoffs' daughters Irina and Tatiana. This is now considered the main Rachmaninoff archive. With material at Villa Senar, Lucerne, Switzerland, due to be released in 2023, the archive is an ongoing project.

Preface

Goodbye Russia is an exploration of Rachmaninoff's departure from Russia in 1917 and his existence thereafter. Rachmaninoff's time in exile has long fascinated me, but relatively little has been written about it. In the face of the global COVID-19 pandemic, during which this book was written, the world, rich, poor, healthy or sick, was in a form of exile from its old ways. It made me think, again, about Rachmaninoff.

Few people foresaw the new catastrophe that would occur at the start of 2022. In Ukraine the cities of Kyiv, Kharkiv, Odesa, places Rachmaninoff knew and performed in, were destroyed by Russian bombardment. Rachmaninoff himself once took personal responsibility for elevating the music school in Kyiv to the status of a 'conservatoire', so that this noble southern city would have recognition alongside Moscow and St Petersburg. We can only wonder what he would have made of Russians destroying Kyiv and Kyivians today. Hundreds of thousands are fleeing the region. Exile, a potent word at any time in history, now has a yet more deafening echo.

Rachmaninoff was able to escape Russia in relative safety, but he left, for ever, all that was familiar. He died in Beverly Hills in 1943, surrounded by émigré Russians. During those post-Russia years, transcriptions and revisions aside, he wrote only six new works. Nearly everything that made his name as a composer, pieces we know and love, already existed: three of the four piano concertos, two of the three symphonies, the solo piano music, all the songs, the *Trio élégiaque* no. 2 in D minor, *The Isle of the Dead*, the Cello Sonata, *The Bells*, the *Liturgy of St John Chrysostom* and the *All-Night Vigil*.

Putting composition, and his parallel life as a leading conductor, to one side, he embarked on a highly lucrative career as a virtuoso pianist. Why? What was this new reality like? This is not a book of musicology or straightforward biography, more a broadly chronological set of impressions and excursions, sometimes looping back and forth. I hope I can take the reader with me. Much has been told comprehensively elsewhere – the history of his recording career, for example (those revelatory aural testaments now mostly accessible via digital platforms). If detailed analyses of Rachmaninoff's compositions are the reader's priority, several excellent studies exist (see Bibliography).

In his lifetime, Rachmaninoff was condemned for being popular, as if that tendency cancels out seriousness or musical genius. This has dogged his legacy in the eight decades since his death. A famous entry by Eric Blom, in *Grove's Dictionary of Music and Musicians* (fifth edition, 1954) scorned him as 'highly gifted, but also severely limited'. Blom summed up the music as a popular concoction of 'artificial and gushing tunes accompanied by a variety of figures derived from arpeggios', which he predicted 'is not likely to last'. Harold C. Schonberg, the waspish New York critic of that era, responded that this was 'one of the most outrageously snobbish and even stupid statements ever to be found in a work that is supposed to be an objective reference'.[1]

Critics, all of us, get things wrong. When I realised Blom, as chief music critic of the *Observer*, was my own predecessor, I felt something of a mission to redress his conclusions.

While I was writing this book, the biographer Janet Malcolm died. One obituary quoted her study of Sylvia Plath and Ted Hughes (*The Silent Woman*) in which she said writers (and readers) of biography were impelled by 'voyeurism and busy-body-ism . . . obscured by an apparatus of scholarship designed to give the enterprise an appearance of bank-like blandness and solidity'. This is remote from, even alien to, my own approach. I am an intrigued outsider trying to understand Rachmaninoff across boundaries of language and culture. What would he be like to know? There is a distinction between interpretation and wild speculation. I have tried to stick to the former.

In one respect I agree with Malcolm. When one of her subjects complained about some errors in her book, she replied that his complaint was an illustration of the impossibility 'of ever getting the hang of it entirely, and the fundamental problem of omniscient narration in nonfiction'.[2] No omniscience is claimed here, only curiosity and fascination, prompted by a love of the music.

Rachmaninoff's English never became fluent. He was more at home in German or French, and of course his native tongue. It is one reason this sensitive introvert was ineluctably drawn to fellow Russian exiles. His manner was cool and distant, yet magnetic, in public; generous, loving and humorous at home. Some said they never saw him laugh; others that his sense of mirth reduced him, and them, to tears of merriment. I particularly like the comment of Nathan Milstein (1904–92), the great Russian violinist. He was a child in St Petersburg when, in 1915, he first heard Rachmaninoff perform as soloist in his Second Piano Concerto. As an adult and fellow virtuoso, Milstein got to know his hero well.

Rachmaninoff, despite his grim appearance, was a merry man. You can hear it in his music. There are powerful lyrical moments when the soul is singing, if I may put it that way. And there are other moments when you can see his humour. He liked to be amused. I adored him and loved to make him laugh.[3]

That paradox is part of the Rachmaninoff enigma.

The tripwires of life make this a book of its singular time. I had imagined travelling to New York and Beverly Hills, following in Rachmaninoff's footsteps. I envisaged hours spent in libraries and archives, chasing a blizzard of fruitful connections. Libraries have been shut or, for other reasons, out of reach. Serious family health issues, on top of the pandemic, have meant instead that I have scarcely gone further than a desk in a garden shed. I did, however, manage to visit Villa Senar, Rachmaninoff's Swiss home on Lake Lucerne, at a vital moment.

Several English-language books have charted Rachmaninoff's music and life, leaving me free to take a more discursive route. Geoffrey Norris's admirable study in the Master Musicians series is a model of its kind, as clear, authoritative and readable now as when he wrote it. He specialised, as scholar and musicologist, in Rachmaninoff when to do so was to court some scepticism. Other studies, by Max Harrison, Barrie Martyn, Michael Scott, Robert Walker, Robert Threlfall and (in French) Catherine Poivre D'Arvor, add insights and depth. Julian Haylock, in his skilful *Essential Guide*, squeezed as much into a few short pages as humanly possible.

Now a fresh wave of scholars is taking the story on: Philip Ross Bullock, Marina Frolova-Walker, Rebecca Mitchell, Richard D. Sylvester, David Butler Cannata prominent among them. The late Richard Taruskin threw his capacious if bristly net over the whole Russian music scene. Each has expanded horizons in a Soviet and post-Soviet era. As historians, musicologists, musicians, their knowledge is invaluable. Two excellent new studies appeared just as mine was finished: *Rachmaninoff and His World* edited by Philip Ross Bullock and published to coincide with the 2022 Bard Music Festival, and Rebecca Mitchell's incisive biography (Reaktion).

I hope that my book can serve as a complementary view. I have followed my own interests, often veering wildly off the main track. At all times I have tried to amplify our understanding of an enduringly elusive figure about whom there is still so much more to grasp.

1915-1918

Revolution, Departure, Arrival

Revolution

On 15 March 1917, monarchy in Russia came to an end. The double-headed eagle, symbol of imperial power, together with other Tsarist regalia, was torn from public buildings, tossed down on the icy streets. Tsar Nicholas II, the last Emperor of All Russia, abdicated, ending the Romanov dynasty's three-hundred-year rule. Little over a year later, the Romanov household – Nicholas, his wife Alexandra, five children and four servants – were murdered in a cellar in Yekaterinburg, east of the Ural Mountains, an event still resonant with horror and fascination.

The man who would order their execution was Vladimir Ilyich Lenin (1870–1924). For now, the forty-seven-year-old revolutionary and political theorist was still exiled in Switzerland, awaiting his moment. In her memoirs his wife, Nadezhda Krupskaya, notes that Lenin was about to go to the library as usual. She was washing the lunch dishes, when a fellow exile rushed in crying 'Have you heard the news? There's a revolution in Russia.'[1]

Lenin and his small band of allies quickly left Switzerland to shouts of 'You'll all be hanged', with loyalists singing the 'Internationale'. Travelling in secret, the party was given safe passage through Germany in a 'sealed' train, like a 'plague bacillus' as Winston Churchill wryly put it. They crossed a stormy Baltic Sea to the Scandinavian peninsula,[2] then joined a ribbon of horse-drawn sledges and shuttled across the frozen Tornionjoki river into Finland, heading for Petrograd. That city would eventually adopt Lenin's name and (from 1924 until 1991) become Leningrad.

Arriving late at night at Petrograd's Finland Station on Easter

3

Monday, 3 April 1917, Lenin was greeted by flags in red and gold, bouquets of flowers, a guard of honour of sailors, a military band and speeches of welcome. Hoisted atop an armoured car, he was driven to the Kshesinsky Mansion, built a decade earlier in opulent Tsarist style. This villa belonged to the ballerina and socialite Mathilde Kshesinskaya, who had before his accession been the mistress of Nicholas II, with two other Romanov Grand Dukes numbering among her erotic entourage. Having seized and looted her home in the February Revolution, the Bolsheviks now occupied it as their base. Their official newspaper, *Pravda*, had editorial offices in its salons. From the mansion's grand balcony, facing Kronverkskiy Prospekt, Lenin addressed the masses.

This collision of old Russia and new could not have been more symbolic. As a star dancer at the Imperial Ballet, the bejewelled Kshesinskaya was associated with Anna Pavlova, Vaslav Nijinsky and Sergei Diaghilev, as well as being on partying terms with everyone in aristocratic circles. She swirled and twirled at the centre of Russia's elite cultural life. The great choreographer Marius Petipa described her as 'a nasty swine', but nonetheless still collaborated with her on many roles.[3] She was a famous Odile–Odette in Tchaikovsky's *Swan Lake* and Aurora in *The Sleeping Beauty*.

One of her celebrity friends was the charismatic bass-baritone Fyodor Chaliapin, a name that will often visit these pages. An imposing figure, distinguished by his preference for a long coat, Russian shirt and high boots, he was unsurpassed in his interpretations of Mussorgsky's Boris Godunov and Rimsky-Korsakov's Ivan the Terrible. He, too, knew every artist, writer, actor, musician, a fluid group associated with the final flowering of Russia's *fin de siècle*, now known as the 'Silver Age': the painter Ilya Repin, the writers Anton Chekhov and Ivan Bunin, the composers Alexander Glazunov, Alexander Grechaninov and Alexander Scriabin. One of

Chaliapin's closest friends, as well as a musical ally and mentor, was the composer, conductor and pianist – our subject here – Sergei Vasilievich Rachmaninoff.

Chaliapin had just had his gossipy, humorous autobiography 'written down by' his friend Maxim Gorky, the prominent writer. They had spent the previous summer at a resort in Crimea, Chaliapin reportedly shouting, laughing and running about in a bathing suit, dictating his life story to a patient stenographer. Gorky later polished this raw material into fine prose. One of the liveliest anecdotes involves Chaliapin's wedding ceremony in a little village church. At six o'clock the next morning, he and his Italian ballerina bride were woken up by 'an infernal din'. Outside a group of rowdy friends were banging stove lids and various kitchen utensils in a crazed, ad hoc concert, hoping to persuade the honeymoon couple out of bed to come mushrooming. 'This ear-splitting clamour was in the capable hands of the conductor, Rachmaninoff.'

Soon, these lives and friendships would be cast to the winds. By November 1917, the country's fate was sealed. The Silver Age was over. Time was running out for the nobility, called by Russians *bélaya kost*, meaning 'white bone', the equivalent of 'blue blood'. Bolsheviks narrowly held the balance of power with Lenin as leader. Landowners were under threat, the old social fabric torn apart, estates razed, an entire social class practically destroyed. In this upheaval, the religion, music, art, literature of the past, so treasured by the now-fleeing educated classes, were considered of no value to the workers. Revolution would purge Holy Russia of its ancient cultural traditions: banned, censored, silenced. Some of its guardians emigrated by choice, others were forced to leave. Soldiers and civilians, businessmen and Russian Orthodox priests, artists and intellectuals, loosely called White Russian émigrés, took various routes, via Finland and the Baltic, via

Istanbul and southern Europe, out of their homeland. Lines grew blurred between refugees hoping for repatriation and émigrés who could never return.[4]

They would form the nucleus of a Russian diaspora, swelling over the next five years and reaching (figures vary) an estimated two million people. Chaliapin, at first lionised by the new Soviet regime, would soon choose exile. Gorky, drawing on his 'proletarian' origins, became a Soviet literary hero, bouncing around the political arena, falling out with Lenin, embracing the orthodoxy of Stalin. Kshesinskaya fled to Paris where she opened a ballet school, with two of the greatest British classical ballerinas of the twentieth century as her pupils: Margot Fonteyn and Alicia Markova (Diaghilev urged the latter to change her birth name, Alice Marks, underlining the assumption that the finest dancers were Russian). Kshesinskaya's mansion became the Museum of Revolution. In 1991 it was renamed the State Museum of Political History of Russia, its gilded Tsarist past, once suppressed, now re-glamorised in Putin's Russia.

One particular journey into exile, a distorted mirror image of Lenin's own, was about to begin. At forty-four years old, three years younger than Lenin, Sergei Rachmaninoff was in his prime. A landowner as well as a musician, he was famous at home and abroad, greeted with respect and ovations. His life, in late 1917, was poised to change beyond recognition. As he described it:

On one of the last days in November, I took a small suitcase and boarded a tram, which drove me through the dark streets of Moscow to the Nikolai station. It rained. A few isolated shots could be heard in the distance. The uncanny and depressing atmosphere of the town, which at that hour seemed utterly deserted, oppressed me terribly. I was aware

6

that I was leaving Moscow, my real home, for a very, very long time . . . perhaps for ever.[5]

From Moscow Rachmaninoff would travel to Petrograd. He was on his way to the very place to which Lenin, a few months earlier, had returned in fevered glory: the Finland Station.

On the Edge

As a performer as well as a composer, Rachmaninoff prized his hard-won balance between busy, public periods of giving concerts and conducting, and the quiet retreat of Ivanovka, his country estate in the Tambov region, five hundred kilometres south-east of Moscow. The estate belonged to the family of his wife, Natalia Satina, and was now an additional responsibility in which he took great pleasure. He enjoyed the many practical challenges of managing the land, as well as supporting the peasant community who lived and worked there. He had come to love, too, the landscape. Ivanovka was a precious retreat. There, with his wife and two growing daughters, Irina and Tatiana, nearby, he could work at his composition.

He and Natalia, herself a trained and skilled pianist, had married in 1902, having battled the highest echelons of the Orthodox Church and the Tsar's authority to gain permission: they were first cousins therefore strictly not allowed to marry. The ceremony took place in an army chapel outside Moscow, in the heavy rain, with the pianist Alexander Siloti a witness to the marriage. Himself a first cousin to both, Siloti gave them tickets to Wagner's *Ring* at the Bayreuth Festival as a wedding present.

At this period, songs poured out of Rachmaninoff: Twelve Songs op. 21 (1902), which includes his famous 'Lilacs', helped pay for their honeymoon to Vienna, Venice, Lucerne and Bayreuth. Among the dedications, one is especially touching. 'Before the Icon', resonant with Orthodox spirituality and the suggestion of tolling bells, is about a woman in prayer: Rachmaninoff dedicated it to Maria Ivanova, the family's loyal housekeeper. Rachmaninoff would leave their Moscow apartment to her care and, after 1917, helped her with money. As we will learn, this was a typical gesture.

An elusive but generous and constant figure throughout his life, Natalia was his support, his companion, a fierce and accomplished critic and his greatest champion. They had known each other since their teenage years. She was not his first romantic attachment. We know this through hints in the letters, diaries and memoirs of the other cousins and via the important figure of Natalia's sister, Sofia Satina, who played a vital role – through her own letters and diaries, or by assisting others in their writings – in chronicling Rachmaninoff's life for posterity. The invaluable and detailed picture we have, almost an authorised version, is in large part thanks to Sofia Satina.

Before their marriage, Natalia suffered as she waited for Sergei to live out his youthful passions. Her constancy was rewarded. He had first fallen in love, under Natalia's nose, with Vera Skalon, youngest and most spirited of the three Skalon sisters, part of the extended family. All were together, sharing the long hot country days in industry and pleasure, in Rachmaninoff's first, happy summer at Ivanovka in 1890. The adults disapproved of the teenaged sweethearts. Vera married someone else and died tragically young. In a memoir written after Rachmaninoff's death, Lyudmila Skalon recounts the romance between her younger sister and the composer and the enduring sadness of a love interrupted:

8

[Sergei] could not have chosen a better wife. [Natalia] had
loved him since her earliest years and won him, if I may put
it that way, through suffering. She was clever, musical and a
deeply endowed personality. We were overjoyed for Seryozha,
knowing to what safe hands he had entrusted himself, and
were very happy that our beloved Seryozha would thus be
staying within our family. [. . .] Natasha dressed for her
wedding at the home of my sister Verochka [Vera], who was
then living in Moscow with her husband. The two cousins
were firm friends and never allowed a trace of jealousy over
Seryozha to overshadow their feelings. Almost three years
before Seryozha's wedding, hence in autumn 1899, Verochka
had married her childhood friend Sergei Petrovich Tolbuzin.
Before her wedding she burnt more than a hundred letters she
had received from Seryozha. She was a loyal wife and a devoted
mother, but until the day of her death she was never able to
forget her love for Seryozha.[6]

By whatever path, Natalia became Rachmaninoff's enduring love
through mutual devotion, shared parenthood, habit, suffering, care.
According to Natalia herself, he used to claim that her opinion was
also his. Years later, when his world and horizons were those of a
different continent, he pondered (in terms allowable then) what
kind of wife a creative artist should have. The artist's axis is small,
he said, revolving around 'his' own work. 'I agree that the wife has
to forget herself, her own personality. She must take upon herself
all the physical care and material worries. The only thing that she
should tell her husband is that he is a genius. Rubinstein was right
when he said that a creator needed only three things: Praise, Praise
and Praise!'[7] He might have agreed with Alice Elgar (1848–1920),
the highly talented wife of Edward Elgar, who wrote in her diary:

'The care of a genius is enough of a life work for any woman.' It was the stance of the time.[8]

Scriabin and Other Friends

1916 had been a period of turbulence, public and private. Russia had entered World War I two years earlier, its military weaknesses exposed, civil unrest mounting. Rachmaninoff's own life was at a crossroads. Unexpectedly, much of his concert season that year had been devoted to the music of Alexander Scriabin. Rachmaninoff's one-time classmate with Zverev at the Moscow Conservatory and fellow pianist-composer had died suddenly, of blood poisoning, in 1915 at the age of forty-three. Fundraising concerts were immediately held to support his impoverished family. In artistic circles his demise was likened to that of Russia's greatest, but short-lived writer, Alexander Pushkin (1799–1837). Had his life not been cut short, Scriabin might have matched Igor Stravinsky or Arnold Schoenberg as one of the twentieth century's great modernists. Instead he has been regarded chiefly as a fascinating maverick who, among many eccentric habits, blithely shunned fashion by walking through Paris without a hat, for reasons of hygiene. That view is now being challenged, his originality celebrated anew: his reputation continues to flourish.

Scriabin was feted by experimentalists: not least those who responded to the mystical philosophy of the artist Kazimir Malevich, whose painting *Black Square* caused a stir at its first showing in St Petersburg in 1915, alongside other abstract works by the group who became known as the 'Suprematists'. Since their youthful rivalry, relations between Rachmaninoff and Scriabin were uneasy, but not as bad as some in the Moscow press tried to make out. Rachmaninoff conducted Scriabin's First Symphony, as well as his Piano Concerto, with the composer as soloist. He would also, in his later career as a pianist, frequently include particular works of Scriabin in his recitals.

At the same time, there were tensions. Scriabin's success as a composer of radical imagination had undermined Rachmaninoff's confidence in his own work. Marie Eustis, first wife of the pianist Josef Hofmann, noted in her diary that Rachmaninoff was depressed, and had considered abandoning composition because he thought 'no one in Moscow wanted to listen to his music any more. He couldn't go on composing just for his wife . . . It is all [the fault of] that crazy Scriabin.'[9] The shock of Scriabin's death, however, had moved him into making a substantial memorial gesture.

Having until this point played mostly his own works in recital, he had spent the previous summer learning Scriabin repertoire sufficient for sixteen solo recitals of the composer's music, which he would give in far-flung cities, involving arduous train journeys and day after day of travel. The gesture did not pay off. Many Scriabin adherents disliked the way he approached the music of their visionary, messianic idol. Some shouted curses at him. The two composers were psychologically and musically ill-matched, Scriabin a dreamer, mystical, experimental, rule-breaking; Rachmaninoff an abundantly gifted melodist, stern, applied, above all rigorous and disciplined. Rachmaninoff turned Scriabin's music into 'his own', accused the critics: 'That super-sensuous melody of Scriabin was brought back to earth, saturated in Rachmaninoff's own melodic style,' read one of the more polite assessments.[10] Rachmaninoff left us one recording, from 1929, of Scriabin's music, wistful and flexible, the right-hand melody brought out but the poetic instability between the two hands alive and daring. At under three minutes, Scriabin's Prelude in F sharp minor, op. 11 no. 8, is not long enough to pinpoint the nature of the noisy complaints.

Rachmaninoff could at least comfort himself with the knowledge that his own compositions were winning followers beyond Russia. The British conductor Henry Wood, who would become a friend and champion, introduced *The Isle of the Dead* to London audiences at the 1915 Promenade Season. Wood had already made an orchestral arrangement of the C sharp minor Prelude (complete with incongruous harp cascades at the end) and a viola transcription of the popular 'Vocalise', the wordless 'song' from Fourteen Romances, op. 34. Even so, Rachmaninoff, who had started complaining of old age when he was in his thirties and never really stopped, was still at a low ebb: pains in his wrists as well as his right temple were among various non-specific agues that dogged him all his life.

In the fashion of the era, but also because he needed a physical rest cure, in May 1916 he went to Yessentuki. This spa in the Caucasus was frequented by many of his friends, including, that summer, Chaliapin. Famous for the medicinal powers of its silty mud cures and carbonated mineral waters, Yessentuki had been a resort since the mid-nineteenth century. It lacked the cosmopolitan flamboyance of Germany's Baden-Baden, but had its own attraction, a state-of-the-art mud bath clinic, built in the grandiose style of Roman baths, complete with columns, portico and stone lions. Descriptions of Yessentuki's bath-houses, pump rooms and elaborate therapies make it sound not only medicinal but also somewhat louche.[11]

Diversions: Nina Koshetz and Marietta Shaginian

Four women had a loyal and constant presence in Rachmaninoff's adult life: his wife, Natalia, his two daughters, Irina and Tatiana, and his sister-in-law and cousin, Sofia Satina. In the period leading up to his departure from Russia he formed close bonds with two others, both younger. One was the soprano Nina Koshetz (1894–1965), an excellent and multi-talented musician, and alluring with it. The other was a poet and intellectual, Marietta Shaginian (1888–1982). 'Close' is not here intended as a euphemism. With Shaginian the relationship was intimate, psychologically deep but with no obvious frisson of sexuality. The alliance with Koshetz is open to question. Urged on by Sergei Prokofiev's scurrilous comments in his diaries, many have assumed Rachmaninoff had an affair with her. Evidence is scant, not surprisingly played down by those loving narrators of his life, his close family and friends. Both women were important to him, and deserve recognition for the part each played, whatever the nature of their friendship.

Shaginian entered his life uninvited in 1912, aged twenty-three. In a flush of enthusiasm, as she put it years later, she sent him a fan letter written in the middle of a snowstorm on a February day, 'as if the whole city had been swept out to the Russian steppes by Pushkin himself'.[12] Pushkin was on her well-stocked mind: Rachmaninoff had just conducted *The Queen of Spades* at the Mariinsky Theatre, Petrograd. Tchaikovsky's opera is based on the poet's short story. Signing herself only 'Re' (as in the second note of the sol-fa scale), Shaginian presented herself as an artistic saviour, an intellectual helpmeet. Her timing was excellent. Rachmaninoff, approaching forty and perpetually riddled with self-doubt, had no shortage of female fans. Prominent among the many was the widowed Thekla Russo, whose grief was assuaged by attendance at one of his concerts, after which, in a conspicuous show of gratitude, she sent him white lilacs wherever he played. Like any star artist, he found some hangers-on far more troublesome than others, offering their sundry services and enthusiasms in no uncertain terms (only later, when Irina and Tatiana were older, did Natalia accompany him on all his tours, which no doubt kept the more ardent groupies at bay).

Shaginian was too smart to make herself a nuisance. Her enigmatic identity may have been part of the appeal. He certainly took seriously her observations about life and art, which always seemed to make him their focus. So began an intense epistolary relationship. He shared his anxieties, even revealing to her that he thought he might one day give up composition and concentrate on being a pianist. Perhaps with a degree of self-mocking exaggeration, he listed his morbid dislike of mice, rats, cockroaches, bulls, burglars, high winds, heavy rain on the windows, being alone. 'I don't like attics and I'm ready to believe ghosts are everywhere.'[13] Shaginian was highly literate, with an intellectual confidence he entirely lacked. They exchanged ideas about poetry and aesthetics, and eventually met in December 1912.

Vitally, she opened his eyes to more adventurous, modernist texts for song settings and scorned his hitherto conservative choices. He bowed to her knowledge, asking for specific suggestions, as long as 'the mood should be sad rather than cheerful'.[14] Bright tones did not come easily to him, he said. Shaginian showed deft assurance in understanding, and probing, his psyche. He in turn must have felt excited by her interest and perception. She widened his hitherto confined literary horizons. He set poems she suggested, and dedicated to her 'The Muse', the first of his Fourteen Romances, op. 34 (1912–15). Would he have been irritated that she sent the same Pushkin poem to the composer Nikolai Medtner, who likewise set it to music and dedicated it to her? Medtner would become a great ally of Rachmaninoff, but only later. For now, the Medtner family were Shaginian's formidable friends, representing a world of intellectualism alien to Rachmaninoff.

If he was a complicated individual, so too was this intense young woman. Before approaching him, and again after, she made similar anonymous overtures to prominent strangers, insinuating herself unbidden into various situations. She challenged the dashing, well-connected young poet Vladislav Khodasevich to a duel over a woman whom she, Shaginian, admired (she knew neither of them personally). Khodasevich declined her challenge on the grounds of not duelling 'with ladies'. Her life was irregular: she lived in a room in a half-ruined churchyard, approached through dark tunnels inhabited by bats and rats, and guarded by a drunk 'gypsy' woman with a beard. Rachmaninoff would have hated it!

Taking the Waters

In 1916, Shaginian visited Rachmaninoff in the spa sanatorium at Yessentuki. He was in his own comfortable rooms complete with a grand piano, but in a state of nervous exhaustion. Remembering that their previous conversations had explored issues of death, artistic disappointment and psychological frailty, she was quite used to his moods and depression. He said he felt a failure as a composer, still crushed by events of his youth including the disaster of his First Symphony, famously mauled by the critics and causing a creative and emotional breakdown. Shaginian knew, too, of his disappointment over the recent Scriabin recitals and the sour critical reaction. He explained to her how he, as a living musician, was trying to bring alive the work of another musician, now gone. Her account is unsparing:

> Rachmaninoff looked haggard and spent . . . for the first time in my life I saw tears in his eyes. In the course of our conversation he several times wiped them away but they welled up again. I had never seen him before in such total despair. His voice broke the whole time. He said that he was not working at all, whereas before he always used to work at Ivanovka in the

15

spring; that he had no desire to work and that what galled him was the awareness of being incapable of creative work and the impossibility of being anything more than a well-known pianist and a mediocre composer . . . He spoke of the impossibility of living in the state he was, and all this in a terrible dead voice, almost that of an old man, with his eyes lifeless and his face grey and ill.[15]

After the spell at the sanatorium, he went to nearby Kislovodsk. There, inexplicably or all too explicably, his spirits soared. The exuberant presence of Chaliapin always cheered him. Stanislavsky, the pioneering theatre director and founder of the Moscow Art Theatre, was there too. The Tolstoys, the conductor-publisher Serge Koussevitzky and the philosopher-mystic George Gurdjieff were among those passing through, meeting and greeting at mud bath or cure. There too was Nina Koshetz. Rachmaninoff had met her in Moscow the previous year when he accompanied her singing at a concert in memory of Sergei Taneyev. (Both of them had studied with Taneyev; Koshetz had also been coached by Stanislavsky.)

While Shaginian could stir Rachmaninoff's mind and soul, Koshetz was a different creature: coquettish, a performer, flirtatious, glamorous, quick to alight on any susceptible male, especially if they could compose a song for her. Rachmaninoff showed Koshetz a playfulness absent in his exchanges with Shaginian. Had his lethargy and agitation with her been the result of an emotional entanglement with Koshetz which, given his marriage and family, or even Shaginian's own hopes, he could not mention? He was soon enjoying spa encounters with Koshetz. The letter he wrote to her at Kislovodsk was frisky (though written in the formal 'vous' not 'tu' voice), and a touch desperate. He hadn't managed to meet her in a 'pleasant pavilion' as planned. Stanislavsky's arrival had quashed his plans:

Dear Nina Pavlovna,

I've had my bath and am now resting. Last evening Stanislavsky dropped in unexpectedly and stayed the whole evening. I am very sorry I couldn't come to you. Today I hoped to see you but the rain came, and stopped, and came again. Perhaps we'll see each other at 5.30 in our pleasant pavilion near Spring no. 3? Or could you come here at 4.30 for supper? All these plans are good. Which do you prefer? Till we meet. I send this with your umbrella – for the rain and to deceive the eyes. I kiss your hands. SR[16]

Why did he have her umbrella? Whose eyes did he wish to deceive? Questions without answers. Koshetz, who might today be described as an 'operator', had already caught the attentions of leading musicians such as Koussevitzky, Tcherepnin, Medtner and Grechaninov. Her charms intoxicated all. Both her parents were opera singers. Her father, who committed suicide when she was a child, was the first in Russia to sing the title role of Wagner's *Siegfried*. An outstanding musician herself, she had studied composition and was a virtuoso pianist: at her graduation concert she played Rachmaninoff's Piano Concerto no. 2. In vocal recitals, her preferred partner was a young, still unknown pianist: Vladimir Horowitz.

With whatever motive or artful ploy, that summer Koshetz engaged in a warm correspondence not only with Rachmaninoff, but also with his wife, Natalia. After Rachmaninoff left the spa and returned home, Koshetz was readying herself to perform Tatyana in Tchaikovsky's *Eugene Onegin*. She wrote to tell the older woman as much. Natalia's response, while encouraging, is also that of the knowing wife. 'Seryozha', she writes, was much improved after his time in Yessentuki, though he was already losing his suntan. Her attitude to Koshetz is camouflaged by wise psychology. Was she maintaining a cordial friendship with the young singer until any passions, hers for her husband or his for her, cooled? Natalia may have stiffened, nonetheless, at a photograph of Rachmaninoff with Koshetz, undated, taken around that time. It shows him, with a hint of a smile rarely caught by any camera, in blithe mood, if cautious in matching his companion's extravagant and flirtatious gaiety.

Back at Ivanovka, Rachmaninoff learned of the death of his father. He had been an absent parent since the composer's childhood, but the emotional attachment between father and son was strong. That year, amid public tumult and personal distractions, he completed only one major composition: a group of six songs, op. 38. The poems were chosen by Shaginian, the songs dedicated to Koshetz. In the new 1916–17 season, Koshetz sang them in recital, with Rachmaninoff as pianist, in Moscow, Petrograd and in the Ukrainian cities of Kharkiv and Kyiv. Shaginian, snubbed by the dedication to Koshetz, refused to come to hear the work in which she had played so vital a part. Little love was lost between poet and singer.

Both Nina Koshetz and Marietta Shaginian, in different ways, exerted their influence on Rachmaninoff in that febrile year before he left his homeland. One friendship, that with Shaginian, would all but end, abruptly. The other, with Koshetz, surfaced at intervals, often awkwardly, until the end of his life. Three days before Christmas Day in 1916, he wrote to Koshetz, a tone of irascibility all too evident, puncturing whatever intimacy they may have had. The brash young singer had shown independence of mind by making a decision concerning a professional contract without consulting him. His letter reads as a snub: 'In such matters you are worse than a child. I am afraid that merely because you've chatted with some acquaintances about an attractive proposal, you are ready to sign anything. This is, unfortunately, very like you . . . Greetings on the approaching holiday.'[17]

Street Mobs, Last Moscow Concerts

At the start of 1917, Rachmaninoff made his last appearance in Russia as a conductor, at Moscow's Bolshoi Theatre. Despite his prowess in this activity, he would not conduct again until 1939, many years into his new life. That programme on 7 January 1917 featured his own works: *The Rock*, a symphonic poem dedicated to Nikolai Rimsky-Korsakov and influenced by Chekhov; *The Isle of the Dead*, inspired by a painting by the Swiss symbolist Arnold Böcklin ('an ordinary print found in every Berlin home', as Nabokov put it in his 1932 émigré novel, *Despair*); and *The Bells*, to poems by Edgar Allan Poe. This last, a choral symphony, Rachmaninoff claimed as his favourite among his compositions. The sound of bells, as he observed, dominated 'all the cities of the Russia I used to know – Novgorod, Kyiv, Moscow. They accompanied every Russian from childhood to the grave and no composer could escape their influence.'[18]

As far as possible, the family stayed inside their Moscow apartment in these difficult days, shutting their doors against protests and riots, trying to make plans. At the same time Rachmaninoff continued to attend concerts. The chamber music of Prokofiev featured in one, on 5 February 1917, entitled 'An Evening of Modern Music'. A fellow composer-pianist, Prokofiev bumped uncomfortably up against Rachmaninoff, first in Russia and later in exile. Still only in his mid-twenties, Prokofiev was already acquainted with Diaghilev; his opera *The Gambler* was about to be premiered (but was postponed, owing to the political situation). His diaries shed light on Rachmaninoff: the two moving in the same musical circles, their activities overlapping, and in one case, their emotions too. Of that chamber concert, Prokofiev noted in his diary that severe weather conditions nearly hijacked it.

Central Russia was blocked by snow; trains were delayed. All the same, the 'whole world without exception' had elected to attend: Rachmaninoff, Medtner, Koussevitzky, Balmont, Mayakovsky, Borovsky, Igumnov, Koshetz – 'in a word, le tout Moscou'.

Prokofiev's autobiography fills out the detail.

Among those invited were Rachmaninoff and Medtner. Throughout the concert Medtner fumed and fussed. 'If that's music, I'm no musician.' Rachmaninoff, though, sat like a stone idol, and the Moscow audience that usually received me well, was confused as it watched its hero's reaction to my music.

Rachmaninoff, he continues, sat near the gangway in the second row next to Koussevitzky, 'immobile as a statue of the Buddha'.[19]

Comparing Rachmaninoff to a statue of the Buddha was almost as commonplace, throughout his life, as likening him to a prison inmate due to his buzz-cut hair. (Vladimir Nabokov calls this kind of style 'hedgehog'.[20]) Chaliapin compared his friend's appearance to that of a jailbird or, when dressed for the stage, that of an undertaker. Years later the record executive, Charles O'Connell, head of artists and repertoire at RCA Victor's Red Seal label from 1930 to 1944, would use both descriptions.

Everyone is familiar with his economical and unromantic haircut which, together with certain other features, brought a suggestion of a newly released convict or even of the hangman himself. His eyes were almost Mongolian in their obliquity and generally inscrutable expression, yet they could light up with the most engaging warmth and friendliness.

Enjoying a glass of Chianti and a plate of spaghetti at a local Italian restaurant, 'Rachmaninoff would lose his customary appearance of a deflated Buddha.'[21]

Of that future life, of new friends and colleagues, Rachmaninoff as yet knew nothing. For now, he was in the midst of civil war on the streets of his home city, but he stuck to his schedule. Two days before the mass demonstrations that led to the abdication of the Tsar, he gave the premiere of his complete *Études-Tableaux* op. 39 – the last of the set, his last completed composition in Russia, finished only a week earlier. He had begun these nine pieces, arguably his most experimental and rewarding solo piano works, in the summer of 1916. Eight of the highly expressive, rhythmically bold études were in minor keys. The theme of the *Dies irae* plainchant, which haunts so many of his works, threads and embroiders its way through these études: conspicuously in the first five, cryptically in the other four. Thoughts of dedicating the *Études-Tableaux* to Koshetz, as he had the op. 38 songs, were abandoned, though they were well within her considerable pianistic range. To put her name on consecutive opus numbers would have drawn unwelcome attention. He decided against.

He gave two more concerts, as soloist with orchestra, before the season ended. The conductor was Serge Koussevitzky, a name that would dominate musical life in the mid-twentieth century. On the day Nicholas II abdicated, a report appeared (15 March 1917) in *Russkiye vedomosti*, a liberal daily paper: 'Free artist S. Rachmaninoff donates his fee for his first performance in this henceforth free country to the needs of the free army.' One week later he played Liszt's Piano Concerto no. 1, also with Koussevitzky. Then on 25 March, he was soloist in a bumper concert conducted by Emil Cooper, a Russian of English origin who later found his niche as a staff conductor at the Metropolitan Opera, New York.

Rachmaninoff took on Liszt's Piano Concerto no. 1, Tchaikovsky's Piano Concerto no. 1 and his own Piano Concerto no. 2 in a single evening. It was his last concert in Moscow, an extravagant farewell.

Spring Awakenings

With no concerts in the diary for the rest of spring, Rachmaninoff went alone to Ivanovka. This was where, over twenty summers, he had written so many works, as well as overseeing the sowing and harvesting. It was inextricably bound to every aspect of his life, his family, his being, everything he loved. He had also, since 1909, invested most of his earnings in the estate, bucking the trend of so many other landed Russian families whose wealth had drained away. He was still left with debts. Ivanovka swallowed money. Typically, he attended closely to new technical developments and costly machinery to try to maintain the greatest productivity standards: a passion as well as an important profession, no mere hobby.

In her short memoir, Natalia Rachmaninoff emphasises her husband's love of the land, writing:

As a child his favourite pastime in summer was swimming, and in winter skating. A little later on, it was riding. He had an excellent, graceful seat on a horse, and generally loved the animal. Of dogs he was somewhat nervous, but at the same time adored his strikingly handsome Leonberger, Levko. Later still his passions were for motor cars and motor boats. During the last three or four years he spent in Russia, he became seriously interested in agriculture; conversation at Ivanovka revolved about ploughing, winnowing machines, ploughs, binders, sowing, weeding, threshing, and so on. Only the Revolution put a stop to this engrossing preoccupation.[22]

Word of Lenin's return to Petrograd had reached the peasant workforce in Tambov, who were already mobilising. Some had signed up to the Social Revolutionary Party. All talk was of shared land ownership. Rachmaninoff later told Oskar von Riesemann: 'The impressions I received from my contact with the peasants, who felt themselves masters of the situation, were unpleasant.'[23] The peasant community had stolen cattle at night, raided stores, charged around drunk and brandished flares. Usually they would have heard their master, Rachmaninoff, practising. Now the big house was silent. Some workers, devoted to their reserved, gifted overlord, who could speak tirelessly about planting, or tilling, or horses, or machinery, urged Rachmaninoff to hasten elsewhere, before the troubles grew worse. 'By March of 1917 I had decided I would have to leave Russia but could not carry out my plan, for Europe was still fighting and no one could cross the frontier . . . I should have preferred to leave Russia with friendlier memories.'[24]

Natalia's reminiscences have a different emphasis:

He set off for Ivanovka in March and stayed there for about two months, after which we went together to spend the summer in Crimea. One day the peasants of the village came to see him in a body. Sergei Vasilievich went out to meet them, and spent a long time answering all the questions they put to him. The peasants behaved with great courtesy, naturally interested mainly in everything to do with the land and who would now be ruling Russia. They then dispersed peaceably and went home. But a few of the older generation soon returned and started urging Sergei Vasilievich not to delay leaving Ivanovka, because there were frequent visits from 'certain individuals, God knows who they are, who upset our people and give them too much to drink. Go away, better to put distance between yourself and this evil.'[25]

Once again, despite worsening circumstances, Rachmaninoff went off for his summer spa cure at Yessentuki. In June he wrote to Siloti, asking a favour, begging him to act as quickly as possible. He was restless, he admitted to his kindly and supportive cousin, quite unable to work, he had to find a way to leave Russia, and go anywhere. The calm centre of his life had collapsed. Everything he treasured about running an estate, the continuity, habit, solace, rhythm of the seasons, was in jeopardy. He must find a new life, as a performing musician. He hoped that an influential friend of Siloti, Mikhail Tereshchenko, now foreign minister in the Provisional Government, might help:

I'll be brief. First a few sentences of explanation. I've spent almost my entire earnings at the Ivanovka estate. It now represents an investment of about 120 thousand rubles. Yes I am ready to write this off, for I see another crash in store for me. Besides, living conditions here seem so much better than there that I've decided not to return there. I have about 30 thousand left – which is 'something' especially if I can work and continue to earn.

But I fear another crash: everything around me affects me so that I can't work and I'm afraid of going completely sour. Everyone advises me to leave Russia temporarily. But where and how? Is it possible?

Can you possibly catch M. I. T[ereshchenko] at a free moment to consult him about this? Could I count on receiving a passport to go at least to Norway, Denmark, Sweden? It makes no difference where! Anywhere! Please talk with him. Perhaps he can suggest something else. He who is at the summit has the widest view! Please talk with him, and answer me quickly. Yours, SR.[26]

Rachmaninoff scrutinised the newspapers, on a daily basis. In Petrograd crowds marched under Bolshevik slogans: 'All power to the people. All land to the people.' Ever more anxious, he wrote once again to Siloti asking for help. Matters with Koshetz, meanwhile, had soured, not helped by a somewhat farcical, lopsided triangular dance with Prokofiev. After Rachmaninoff left Yessentuki, Prokofiev had arrived, renting a 'marvellous four-roomed dacha' near his mother. He was delighted to be in the sunshine and 'under the southern stars' as he recorded in his diaries, and on the look-out for Koshetz. She told him of her impatience for his arrival and passed on Rachmaninoff's less than flattering remarks: that Prokofiev was, of course, talented but had not yet reached his potential.

'By this last I was given to understand that I had not attained that sphere to which he, Rachmaninoff, had compositionally speaking, access.'[27] In Prokofiev's dacha Koshetz wrote in his special notebook he was compiling devoted to insights on the sun 'that of the two suns that bestowed their rays upon her she wished to be warmed not by the old, long-standing one but the young one. As decoded, Rachmaninoff and Prokofiev.' Koshetz and Prokofiev dallied in the park – presumably the park with the 'pleasant pavilions' to which Rachmaninoff, with a certain pathos, had referred the year before – and generally enjoyed each other's company.

She was singing in Halévy's *La Juive* in Kislovodsk. Prokofiev went along too: he hated the piece but agreed that she had triumphed. The train journey back to Yessentuki, brimming with all her floral tributes, was 'like the garden from Kitezh', he wrote. Next morning he went to her lodging and found her in a state of *en déshabille*, surrounded by seven trunks, hat boxes and 'forty or

so' dresses, packing for Moscow and apologising for her 'whirli-
gig gyrations'.[28] She wanted Prokofiev to dedicate his Akhmatova
songs to her, adding to the catalogue she had already inspired
(including Scriabin's only song, 'Devotion', also dedicated to her).
He was not keen:

> I had not wanted to create an unfavourable comparison with
> another set of songs dedicated to her. I was hinting at the
> very good songs Rachmaninoff had dedicated to her. Koshetz
> said 'you're so cheeky but I like that'. It was indeed a cheek
> to compare them to the best songs of the ineffably divine
> Rachmaninoff! I love his songs very much, but as a matter of
> fact mine are better.[29]

Ready to depart, Koshetz requested he travel with her, discreetly,
on the local train as far as her connection with Moscow. Then she
revealed that she had made the same journey herself, exactly one
month earlier, to wave off 'someone else': Rachmaninoff. As a final
gesture, ever the minx, she gave Prokofiev a photograph of herself
on which she had written (in French) the saying: all passes, all
breaks, one tires of everything. This was a reference, she said, to
her association with Rachmaninoff which was now over.

The Moscow train began to pull out. Prokofiev ran along trying
to keep up. As a parting shot, she invited him to tour with her that
winter. Was it all a repeat of her behaviour with Rachmaninoff? She
implied to Prokofiev that the narrow-minded, 'bourgeois' attitudes
of Rachmaninoff's family, and of 'the man himself', had brought
relations to a close. Rachmaninoff may simply have tired of her
frolics. She was exhausting company. After the 'fantastic, volcanic'
Koshetz had gone back to Moscow, Prokofiev, no slouch, spent two
full days recovering. It seems that she had worn him out.[30]

Rachmaninoff saw Shaginian, too, that summer, their last encounter. The occasion was a charity gala concert, in Kislovodsk. Koshetz was down to sing as well. Shaginian had recently married. The night was hot, the insects swarming. 'Sitting next to my husband in the last row, I felt as though I were looking at the stage through the reverse side of binoculars, looking at the diminutive picture of something endlessly far away, disappearing, gone.'[31] Shaginian, not one to miss a chance to needle, and still irritated by Koshetz, describes an unpleasant situation:

> Next, Rachmaninoff appeared, dressed in tails with a white cape over his shoulders, nervous and seething with anger. Rachmaninoff did not want to accompany Koshetz, and Koshetz pouted and refused to sing without him. Rachmaninoff finally consented.
>
> We saw him in the intermission. That night in Kislovodsk was full of peculiar smells – a smell of roses and the southern earth was mixed with perfume, a smell of cigars with poplar trees. Swarms of midges were fighting in the bright light. The members of the orchestra paced back and forth on the stage, waiting for the second part of the concert.
>
> Rachmaninoff was scheduled to start it with the Marseillaise, but he purposely drew out the intermission, while he sat with us on a bench in a garden. Somehow he could not find the courage to say good-bye. I never saw him again.[32]

Aware of his celebrity, she wrote to Rachmaninoff in 1921, in despising tones, asking how he could bear to live this life of success, idolised but not engaged in composition. Shaginian's own future lay elsewhere. She took up many Communist causes and hero-worshipped Stalin, to whom she also wrote out of the blue, asking him for a foreword to one of her novels. He declined. Her seventy-nine books included Soviet detective thrillers. At her death, aged ninety-three, the Soviet leader, Leonid Brezhnev, praised her four-volume work on Lenin's family, for which she won the Lenin Prize in 1972. She was not universally popular. In *Hope Against Hope*, a memoir about life with her husband (the poet Osip Mandelstam) under the Stalinist regime, Nadezhda Mandelstam wrote scathingly of Shaginian, intimating that she was a Soviet puppet. In the final years of the USSR, she still had some cachet: in 1988 she featured on a postage stamp to mark her centenary.

Oddball she may have been, yet something in her youthful persistence had touched Rachmaninoff. The eventual publication of his letters to her occurred only after his death. His niece Zoya Pribytkova, on reading them, realised Shaginian's importance at this period of Rachmaninoff's life:

Very few people knew the real, essential Rachmaninoff. But there were those who became real friends, to whom he was not afraid to reveal his true self, and who straight away became close to him. Sergei Vasilievich talked to me about his correspondence with a certain 'Re'. He said that he did not know her personally but her letters were full of interest and substance, and she was able to give him advice about texts for songs, and indeed provided him with some actual texts. I could see that he entertained warm feelings for this unknown girl, and that that he revealed to her aspects of his real 'I' that he otherwise jealously withheld from everyone.

At a certain point I came across a copy of one of the *Novy Mir* journals and saw an article with the heading 'My Recollections of S. V. Rachmaninoff', by Marietta Shaginian. I started reading it and realised that 'Re' was none other than

Marietta Sergeyevna Shaginian. And I was overcome by feelings of such warmth and truthfulness emanating from her words about someone so eternally dear to me.

From what she wrote about Rachmaninoff, and from his letters to her, I realised that Marietta Shaginian was one of the very few people whom Sergei Vasilievich admitted into his inner world as a true and close friend, and with whom he could be the simple, gay, wise – in other words *real* – person that he really was.[33]

Last of Russia: Clouds of Wisteria

Rachmaninoff was depressed about the fate of Ivanovka, worried about his daughters' future, fearful of being left destitute. The decision was made. They would go abroad. How to achieve this was problematic. First, he and the family went to a Black Sea resort on the Crimea peninsula. Natalia's family had a house there. Her niece, Sophia Satin (1915–96), a very young child at the time (and not to be confused with Natalia's sister, Sofia Satina), describes it in her memoir: 'The house was built of white marble and situated at the top of a hill overlooking the port. It was surrounded by a large garden. I can still see the pergola covered with lilac coloured clouds of wisteria blooms.'[34]

She remembers, too, a gramophone with its large horn and, in particular, one record of a political song, probably performed by Chaliapin. That summer of 1917, the Chaliapins were by the Black Sea with the Rachmaninoffs, adding cheer. Chaliapin was by now maintaining two families and several children: it is not known which were there that summer. Rachmaninoff was preoccupied with work. At the end of the holiday he had a concert in Yalta, up the coast. Years before, he had met Chekhov in his White Dacha there, where Chaliapin, Tolstoy and Gorky were frequent visitors. Chekhov, who would remain among Rachmaninoff's most treasured writers, had foretold the young composer's artistic success, saying, 'It is written in your face.' Chekhov's sister, preserving her dead brother's memory, still had the house, but the parties were over. In Yalta, on 5 September 1917, Rachmaninoff gave his last concert in Russia, as soloist in Liszt's Piano Concerto no. 1.

The Rachmaninoff family went home to Moscow. Food and fuel were in short supply. A responsible citizen, Rachmaninoff went on duty each night as a civil guard to the block in which they lived. In the 'October Revolution', the Bolshevik Party confirmed its hold over Petrograd, seizing the Winter Palace and announcing an end to private property and the redistribution of land among the peasantry. The Bolshevik Red Army then turned its attention to Moscow. All but confined to his apartment, Rachmaninoff took up a long-deferred task: the revision of his Piano Concerto no. 1, composed in 1891, at the age of eighteen:

> I had started to rewrite my first Concerto for pianoforte, which
> I intended to play again, and was so engrossed with my work
> that I did not notice what went on around me. Consequently,
> life during the anarchistic upheaval, which turned the existence
> of a non proletarian into hell on earth, was comparatively
> easy for me. I sat at the writing table or the piano all day
> without troubling about the rattle of machine guns and rifle-
> shots. I would have greeted any intruder with the answer that
> Archimedes gave the conquerors of Syracuse.*[35]

* Archimedes, deep in mathematical rumination, failed to notice the Romans had stormed the city. Ignoring a soldier's command to accompany him, he was struck dead.

The First Piano Concerto, his opus 1, was written at Ivanovka. Rachmaninoff had made his British debut in the concerto, on 19 April 1899, at Queen's Hall under the baton of Henry Wood. Since as long ago as 1908 he had been wanting to rework it, a lifelong habit visited on most of his major compositions, and sharpen its focus. He considered his revamped, streamlined version successful. He signed the score with the date 10 November 1917. Within six weeks, he would leave Russia. The last music he wrote before leaving his homeland consisted of three miniatures: 'Oriental Sketch', a bleak prelude in D minor and some sombre 'Fragments', just twenty-six bars, all dated mid-November 1917.

His account of those last days in Russia, a country now heady with false hopes of Utopia, continued:

I saw with terrible clearness that here was the beginning of the end – an end full of horrors the occurrence of which was merely a matter of time. The anarchy around me, the brutal uprooting of all the foundations of art, the senseless destruction of all means for its encouragement, left no hope of a normal life in Russia, I tried in vain to escape from this 'witches' Sabbath' for myself and my family.[36]

Exodus

The chance for that escape came unexpectedly: an invitation to give a short series of concerts in the politically neutral countries of Scandinavia, his first offer of a tour abroad since the start of World War I. This entitled him to apply for visas for himself and his family. Later he learnt they were the last to leave the country legally. He travelled ahead to Petrograd. For an anxious few days, he waited for his family. The British writer Watson Lyle, an early biographer, gives a touching pen portrait of Rachmaninoff's wife. 'While it was quite possible that [the family] might not arrive, such a contretemps was unlikely. Madame Rachmaninoff is a woman of wit and resource, an experienced traveller and, on that journey, impelled by the strongest of all incentives to win through – love of her family.'[37]

They were allowed to take personal luggage and a restricted amount of money. No one waved them off at the Finland Station, though Chaliapin sent caviar and homemade bread for the journey. A newspaper reported that Rachmaninoff was giving concerts in Norway and Sweden, but in the midst of so much political upheaval, not least the first stages of Russia's withdrawal from World War I, little attention was paid. On 23 December 1917, the family at last left Russia. They were accompanied by their close family friend, the composer turned publisher Nikolai von Struve. The train, crowded with refugees, was uncomfortable, but they had minimal difficulties with frontier officials. Some of the guards recognised Rachmaninoff's name and wished him well. In his suitcase he carried the libretto, some sketches and the vocal score to Act I of his incomplete opera, *Monna Vanna* (which he would never finish), Rimsky-Korsakov's *Le Coq d'or* and a copy of the newly reworked Piano Concerto no. 1 (he had also sent the manuscript to his Russian publishers, Koussevitzky's Éditions Russes de Musique). He left behind many members of his family, his fortune, his apartment in Moscow, the estate of Ivanovka, his land, his horses, the trees he had planted, the lilacs he loved, his pianos, his personal belongings, the world he knew and loved. In terms of worth, his most precious unintended legacy to the new Soviet regime was all his other existing manuscripts, published and unpublished.

The journey into exile was long and uncomfortable. The train stopped at the Finnish border. The family travelled over the frozen snow to the Swedish frontier on a horse-drawn sleigh, known in Finnish as a 'hen basket'. They went by train to Stockholm, woken up from a sleeping carriage before dawn and forced to move compartments, arriving in the late afternoon to a city in festive mood. It was Christmas Eve.

Many of their circle disapproved of this departure. Rachmaninoff received a New Year's message, dated 1 January 1918, from Olga Knipper-Chekhova, the widow of Anton Chekhov. An actress and musician, founder member of the Moscow Art Theatre, and the creator of the role of Masha in *Three Sisters*, Olga made no attempt to hide her pique: 'You abandoned Russia.' She still 'for some reason wanted to write a few words', with the fervent hope that when life improved, he might return to Russia.[38]

For now there was no prospect of returning. The Rachmaninoffs decided to settle in Copenhagen where the Struves were based. The house they rented was cold, life dismal. Rachmaninoff spent hours each day practising. Lyle writes:

> Their daughters went into town on push-bikes to do the family shopping, while Mme Rachmaninoff became cook and housekeeper, the composer doing his share of the housework to the extent of getting up first in the morning to set alight the badly-drawing and damnably troublesome stoves.[39]

The concerts Rachmaninoff played in Scandinavia in 1918 were a success but he was left with a clear realisation. He would have to find a new way of life, as a virtuoso pianist, to support his family, educate his daughters and survive financially in a foreign land. He was already in debt. Composition would have to be put to one side, for how long he had no idea. Used to playing mainly his own compositions, he would have to build an entirely new repertoire of solo works and concertos. Offers of prominent conducting jobs, as music director, came in from the Cincinnati Orchestra and the Boston Symphony Orchestra. He declined, considering his repertoire too limited, with no time for the preparation needed.

A third invitation also came from the USA, to perform twenty-five recitals as a solo pianist. The fees were high. His mind was made up. His future lay in America. He borrowed money to pay for the family's Atlantic crossing. On 1 November 1918, they set sail from Oslo bound for New Jersey. Ten days later, they arrived in the New World.

REWIND

Life before Exile

Early Years

I remember when I was four I was already being asked to play for guests. If I played well I was rewarded generously. From the adjacent room the 'public' would throw me all sorts of pleasant things – sweets, paper roubles, and more. I was overwhelmed.[1]

We leave Rachmaninoff, in middle age, newly arrived with his family in exile in New York, speaking limited English, with few possessions and little money, and facing a dramatic shift in his career. He had left behind an enviable existence, at least in terms of material comforts and – the musical season aside – a pattern of life governed by the seasons of nature at Ivanovka. In the decades since completing his conservatory studies in 1892, covered in Gold Medal glory and awarded an extra exam distinction by Tchaikovsky (who added a plus sign to the highest mark available, 5), he had established an illustrious career. He conducted at the Bolshoi Theatre and elsewhere. His conducting repertoire extended beyond the Russian circle (Borodin, Glazunov, Mussorgsky, Rimsky-Korsakov) to include Berlioz, Bizet, Haydn, Dvořák. He also experimented, in a limited manner, with the music of his near-contemporaries Richard Strauss, Debussy and Ravel. He had made his UK debut at Queen's Hall in 1899, and toured to America in 1909. Siloti had gone on ahead, on his own tours introducing the world to his cousin's youthful C sharp minor Prelude, both a useful calling card and, as Rachmaninoff would come to consider it, a permanent curse. Before he had set foot in another country, he was famous on account of sixty bars of music, written when he was nineteen years old, which quickly acquired a fertile mythology. As the distinguished critic of *The Sunday Times*, Ernest Newman, would later remark, Rachmaninoff was 'that Prelude', just as Charlie Chaplin was a pair of baggy trousers and hypertrophied boots, and George Robey a pair of arched eyebrows.[2]

Now this life, and the reassurance that went with it, had been shattered. It was not the first time he had experienced a seismic emotional rupture. Rachmaninoff's childhood had been chaotic – in today's terminology, dysfunctional. Born in the Novgorod region south-west of St Petersburg, he was the fourth of six children. On both sides there were military and musical links. His mother, Lyubov Petrovna Butakova, the daughter of a general, was a good pianist. She came with a dowry consisting of five estates from her family lands. (A familiar pattern: in Chekhov's *Uncle Vanya*, Serebryakov lives comfortably for years on the income from his wife's estate.) The family of his father, Vasily Arkadyevich Rachmaninoff (1841–1916), also had military and musical links. Vasily's own father, Arkady Rachmaninoff, had studied with John Field, the Irish composer-pianist who became famous for 'inventing' the nocturne form (and who earned a walk-on part in Tolstoy's *War and Peace*).

A tradition long maintained by aristocratic families was that their lavish lifestyles in Moscow or St Petersburg would be supported by income from country estates. The power of that lineage was fading. Serfdom had been abolished, but emancipation led to economic chaos for all. The plays of Chekhov are as much about lack of money as about love. *The Cherry Orchard* (1903) is propelled by the need to sell up to pay the mortgage. Rachmaninoff's family faced the same crisis. In his time in the Imperial Russian army, Rachmaninoff's father had been a wastrel. Later, he chased fruitless business ventures and whiled away hours at the piano. One by one, his wife's estates had to be sold. In 1882 the family was forced to move to cramped quarters in St Petersburg. The marriage ended. Adding to the trauma of separation, Rachmaninoff was sent for a time to live with an aunt and uncle, to relieve the strain of life in the crowded flat. Soon he lost his sister Sophie, who died from diphtheria, then Yelena, his musically gifted older sister, also fell ill and died. All sense of family security was overthrown.

The expected army career at an elite military establishment was beyond the family's financial means. Rachmaninoff's fate was dictated when he won a scholarship to the St Petersburg Conservatory. By this time, his maternal grandmother lived with them and supported the family financially. With his father gone and his brother away, he was the 'man' of this female-dominated family:

Of my parents, who often disagreed, we loved our father the better. This was probably unfair on my mother; but as the former had a very gentle, affectionate manner, was extremely good-natured and spoiled us dreadfully, it is natural that our childish hearts, so easily won, should turn towards him. Our mother, on the other hand, was exceedingly strict. As our father was generally absent, it was she who determined the routine of the household. From our earliest days we were taught that 'there was a time for everything'. Besides a detailed plan for our lessons, regular hours were set aside for piano playing, walking and reading, and these were never violated except under special circumstances. This careful planning out of the day I have now, by the way, readopted, and appreciate its value more and more; but at the time I was unable to realise it and disliked the constraint imposed.[3]

Bells, Trams, Truant

The boy and his maternal grandmother spent many hours together, including summers at her estate near Novgorod. One of his most treasured activities was to go with her to churches and monasteries in the region: anywhere with the sound of Russian bells, and of Orthodox chant. These tollings and chimes, un-pitched, metallic, would live with him as aural fingerprints for ever. So too would the rituals of *a cappella* voices united in singing choral liturgy (in which the use of musical instruments was prohibited).

In her memoir, Rachmaninoff's sister-in-law Sofia Satina sums up that period:

> Only when his grandmother Sofia Alexandrovna Butakova came to visit did Seryozha's comportment become less manic, and he spent a great deal of time with her. In the warmth of her love he was concerned to be kind and helpful to her.
>
> When spring came, and with it the end of Seryozha's first year of studies at the Conservatoire, Butakova decided to take her favourite grandson to stay with her. All that summer he spent with his grandmother in Novgorod, and the two succeeding ones on the small estate of Borisovo not far outside the city – an estate she had acquired as a result of her grandson's insistent suggestions and pleadings. These two summers were unquestionably the happiest months of his entire childhood.
>
> He now found himself enveloped in an atmosphere of love and solicitude, complete freedom, unclouded by fear of punishment. Naturally it produced the strongest of impressions on a young boy who had never hitherto been spoiled by excess of loving affection and attention.

Most of the time he roamed about at will, taking a canoe out on the Volkhov River, swimming and generally romping around. Only once in a while, when his grandmother had guests, was he obliged to sit down at the piano and play to them. For the most part he improvised, pretending that he was performing compositions of well-known composers. His undemanding listeners were quite unaware of the deception.

Grandmother loved to visit churches, and he would make her take him to services, beginning to pay heed to the singing of the liturgy and luxuriating in the music. But an even more profound impression was created by the ringing sound of the bells and the services in the monasteries and cathedrals of Novgorod to which he persuaded his grandmother to accompany him.[4]

His indulgent grandmother did little to curb his laziness or bad behaviour. He played truant from the St Petersburg Conservatory, preferring to hone his ice-skating skills or risk life and limb jumping on and off horse-drawn trams on the city's main boulevard, Nevsky Prospect. His mother lost patience and sought help from Alexander Siloti. These two pianist cousins shared, in Arkady Rachmaninoff, that same grandfather who had been a pupil of Field. Siloti had graduated, in glory, from the Moscow Conservatory the previous year, 1881. He in turn had studied with Nikolai Rubinstein and Tchaikovsky and was about to go to Weimar where he would become one of the most brilliant students of Franz Liszt, as well as the last. As pianist, composer, impresario, helped in no small way by a successful marriage to an heiress, Siloti would become a leading light in Russian musical life. As a cousin, friend and teacher of the youthful Rachmaninoff, he played a vital role.

One of Siloti's first influences at the Moscow Conservatory had been Nikolai Zverev (1832–93), disappointed in his own career as a pianist but a charismatic teacher, authoritarian, impatient, with a touch of the Svengali about him. He was capable of violence, but also of great affection and generosity. Habitually he had a few students – his 'cubs' (a wry self-reference: 'Zver' means beast) – living in his house, which was run under the iron rule of Zverev and his sister.

Sergei Rachmaninoff now joined this elite band. In 1885, he left his grandmother's estate in Novgorod, on his own admission boarding the train in tears. A short and carefree period of his young life was over.

Zverev and His Cubs

Zverev's approach was one of tough love. Early-morning practice supervised by his sister was followed by formal lessons at the Conservatory. Then came pleasure: concerts, opera, ballet, theatre. The students were at every 'first night'. Their teacher was popular in society, numbering Dostoyevsky among his friends. At local restaurants the 'cubs' heard gypsy folk music and gypsy singers and dancers which, in their emotion and immediacy, left an impression on Rachmaninoff. His early opera *Aleko* (1893), taken from Pushkin, was a story of gypsy life. *Capriccio on Gypsy Themes*, op. 12 followed the next year. He dedicated it to his hard-drinking friend Pyotr Lodyzhensky, an occasional composer. It is an indifferent work which left the penniless Rachmaninoff depressed and wanting to do nothing but, he recalled, suck his finger like a child.

By all reports he had fallen for Lodyzhensky's wife Anna, a few years his senior, in her mid-twenties and of gypsy extraction. To her he dedicated his song 'Oh no, I beg you do not leave', op. 4 no. 1, and his First Symphony in D minor – her identity cryptically indicated as 'A. L.'. On the original manuscript he also wrote: 'Vengeance is mine, I will repay', a phrase which occurs three times in the Bible and once at the beginning of Tolstoy's *Anna Karenina*. Since the novel centres around an extra-marital affair, a connection with Rachmaninoff's own circumstances has been assumed. Assumption, or presumption, it can only be. No details of a relationship survive. More likely is that he admired her from afar, fascinated by her, and the world she represented. He dedicated another op. 4 song to Anna's sister Nadezhda, a gypsy singer, in thrall to the lure and other-worldliness he perceived in both women. The Lodyzhensky sisters were thought unsuitable company by his family and cousins, yet they, and importantly Pyotr Lodyzhensky too, remained friends with Rachmaninoff, who later helped Pyotr financially.

At Zverev's Sunday salon, the 'cubs' encountered the fabled figure of Anton Rubinstein, the composer, pianist and conductor whose playing Rachmaninoff revered all his life. Rubinstein's concerts, surveying piano music from Elizabethan virginal works forward, made an impact on the young student: here was an exemplar of virtuosity, technique, musical insight. He had what the adult Rachmaninoff would call a 'vital spark'. Rubinstein's artistry and influence shaped Rachmaninoff's ideas throughout his life. Disciplined at last, he made rapid progress. He had begun to make some first real efforts at composition, with a piano piece (now lost, from 1886): an Étude in F sharp, which he dedicated to his fellow cub Matvei Presman. Presman's memories of that summer are vivid: for several days, Rachmaninoff was pensive, a loner, walking around whistling and humming in a world of his own, and secretive about his endeavours. Then it turned out that in fact he was writing music.

After his academic success, Rachmaninoff was allowed to visit his family for the first time since his arrival in Moscow. Growing up and now taking his compositions seriously, he wanted his own room, which led to an argument with Zverev in which the older man raised his hand in anger. Speculation over the exact nature of the argument varies, with Zverev's homosexuality cited in vague terms. Rachmaninoff recalled beatings and arguments. The rift eventually healed. Zverev gave him his own gold pocket watch, in itself remarkable given the number of accomplished pupils he could have chosen to honour in this way. Rachmaninoff treasured it until the end of his life (in hard times having to pawn it) keeping to the end that potent link with this irascible but important figure of his youth.

Rachmaninoff went to live with his cousins on his father's side, the Satins: four children including Natalia (Natasha), four years younger and a talented pianist, who would become his wife, and her sister Sofia, eight years younger, friend, ally, chronicler. After initial hesitation, they embraced this unusual young man into the warmth of a family life he had never experienced. In 1890 and 1891 he spent his summers at Ivanovka, their family estate which he would eventually run himself: two houses, a park in the English style, orchards, a dairy, a stud farm and offices. Already, he had forged an unbreakable connection with Ivanovka:

I grew fond of the broad landscape and, away from it, would find myself longing for it, for Ivanovka offered the repose of surrounding that hard work requires – at least for me. There are none of the beauties of nature that are usually thought of in this term – no mountains, precipice, or winding shore. This steppe was like an infinite sea where the waters are actually boundless fields of wheat, rye, oats, stretching from horizon to horizon. Sea air is often praised, but how much more do I love the air of the steppe, with its aroma of earth and all that grows and blossoms – and there's no rolling boat under you either.[5]

Such was the landscape whose loss he would mourn for the remainder of his days.

From Silence to Redemption

Before 1917, Rachmaninoff had written more than eighty songs, as well as chamber music and solo piano works. Despite the crisis following the disastrous performance of his youthful Symphony no. 1 in D minor (1895), he regained his nerve and courage, with the cello sonata, another symphony and two more piano concertos (he would write four in total). The story of that First Symphony premiere, frequently held up as one of classical music's great fiascos, will be kept brief: the conductor was Glazunov, Rachmaninoff's senior composer colleague, who made heavy cuts and alterations. On the night of the concert he was reportedly drunk. The young composer, listening outside the auditorium in terror, fled as the final note sounded. The critics, some of them fellow composers, were merciless. César Cui, the least talented of the nationalist group known as the 'Mighty Handful' (the others were Balakirev, Mussorgsky, Rimsky-Korsakov and Borodin), achieved minor celebrity with his toxic remarks. He compared the young man's symphony to the Seven Plagues of Egypt, damning it as suitable enchantment for souls in Hell.

Three years of depression and compositional silence followed for Rachmaninoff. Today, with greater awareness of mental health issues, we would be less shocked, or puzzled, by his low mood. Writing to a friend about the symphony after the premiere, he maintained it was disappointment in the work itself, not its poor reception, which had preyed upon his mind. A great reviser of his own music, he never went back to that symphony – though a reference to it would appear, transformed, in his last orchestral work. He withheld the symphony's score from public use. His sister-in-law, Sofia Satina, locked it in a desk drawer for safekeeping, but after she too left Russia in 1921, passing key and desk to the family's much-loved housekeeper, it disappeared.*

On two occasions, the second with Chaliapin, Rachmaninoff visited Leo Tolstoy, to whom he was introduced via his aunt Varvara Satina. The hope was that the great writer might offer wise counsel to the depressed young composer, who reportedly spent hours of every day on the couch, communing chiefly with his dog, Levko. The meetings should have gone well. Tolstoy was a friend of Rachmaninoff's teacher, the composer Sergei Taneyev (1856–1915) – or he was until his wife took something of a fancy to Taneyev. Tolstoy had strong views on music, but he was a good pianist, and had even written his own waltz. Two grand pianos and a gramophone have pride of place in the dining room at Tolstoy's estate, Yasnaya Polyana. If anything, however, the encounters had the opposite effect. Tolstoy first merely shooed the young man away, saying that the life of an artist was hard, that he had to pick himself up and keep going. When Rachmaninoff and Chaliapin performed the song 'Fate' (op. 21 no. 1) to him, Tolstoy, silent for a long time, announced to Rachmaninoff that he disliked it, and asked what the point of such music could be.

A new approach was necessary. On the advice of his cousins, the Satins, from January to April 1900, three years after that nightmare

---

* After Rachmaninoff's death, the original orchestral parts were found in the library of Leningrad Conservatoire and reconstructed – in part thanks to the composer's own version for piano four hands – by Alexander Gauk, who conducted the second performance of the work on 17 October 1945 in the Great Hall of Moscow Conservatoire. The first performance outside Russia was given by the Philadelphia Orchestra, conducted by Eugene Ormandy, on 19 March 1948.

premiere, Rachmaninoff underwent hypnotherapy treatment with Dr Nikolai Dahl, a physician and amateur viola player. Dahl specialised in curing alcohol addiction, as well as other conditions. One of Rachmaninoff's first biographers, Victor Seroff, notes that 'these years of the composer's life were later carefully screened': the associations of depression and drinking were not necessarily the image the family wanted to portray.[6] Rachmaninoff himself told Ivan Bunin, the writer and poet, that in this period, he did nothing in terms of work, and drank heavily. Later there are frequent mentions of his noticeably modest consumption of alcohol, though he never abstained completely (claiming, decades later, that he drank a glass of *crème de menthe* to fortify him before playing his own *Rhapsody on a Theme of Paganini*).

Eventually, creativity returned. Rachmaninoff always credited Dahl and hypnotherapy. This episode has been chewed over endlessly by psychologists both amateur and professional, without firm conclusions. Whatever the correct interpretation, Dahl appears to have helped rouse Rachmaninoff out of his gloom. (Their sessions were dramatised in a 2015 off-Broadway musical, *Preludes*, by Dave Malloy.) The work with which he broke that first long silence, completed in the spring of 1901, would prove his most famous: the Piano Concerto no. 2, op. 18, dedicated to Dahl.

Rachmaninoff's grandson Alexander Conus-Rachmaninoff, perhaps wishing to dispel any 'black dog' stigma, used to explain that his grandfather was not really unwell but was in love with Dahl's daughter, hence the urgency and regularity of his visits. Dahl only had a son.* We must make of that what we will.

* Elger Niels, a musician and long-standing researcher for the Rachmaninoff Foundation, wrote to me in August 2022: 'Like all other witnesses belonging to Rachmaninoff's inner circle to whom I have had the pleasure to talk in person, Alexander Conus-Rachmaninoff was deeply annoyed by the

Episodes of depression occurred throughout Rachmaninoff's life, but never to such an extent. Once he left Russia, a different crisis, a different silence, as well as a disruptive and exciting new mode of life, would envelop him. Were his years as a composer over?

---

stigmatisation of his grandfather as a depressed person. During a walk in Codsall Wood, Staffordshire, in 2003, he voiced his irritation about an article I had written about Nikolai Dahl's therapy. He equated me with all the many other biographers who thoughtlessly elaborated on the myth about Dahl. So I asked him if he had read the article at all. Alexander then showed the honesty to admit that he hadn't, because the subject alone irked him. So I explained to him that precisely by seriously studying the applied treatment (post-hypnotic suggestion), the article shows that Rachmaninoff's psychological problems were incidental in nature and that there were no structural personality problems behind them. To me Alexander did not repeat his statement about Dahl's supposed daughter, but said: 'Better a good story than a true story.' To which I replied: 'A true story provides more answers and will last longer.'

1918-1930

America, the Glory Years

Armistice. Rachmaninoff is Here

The headlines in the *New York Times* of Wednesday 13 November 1918 declared: 'Emperor of Austria Finally Abdicates; German Crown Prince Now Reported Dead.' 'Germany Surrenders All Her Submarines and 150,000 Railway Cars.' 'Cheering after Last Shot.' Two days earlier, on 11 November, in a French railway carriage – 'le Wagon de l'Armistice' – in the forest of Compiègne, an armistice had been signed. After four years, from the North Sea to the Swiss frontier, fighting was at an end. A report from Paris describes the last moments of gunfire. 'At exactly one minute of eleven, like a final thunder crash at the clearing of a storm, the guns on both sides abruptly ceased.'[1]

Jubilation was tempered by sorrow for the dead and wounded. Nevertheless Paris was *en fête*, singing the 'Marseillaise'. In London, munition girls danced in the street. King George V drove along Fleet Street, crowds jostling, bells pealing, a military band playing. Everyone joined in 'God Save the King' as well as the newly popular 'Star-Spangled Banner'.

Did they know the words to this American song? Unlikely. It was not yet the official US national anthem, but in 1917 President Woodrow Wilson had endorsed it as the choice of music for official military events. Composed in the nineteenth century by John Stafford Smith, a one-time organist of Gloucester Cathedral, the English tune had become an American favourite. In the large and virtuosic hands of a new exile, it would soon have a Russian champion too.

The impact of war also dominated the inside pages. The labour market was depleted. Advertisements appealed to women to become waiters and cooks because of the scarcity of a male work-force. Culture, at least, was alive again: the tenor Enrico Caruso (1873–1921) was to star in *L'elisir d'amore* at the Metropolitan Opera and the famous American soprano Geraldine Farrar (1882–1967) would reprise the title role in Puccini's *Madama Butterfly*, which she had created for the Met in 1907.

Into this post-war world, amid the roar of hope and celebration, came Rachmaninoff, with his own newspaper headline:

RACHMANINOFF IS HERE

Composer Escapes from Russia to America to Rest and Work

Sergei Rachmaninoff, the Russian composer, arrived with his family at an Atlantic port recently and was registered yesterday at the Hotel Netherland, in this city. Beside the musician and his wife, the party included their two daughters, 16 and 14 years old. They escaped from Russia to Sweden and thence from Stockholm by steamship to Copenhagen and across the Atlantic. Mr Rachmaninoff was welcomed by the colony of Russian artists now in New York, including the young composer, Sergei Prokofiev, who got here before him by coming the other way round the world, by Siberia and the Pacific. 'I have come to America to rest and work,' Rachmaninoff told his callers yesterday. He referred to a former visit in times of peace, when he conducted his music here with the Boston Symphony Orchestra. The composer is 43 years old now. His previous visit to the country was in 1909–10 and he has since been chief conductor of the opera in Petrograd.[2]

On 14 November 1918 the *Musical Courier* carried an article describing his concerts in Scandinavia; his decision to turn down the offer to become conductor of the Boston Symphony Orchestra; his high opinion of the orchestras in America; his view of himself, now, as above all a pianist-composer; and the fact that he had left most of his manuscripts behind in Russia except his revised Piano Concerto no. 1, op. 1. He expressed surprise that the Bolshevik regime had lasted so long but said nothing about expecting to return home. Finally he gave his impressions since landing in America:

> Well, I must admit that my first impressions, at least of New York, were most remarkable ones. Monday morning I went out soon after ten for a walk of half an hour. You know what a crowd we had here that morning! Unfamiliar with the English language, your methods of transportation and of course, with the exuberance of such a vast throng as was celebrating the greatest day in the world's history, my little walk stretched into an excursion which lasted against my wishes until 4 o'clock in the afternoon, when at last I was able to rediscover the hotel and to have some luncheon and a nap that I sorely needed after my unprecedented adventures of Victory Day!

Flu Epidemic

The Rachmaninoff family had sailed into New York on the Norwegian-American liner SS *Bergensfjord*. The ship docked at Hoboken, New Jersey, on 10 November 1918, the eve of Armistice. America, like much of Europe, was in the midst of a flu epidemic, the 'Spanish' influenza, which ebbed and flowed throughout 1918. Troop ships and trench warfare hastened the spread of the disease, possibly a form of avian or swine flu. This particular strain attacked, above all, those humans in the prime of life: casualties were highest among men in their forties. Cases soared during the month of October 1918. In the week the Rachmaninoffs arrived, the Weekly Bulletin of the Department of Health, City of New York (9 November 1918), showed on its cover a cartoon of a sick man, his nose a water sprinkler spurting forth, with the slogan, 'How disease is spread: sneeze but don't scatter.'

On top of the expected respiratory tract infection, this flu left lasting effects on the heart, lungs and brain. President Wilson suffered a bad dose, his inner circle afterwards noting his change of personality, and wondering if his intellect had been impaired. Schools and shops mainly stayed open, with scheduled times to reduce crowding. Street workers, policemen, office staff wore masks. As casualties rose, so movie theatres, concert and dance halls were forced to shut, not least because no one would come. In an effort to locate the original spread of the infection, a city doctor, from the Medical Society of New York County, registered a complaint to the health department: every passenger on the *Bergensfjord*, on its arrival back in August 1918, should have been quarantined.

The very ship which, three months later, carried the Rachmaninoffs to their new life, was attributed as having introduced the first case of flu to the city. Eleven crew and ten passengers had been affected. The ship was met at the pier by ambulances and health officers from the Port of New York. In September the whole Port of New York was put under quarantine, but by now it was too late: the epidemic was raging.

Did Rachmaninoff know he was aboard a ship with this unhappy pedigree? He may have contracted flu during the voyage. He, and both his daughters, fell prey to the infection within days of their arrival in America, where they had checked in at the fashionable

New Netherland Hotel on the corner of Fifth Avenue and Fifty-Ninth Street. There, ill or not, they were greeted by a procession of musician friends and fans.

The twenty-seven-year-old Prokofiev had arrived in New York two months earlier from the 'other direction', via Honolulu, San Francisco and Chicago. As yet he had failed to make the desired impact on the concert stage because of flu cancellations. He wrote crossly in his autobiography: 'To fly from the Bolsheviks to die from Spanish flu! What sarcasm!' And now he found that Rachmaninoff had arrived in town too. The rival composer-pianists soon met, after Prokofiev had given a solo recital at Aeolian Hall in which he played three of Rachmaninoff's preludes, surely intending a friendly gesture. He noted in his diary on 20 November 1918: 'The Rachmaninoff I played very well, there is simply no other word for it, but the Scriabin was less scrupulous in terms of accuracy.'

Revelling in eleven generally flattering press reviews, Prokofiev had lunch at Steinway's next day in the company of Rachmaninoff, 'who observed with a benevolent smile: "I should have liked to come to your concert, but you did not send me an invitation, so I concluded you did not want me to come."' Prokofiev retorted: 'Sergei Vasilievich, I would have been so nervous at playing your Preludes in your presence that I am glad you were not there to hear it. And my own compositions do not, of course, interest you.'[3] Rachmaninoff's reply was to laugh and observe drily that it depended on which compositions he was talking about.

On Sunday 24 November, the *Washington Post*'s Olin Downes wrote a discursive article on the newly resident Russian celebrity. Nicknamed 'Sibelius's apostle' for his espousal of that Finnish composer, Downes was both opinionated and influential, though his views were not always nuanced (Elgar's music was all 'antimacassar and pork-pie bonnets' while Webern's modernist achievements were 'clucking, pecking . . . small and futile'). As Downes wrote, Rachmaninoff had already signed up with an agent:

> [He] will manage a tour of the Russian composer, who lately arrived in New York, and now will give a series of piano recitals through the United States. Mr Rachmaninoff left Russia soon after the Bolsheviki had come into power. He waited outside that forlorn land for a time, doubtless expecting, as everyone else did, that Bolshevism would soon vanish into the Russian discard, with a possible return to more stable conditions in the land of the czars. [. . .] Mr Rachmaninoff was among the conductors who were approached for the post of the leader of the Boston Symphony Orchestra . . .
>
> With a modesty as rare as it was extraordinary the Russian declined the high honor offered him by the trustees of the Boston Orchestra, on the grounds that with the brief period between the offer and the beginning of the concerts he would not have time to prepare and master the enormous amount of orchestral music, much of it of the greatest difficulty, which the conductor of a season of Boston Symphony concerts is called upon to interpret in the course of a season. Mr Rachmaninoff is not a professional conductor, although he led the performance of his own tone poem *The Isle of the Dead* when invited to do so as the guest of the Boston Symphony Orchestra in 1909, the year of his first tour of this country. Neither is Mr Rachmaninoff professionally a pianist, though he admitted when he arrived in New York that he had been practising of late.

Downes offset his remarks about Rachmaninoff as conductor and pianist with comments on his status as a composer:

> He is gradually being appraised as a composer at his true value
> in America, a country where for years he was known principally
> and almost entirely as the author of that piece of portentous
> Siberian gloom, the 'Prelude in C sharp minor'. It is not a bad
> composition, if somewhat over-rated . . .

In an interview some years earlier, Rachmaninoff had obligingly
explained the entire background to that piece of overrated gloom:
that he sold it for a mere forty roubles and that it had no program-
matic narrative but was absolute music. He then proceeded to give a
detailed analysis, for all America's countless aspiring C-sharp-minor-
prelude pianists, of how the work should be approached, starting
with the three opening chords which should 'boom solemnly and
portentously'.[4]

The news wires celebrated Rachmaninoff's 'entirely unheralded
and unexpected' arrival in America, reporting that 'he is not fluently
conversant' in English and conducted his interviews in French.
After the difficulties of musical life in Russia, he said conditions in
the neutral Scandinavian countries were 'quite normal' with many
concerts on offer. Now he wanted to get back to composition,
having had to neglect his work 'owing to the disturbed conditions'
in Russia and throughout Europe. The *Philadelphia Inquirer* noted:

> An exile from his own country under the hardships of war and
> revolution, Sergei Rachmaninoff, the noted Russian pianist,
> composer and conductor, has returned to America after nine
> years of absence. Again he will make a short tour of a few cities
> under the management of Mr C. A. Ellis. Though recent events
> in Russia have not dealt kindly with him, Rachmaninoff comes

back to America in the prime of his years, in the full maturity and exercise of his powers, and at the height of his reputation. Hardly another Russian musician is so many-sided or enjoys such international fame.[5]

Roof Raising and Flappers: First Concerts

Despite flu and less than a month after his arrival from Europe, Rachmaninoff gave his first concert in America as an exile in Providence, Rhode Island, on 8 December 1918. To his audience's delight, he played his own arrangement of 'The Star-Spangled Banner', a tribute to his new home. Plain and dignified, his version could scarcely be less showy. (His performance, preserved on a piano roll, can be heard on YouTube. He ran into none of the difficulties faced by Igor Stravinsky, whose World War II version triggered a visit from the Boston police, allegedly because of the trespassing inclusion of a 'jazzy' dominant seventh chord.)

Rachmaninoff opened his next concert, at Symphony Hall, Boston, with the same anthem, playing to what the Boston critic Philip Hale called 'a very large and bronchial audience'.[6] H. T. Parker, another front-line critic in an era bustling with sharp pens, was lyrical in the *Boston Evening Transcript*. His account of Rachmaninoff's physical presence might be seen as a prototype for descriptions over the next quarter of a century. He compared this appearance with that of Rachmaninoff nearly a decade earlier. Back then, the composer could scorn America and its brash ways, knowing he would soon return home to Russia. Now life was different:

Nine years of absence had dimmed memories of his aspect, perhaps materially altered it . . . His height nearly topped the doorway through which he entered; the breadth of his spare body nearly fitted it; the black that clothed him heightened this austerity of presence. As of old, the head, the face were unmistakably Russian from the close cropped dark hair to the long jaw, the firm chin. The well-remembered brown colour had not turned to pallor; the forehead sloped upward, broad and high; the eyes kept the old gravity of contemplation – deepened. Plainly the past had worn him, yet had not left him in the present wearied.[7]

On 21 December, he performed at Carnegie Hall, New York: 'Rachmaninoff Raises the Roof', ran the *New York Times* headline next morning. But there was a dreadful omission:

No, he did not play it at Carnegie Hall yesterday afternoon. That is, Sergei Rachmaninoff, double distinguished composer and pianist, did not play his celebrated Prelude in C sharp minor, though the Rachmaninoff 'fans' – and there were thousands of them in the audience – clamoured for the favourite piece of Flatbush 'flappers'. They surged toward Sergei in serried masses. They clustered about the stage. They raised aloft their arms as they supplicated the Russian . . . He played five encore numbers, one being the Prelude in G minor, first made known here by Josef Hofmann, who does not play it so rapidly, thereby getting a more sonorous tone. It is dangerous, however, to criticise the interpretation of a composer. He ought to know what he wishes. So please do not accept our opinion as official.

Rare but refreshing to hear a critic volunteer that his opinion may not be 'official'!

Josef Hofmann's motto was 'an aristocrat never hurries'.[8] The Polish-born pianist (1876–1957), greatly admired by Rachmaninoff, was the dedicatee of his Piano Concerto no. 3. He never played it, however. The relative smallness of his hands has been given as one explanation for his shunning the work, though many 'small'-handed pianists have played it since. It may have been the work's notorious difficulties. He may simply not have liked it.

Shared pianistic brilliance aside, Rachmaninoff and Hofmann, close friends, had plenty in common. Hofmann's posthumous assessment of Rachmaninoff still burns bright: 'Rachmaninoff was made of steel and gold: steel in his arms, gold in his heart. I can never think of this majestic being without tears in my eyes, for I not only admired him as a supreme artist, but I loved him as a man.'[9] Away from the concert platform, Hofmann was an inventor, with more than sixty patents to his credit including shock-absorbers and automobile appliances such as wind-screen wipers. Rachmaninoff, with a passion for any kind of vehicle that moved fast, loved inventions and gadgets that aided velocity.

Every leading critic had something to say about Rachmaninoff, good or bad. The *New York Times* reviewer, James Gibbons Huneker, appreciated the 'Humoreske', one of Rachmaninoff's early 'Ten Salon Pieces' (1894), once again commenting on an absence:

It is truly humorous, with more than a moiety of the devilry
that lurks in the dark forest called the Russian soul. The
other three encores were salon music, clever, not very
original though effective. But the chief thing is the fact that
Rachmaninoff did not play *it*. All Flapperdom sorrowed
last night, for there are amiable fanatics who follow this
pianist from place to place hoping to hear him in this
particular Prelude; like the Englishman who attended

every performance of the lady lion tamer hoping to see her swallowed by one of her pets.[10]

A conservatory-trained pianist, Huneker made a detailed, acerbic assessment of Rachmaninoff's pianism. A fan of Hofmann and of Anton Rubinstein, whom he praised for their colour, their glow, he was not won over by Rachmaninoff's touch, which he described as 'like a boulder of granite' and not 'velvety'. He remarked that the 'cold white light of analysis, the incisive touch, the strongly marked rhythms, the intellectual gap, the relative importance in phrase groupings proclaimed that Rachmaninoff is a cerebral, not an emotional artist. Not Woodrow Wilson himself could have held the academic balance so dispassionately.' Rachmaninoff's Beethoven and Mozart 'were as clear as dry-point etching', though Huneker would have preferred there to be no repeats.

On and on Huneker went. He found the Presto of Beethoven's Sonata op. 10 no. 3 far too fast, 'taken at a prestissimo, plus a prestissimo', even its perfection and clarity detracting from the weightiness of the piece. Chopin's C sharp minor Nocturne (op. 27 no. 1) was thoroughly satisfactory because of its 'superlatively fine' adjustment of tonal dynamics, but it reached the head, not heart. Chopin's A flat Waltz op. 42 was brilliant, the elegiac C minor Polonaise the best of the group, its melancholy muted, 'its resignation worn like crêpe in every bar'. Apart from the Chopin Polonaise, he was most impressed by the Allegretto from Beethoven's Sonata in A flat, op. 110, played as an encore, though again he found it too fast. (One suspects, given the nature of his complaints, that he would have hated Rachmaninoff's Scriabin playing in that fated 1915–16 season in Russia.)

Prokofiev and Provocation

As the calendar turned from 1918 to 1919, the new exile Rachmaninoff and the scarcely more established Prokofiev pirouetted
around each other, at once smiling and baring their teeth. Prokofiev's attitude was part envy, part derision and, puzzlingly, part
affection. Scorning Rachmaninoff in private, he was charm per-
sonified in public. Often, too, almost despite himself, he admired
Rachmaninoff's work. Prokofiev heard his Symphony no. 2 in E
minor, op. 27 'with much enjoyment' at Carnegie Hall. 'At the end
of the performance [Rachmaninoff], trying to hide behind his wife,
was identified and made to stand up and acknowledge an ovation.'

The symphony was programmed alongside Prokofiev's Scherzo
for Four Bassoons and, more importantly, the American premiere of
his Piano Concerto no. 1 in D flat. A second concert the next night
featured more of his music. Rachmaninoff did not attend 'as he was
not well' – still recovering from flu. Nonetheless he sent a message
asking why Prokofiev had forgotten him. Had he been able to read
the younger man's diaries, he would have found that Prokofiev's
frantic love life in recent weeks had pushed aside any non-urgent
activity, though to be fair he had also been away in Chicago. Rachmaninoff asked, too, for Prokofiev's telephone number. 'Coming
from Rachmaninoff I am very touched by this,' Prokofiev noted.[11]

A few weeks later, at Carnegie Hall on 28 January 1919, with
Modest Altschuler and the Russian Symphony Society of New York,
Rachmaninoff was the soloist in the premiere of his revised Piano
Concerto no. 1, the score that he had reworked in his final days
in Moscow. (Altschuler, a fellow Moscow Conservatory student
and exact contemporary of Rachmaninoff, had been promoting
Russian composers since his emigration to the United States in
1893.) Prokofiev was there and committed his usual waspish and

contrary views to his diary. He loved the first movement but found the work 'naive and poetical if a little long'. Everything is skilful, 'but when Rachmaninoff decides to insert a touch of modernism in the shape of consecutive triads with parallel fifths, it jars unpleasantly on the ear; it's not at all stylish'. After more insults he calls the finale 'as bad as ever' and full of repellent bluster. He adds, as an afterthought, that the influenza shows no signs of abating: 'there are three hundred new cases every day . . .'[12]

It might have amused Prokofiev to read the snooty criticism of the American critic and journalist Paul Rosenfeld. Its tone set a trend that would, alas, dog Rachmaninoff's years in America, and for decades after his death. Considered an intellectual heavyweight, Rosenfeld moved in a smart set which included the writer Edmund Wilson and the artist Georgia O'Keeffe. In his *Musical Portraits, Interpretations of Twenty Modern Composers* (1920), Rosenfeld included a chapter on Rachmaninoff, who 'comes amongst us like a very charming and amiable ghost'. Referring to Rachmaninoff as a ghost – he would use the expression himself – became quite a habit. The implications are not hard to identify: here was a composer whose music sounded old and whose formal, unflashy manner seemed rooted in the past. Rosenfeld finds the Russian's music cautious, traditional, lacking boldness, smooth, soft, elegantly elegiac, dull, polite, a tepid bath. The entry is short, brutal, and pleased with itself. The Second Piano Concerto is a 'mournful banqueting on jam and honey'[13] (Virgil Thomson later called the same work 'mud and sugar'[14]), while *The Isle of the Dead* lacks 'vitality', an odd line of attack given the work's threnodic subject-matter. Few compositions conjure the mystery of death with quite such abstract and gaseous force.

Red Scare, Tin Pan Alley

The wider context into which the exiled Rachmaninoff family had to fit was troubled and uneasy. From around 1900 to 1925, an estimated three million Russians emigrated to Western Europe and North America. They came from every class of society, alarmed by Bolshevism, at risk for supporting the Tsarist regime, or aghast in a less specific manner at the changes wrought by the Revolution. Jerome Davis, the American sociologist who observed this particular immigration history – at the time it happened, with the biases that implies – wrote in *The Russian Immigrant* (1922): 'In spite of all America gives, we have seen that the great majority of Russian immigrants are isolated and remain almost totally unlike the American people . . . As might be expected of two groups reacting on each other, segregation and mutual non-comprehension result.'[15]

Stereotyping and xenophobia prevailed. The Red Scare, a mood of national hysteria which surfaced around 1920, reflected the American fear of political radicalism, Bolshevism, Communism: all words with pre-echoes of concerns that would surface in the Cold War, and the 'second Red Scare' of the 1940s and 1950s, characterised by the so-called 'McCarthy years.' Irving Berlin, himself a Russian immigrant, composed the song 'Look out for the Bolsheviki Man' in 1919, one of many lyrics in that mode. Rachmaninoff felt the same muddled, generic prejudice when he was in Paris (as reported in *Vogue*, April 1943): 'I was once on a street in Paris with my wife when a cab-driver, who heard me speaking to her in Russian, leaned out and spat at us, "*Sales étrangers!*" [Filthy foreigners!].'

As the immediate anxiety dwindled and it was clear America might not, after all, be ravaged by Bolsheviks, Russians became a butt of humour. Tin Pan Alley music, which had originated some three decades earlier in the publishing houses around New York's

Flower District, had its own strain of songs relating to Russianism in general, with an underlying anti-Bolshevik attitude in particular.[16] 'Russian nostalgia', consisting of lullabies and gypsy songs, tea rooms, beards, flowered headscarves, vodka, samovars and balalaikas, all filtered into popular culture. Rachmaninoff found his by now wearying Prelude at its heart. Among the most popular songs of 1918 was 'Russian Rag: Interpolating the World-Famous Prelude by Rachmaninoff' by George L. Cobb. One account describes how Cobb sat down and offered a ragtime version of the Prelude, having heard it played by an orchestra in a restaurant, only to find Rachmaninoff himself was there as a fellow diner and that it had been played in his honour.

This may well have happened, but the original sheet music for Cobb's version was published in April 1918, a full seven months before Rachmaninoff's arrival in America. It opens with the momentous three-note figure (A–G sharp–C sharp in the original, now transposed to B flat–A–D) before tripping off into a cheeky rag, only the three notes staying intact. Nor could Cobb, who enjoyed enormous success from his energetic pianistic skit, let the Prelude go. A second version, *New Russian Rag* (1923), is more technically ambitious. Was he parodying the solemn Russian virtuoso or paying homage?

A version by James Reese Europe and the 'Hellfighter' band turned the Prelude into a foxtrot. It enabled Rachmaninoff's Soviet accusers to accuse him, as a servant of 'world Bourgeoisie and world capitalism', of being a 'manufacturer of foxtrots'![17] As it happened, Rachmaninoff *did* have a taste for foxtrots, telling a journalist in 1919 that he had 'never heard any rhythm like it before' (though later making it plain he had never written a foxtrot himself). The vamping and jazzing of the Prelude would form a secondary backbone to Rachmaninoff's American years. By the time the habit of 'jazzing the classics' was established in the 1930s and 1940s, partly thanks to the African-American Broadway composer-arranger, Chappie Willett, the Prelude was regarded as a free-for-all. After Duke Ellington's jam session was broadcast live from New York's Cotton Club in 1938, the press reported that he had played a swing version of the 'immortal Prelude in C sharp minor', an old piece written by Rachmaninoff 'in the eighteenth Century'. To some, the ghostly Rachmaninoff was dead already.

That first American season, nonetheless, was a triumph. Rachmaninoff gave twenty-two solo recitals and twelve concerto performances. He built up his repertoire, earned large sums and now had the all-powerful Charles Ellis as agent. Ellis already managed the violinist Fritz Kreisler, and the soprano star Geraldine Farrar, as well as Ignacy Paderewski (1860–1941), until the celebrated pianist-composer returned to his homeland to become President of the new republic of Poland. Paderewski was the performer to whom Rachmaninoff was most often compared, commanding extortionate fees and playing to vast crowds (an estimated twenty thousand) in Madison Square Gardens. For five years from 1919, until he returned to performing in 1924, Paderewski was off the concert scene, leaving the limelight and grand remuneration to Rachmaninoff.

Within a year, Rachmaninoff had become a cover pin-up. In its October 1919 issue, *Etude* magazine (an American music journal published 1883 to 1957) for the first time devoted the bulk of its editorial content to a single musician. Calling it the Rachmaninoff Number, the journal depicts the composer on the cover, sitting solemnly, playing, at a grand piano. The introductory article reads:

That we have now residing in America a great master – one who in future years will stand out on the pages of history, as stood his great predecessors – is in itself an honor we should not ignore. Not since Rubinstein visited America has any European composer-pianist of the stature of Sergei Rachmaninoff been with us. Simple, sincere, earnest, intense, granite in strength, yet fern-like in delicacy, the works of Rachmaninoff rank with the great music of all time.

'Fern-like in delicacy' is a pertinent phrase to remember.

He had made another recent appointment: his secretary, Dagmar Rybner, a pianist herself, as well as a composer. (A song of hers was premiered at Aeolian Hall in October 1918, shortly before Rachmaninoff's arrival in the US.) The shy Rachmaninoff, according to her own account, had to be summoned by his wife from behind the room's dividing curtain to greet his new employee. That summer, the Rachmaninoff family took a house on the Pacific West Coast, at Palo Alto, on the south-western shores of San Francisco Bay. The air, as he wrote to Miss Rybner, was 'heavenly'.[18]

'You Know What Means to Me a Car'

Cars were Rachmaninoff's passion. Only his wife and children got more attention. In Ivanovka he had been a pioneer driver, owning a jaunty Loreley Tourer, with a right-hand drive. The unexpected spelling is easily explained: the German car company, Ley, saw the potential for uniting its own name with that of Lorelei, the legendary Rhinemaiden whose singing charmed passing sailors. The marque had particular success in the Russian empire. In Moscow in 1911, twenty-three out of 826 registered cars on the road were Loreleys. This tiny number of vehicles confirms the novelty of an automobile in the Tambov region a year later when Rachmaninoff acquired his: 'When I become too tired to work, I get into my car and speed some fifty versts away [thirty-three miles] . . . I take deep breaths and praise the freedom and the blue skies. After this air bath, I feel strong again and full of life.' As he recalled, even the dogs and horses were frightened. When they stopped, people crowded round: 'Driving around a shed, we hit a pothole and the car jolted. At this moment, a dog jumped out of its kennel, barking ferociously. When it saw the extraordinary monster roar at it, the dog got so frightened that it plummeted into the tall grass. Wherever we went we sowed terror and astonishment.'[19]

His saga continues: at last they were out on a level road. 'The car started riding so fast that the wind hummed in our ears. Seeing a car for the first time, a herd of young horses scattered in different directions with their tails and manes streaming behind them.' Rachmaninoff humorously compared (recorded by Riesemann) a good conductor with a good driver. 'The qualities that make the one also make the other. They are concentration, an incessant control of attention, and presence of mind: the conductor only has to add a little sense of music.'[20]

In America he was obsessed, scarcely too strong a word, with the ever more luxurious and technically advanced limousines appearing on the domestic market. The care and safety of his own vehicles would become a preoccupation, as his poor, put-upon agents would learn, very nearly as vital as his concert programme or having the right piano at a given venue. When he sailed to and from Europe, his latest deluxe model Lincoln came with him. Rachmaninoff's correspondence with his London agent, Robert Leigh Ibbs of Ibbs and Tillett, reveals his order of priorities. In 1930, his motorcar was to sail across the Atlantic. An important part of his entourage was to go ahead of him on the SS *Lancastria*. Rachmaninoff recorded his concerns about the precious cargo:

505 West End Avenue, New York City
5 March 1930

My dear Mr Ibbs,

On March 22nd, on SS *Lancastria*, I will ship my new
Lincoln car to Le Havre, France. I would appreciate it if you
call on the Secretary of the AA Association and ask him to
instruct their agent at Le Havre to take care of my car upon
its arrival at Le Havre. As I am sailing on SS *Mauretania* on
April 9 to Cherbourg, I could come from Paris to Le Havre
on April 17–18 only and take delivery of my car. Therefore I
would prefer that my car should be in care of the Automobile
Association's agent from the time of its arrival up to the day
when I will take it. You know what means to me a car, and
especially a new car, and you will understand that I could not
sleep quietly if I would not know that my car is in a safe place.
Kindly let me know the name and address of the agent at
Le Havre, as I shall communicate with him immediately upon
my arrival in Paris.

505 West End Avenue, New York City
6 March 1930

My dear Mr Ibbs,

Referring to my letter mailed to you yesterday, I forgot to
tell you that I overlooked to pay my membership fees to the
Automobile Association. Will you [be] so kind as to pay it for
me and charge my account with you. One more request: kindly
ring up Mayfair 3119, Pharmacy Nelson & Co., 73 Duke
Street, and find out if there is any outstanding bill for me. If so,
kindly pay that bill too.

Sincerely yours,
S. Rachmaninoff.

Telegram dated 1 April 1930 from New York to Ibbs and Tillett:
Have you arranged Automobile Association regarding my car
shipped March twenty-second to Havre. Rachmaninoff[21]

The Rachmaninoffs were sailing on the SS *Mauretania*, elderly
but still fast, with a grandeur described by Franklin D. Roosevelt
as 'having a soul you could talk to'. The novelist Theodore Dreiser
revelled in its luxurious Edwardian interior: 'It was a beautiful thing
all told – its long cherry-wood panelled halls, its heavy porcelain
baths, its dainty state rooms fitted with lamps, bureaus, writing desks,
wash-stands, closets and the like.' A bugler signalled guests to dinner
'as if to say "This is a very joyous event, ladies and gentlemen. We are
all happy."'[22] All, that is, except Rachmaninoff. From Paris he immediately wrote again to his agent. This time he addressed Mr Tillett,
Mr Ibbs having sustained a cricketing injury ('Please do not play
again that awful game that was so bad for you,' Rachmaninoff urged
him). After some minimal business niceties, he gets to the point:

May I ask you to see the secretary of the AA Club again and to
tell him that I got my car in perfect order, but was surprised
to see that the plates were given out in France instead of Gr.
Britain, which I do not like for many reasons. (F No . . . Instead
of G.B. No . . .) Could these be changed for G.B. ones or have
the French plates already been registered?

The car anxieties never ceased. To Somov from Manchester on
20 April 1935 he wrote:

That's all for today. There are exactly four weeks to go until the end of my concert season. May we live to see it! I'm waiting for my car. They are checking the dynamo. Might it be a good idea to charge it up again? Please do!

To Somov, that loyal friend and patient employee with whom one has increasing sympathy, he wrote from San Francisco in 1937:

It doesn't seem to me as though Charlie [Foley, agent] has done anything about my car, otherwise I would surely have heard something about it, and because I won't have either time or opportunity during the three days I shall be in New York to do anything about it myself I have decided to stick with the old one, and therefore would like you *immediately* to take care of what needs to be done. Please take it to the Lincoln dealer and, if possible, go for a test drive yourself with the mechanic. I'm worried about the following things:

1) it is very difficult to start, and therefore 2) the carburettor must be examined, as was suggested to me by Mercedes in Germany, and 3) it pulls very sluggishly. 4) The steering must be adjusted and tightened up, as it wanders. 5) Take out and throw away the radio; they advised me in Europe it's the reason why the clock has not been working all summer. In any case the radio itself is not worth a row of beans. 6) Either have it mended, or, better, install a new clock. 7) Renew all six outer tyres. 8) If there can be found in New York *inner* tubes *equivalent to those that are currently on my wheels*, have them replaced. If there aren't any, please have the present ones checked, as I should prefer to keep them rather than replace them with new tubes that are susceptible to punctures. 9) The car should be sent to Europe no later than

15th March, so you will have to get on with the trip ticket right away. Which line? Doesn't matter, but I would prefer an American line going to Le Havre. And finally, 10) If Lincoln could have the car resprayed in black steel colour in time, this should be done.

I think that is everything. If you could take this on with your customary energy, I should be very grateful.[23]

Anyone lacking a knowledge of carburettors, steering mechanisms or inner tubes would have been unwise to engage in a car conversation with Rachmaninoff.

Home Thoughts

Conceivably his more than hobbyist fixation with cars took his mind off memories of a Russia which no longer existed. A Soviet country now stood on the same land, with the same vistas and cities, but all else changed. As the *New York Times* reported on 12 April 1925, in a feature on these new Russian arrivals to America: 'They forget the present and through their artists and their singers go back to the days that are forever ended. Their artists, like themselves, are refugees. They meet to live over the life they have left.' A new shadowland was taking shape: Russia Abroad, complete with clichés, stereotypes, fashions, prejudices. In early 1920s New York City, clusters of 'first wave' White Russians in exile began to gather, in Hamilton Heights and across what became 'Russian Harlem', around Mount Morris Park, now Marcus Garvey Park, leaving an imprint in streets, shops, cafes, theatres, churches. (The 'second wave' would come after World War II, with a third in the 1970s, colonising at Brighton Beach. The impoverished Jewish Russian community, another story, favoured the Lower East Side.)

Russian bookshops, restaurants and food shops opened. New York's famous Russian Tea Room, near Carnegie Hall and founded by former members of the Russian Imperial Ballet, welcomed its first customers in 1927. Every Thursday, the basement of the Episcopal Church of St Andrew, on 127th Street, became a weekly rendezvous for gatherings of these new residents. As the same *New York Times* article reported, this was a coming together of 'the Russian colony of aristocrats, intellectuals and artists now in New York' (Rachmaninoff could fall into any of those categories). Most had been in the country only a year or two, all remnants of 'an empire and a period to which 'finis' has been written'. Rachmaninoff, with several fellow musicians, was one of the first to donate to Christ the Savior Russian Orthodox Church when it was founded in 1924. Its Russian Club, in the building next door, held its own weekly evenings of folk and gypsy music. Russia in American eyes was a world of Imperial Theatre ballet, fur hats, pure snow-covered landscapes. Its other side was dark, mystical, with a brooding, sensual eroticism associated, in the vaguest, least understood or acceptable and most stereotypical way, with gypsies, Tatars and a generic Asiatic-Russianness. Tsar Nicholas II's mystical adviser, Grigori Rasputin, seen as a holy devil, epitomised that kind of exotic-erotic, almost fantastical Russia.

The Russian landscape, too, had acquired its own, hyper-real character, intensified through English-language fiction. Virginia Woolf, through Sasha in her novel *Orlando*, conjures a potent Russia of long sunsets, frozen rivers ten miles wide, wild horses, men who gashed each other's throats open and million-candled Christmas trees 'hung with yellow globes, incandescent enough to light a whole street by'.[24] In the introduction to *Ashenden: or The British Agent* (1928), Somerset Maugham would recall his journey to Russia in 1917. 'I was sent to prevent the Bolshevik Revolution and to keep Russia in the war. The reader will know that my efforts did not meet with success.' He describes a train journey through Siberia where, stopping at 'some station', he encountered several war-weary soldiers. One of them, who had been blinded, began to sing, accompanying himself on an accordion.

> I could not understand his words, but through his singing, wild and melancholy, I seemed to hear the cry of the oppressed: I felt the lonely steppes and the interminable forests, the flow of the broad Russian rivers and all the toil of the countryside, the ploughing of the land and the reaping of the ripe corn, the sighing of the wind in the birch trees, the long months of dark winter; and then the dancing of women in the villages and the youths bathing in shallow streams on summer evenings.[25]

All this filtered into the cinema, from the early 1920s onward. Cecil B. de Mille chose the name of a popular song for his silent film *The Volga Boatman* (1926). The film is set in the Russian Revolution but 'it pleads no cause, takes no sides'[26]; DeMille had no wish to be mistaken as a Communist. In the wake of the film's release, both Kreisler (in a violin version) and Chaliapin made new recordings of the Russian song.

Naturally the plot revolves round a White Russian prince in the Tsar's Army, a princess with whiter-than-white skin, a bare-chested Bolshevik boatman, a gypsy who can wolf-whistle and a mute, child-of-nature blacksmith. This last was played by the alluring Muscovite Theodore Kosloff, one of Diaghilev's dancers and, given his looks and physique, quite a matinee idol. At Kosloff's death in Los Angeles in 1956, a baby grand piano was left behind in his house which had been played, according to hearsay, by Rachmaninoff. It probably had. In those close émigré circles, everyone knew everyone and no doubt many had pianos.

Making Myths

In smart salons across New York, America's super-rich were beguiled by pre-Revolutionary Russian fashion, as if imagining a return to a Tsarist world of fur-trimmed, bejewelled glamour. Some purchased the black-market gems and jewels being sold up and down Fifth Avenue, with labels such as 'Tsaritsa' or 'Romanov' attached. One such precious item, bearing the insignia of Catherine the Great, was bought by a monied automobile industrialist. (Founded in mid-nineteenth-century Kyiv, the New York antique store À la Vieille Russie, with its paintings of Russian nobility and Fabergé collection, is a vital remnant of that world.)

High-society women with wealth at their disposal, such as Mrs Theodore Roosevelt Pell and Mrs Cornelius Vanderbilt, involved themselves in organising Russian-themed balls, from around 1922 onwards. On occasion, Rachmaninoff featured as honoured guest and performer. Newspapers carried long articles on the influx of White Russian nobles whose status had been ripped from them: the duke who once rode down the Nevsky Prospect, gold jingling in his pockets, now struggling to pay his rent in Brooklyn; the young lieutenant forced to take work as a docker; the elderly colonel doing shifts at a bakery. So many had never had to think about earning money before, their hands used only to twiddling 'the pommel of a sword or the tassel of a fan'.[27]

A princess, a real princess in a land without its own royal family, was known to be waiting at table in a Russian restaurant.

They tell you how she used to sit at her own board in far-away Russia, with the snow piled up at the windows, the sleigh bells tinkling in the winter air and the guests arriving for dinner. Looking at her, it is easy to call up the smoking boar's head on the table, the roaring fire on the hearth, the sparkling wine in the thin glasses, the servants awaiting her nod. But today she is serving a few tables in one of the city's new colourful Russian corners.

With the pity came an irresistible romance, for these people were perceived as intellectuals, superior beings in the eyes of a young country like America. They brought with them 'their art of the stage and brush, their sad, heart-touching music, and a certain devil-may-care good fellowship in the face of adversity that is not to be dented'.[28] Dancers were flooding in, hoping to steal the stage from their American counterparts, meanwhile working as seamstresses or scenery painters. So too were musicians from the imperial orchestras, 'coming by every ship', bringing training and technique of the highest Europe could offer. They arrive and find jazz and the saxophone, noted the *New York Times* reporter. One musician, fearing the 'prostitution of his art', unable to give up Tchaikovsky, had committed suicide. For Russians, music was as important as bread and borscht. These were, in part, Rachmaninoff's audiences. With scarcely enough money to buy food, they turned up to every concert given by one of their fellow countrymen, sitting in the back rows and dreaming, 'looking across the expanse of ocean and Europe and wasted homeland to the St Petersburg that used to be and the Moscow that never will be again'.[29]

Moscow, however, still had its own memories of Rachmaninoff and, belatedly, celebrated his fiftieth birthday. Larger than life-sized posters of him were on display.[30] All three piano concertos featured in one concert. His old Conservatory allies – Alexander Goldenweiser, Samuel Feinberg and Konstantin Igumnov – were now leading figures at the Moscow Conservatory, championing a new Soviet piano tradition which was, in reality, an old Russian one. Their names may mean little today but they were part of Rachmaninoff's Russian heyday: Goldenweiser had been his duet partner, and dedicatee of his Second Suite for two pianos. Igumnov had taught both Rachmaninoff's wife, Natalia, and the soprano Nina Koshetz. He would one day co-edit a posthumous Soviet edition of Rachmaninoff's piano works.

These friends were keeping the flame alive. They might have had hopes that Rachmaninoff would still return home. They knew the burden of exile was stifling his energies; surely even this new Soviet existence would suit him better? In 1922 he confided to Vilshau that he was only playing the piano and had not composed 'one line' (in fact he made a cadenza for Liszt's Second Rhapsody that year). At the end of the season he told the same friend that his hands were nearly paralysed and he couldn't write. Whether from fatigue or from a loss of habit, he was 'not drawn' to composition. It was five years since he had worked on anything major.

Deals and Contracts

From his first reappearances in America Rachmaninoff, unlike most fellow exiles, had a high earning capacity. He was courted by managers and concert bookers, as well as piano companies pledging money if he would agree to play their instruments. He opted for Steinway & Sons, which offered no payment but served, and was trusted by, his pianist colleagues. The company's then director, Frederick Steinway, became a friend, and Rachmaninoff remained loyal to the firm throughout his career. However withdrawn or shy Rachmaninoff was in so many aspects of life, he was not hesitant in trying to secure high fees. In 1919 his American recording career took off: the labyrinthine history of what he recorded, for whom, with whom and on what, is assessed in detail by Max Harrison in *Rachmaninoff: Life, Work, Recordings*.[31]

To tell this early stage briefly: a session with Ampico, the American Piano Company, makers of player pianos and reproducing pianos, resulted in nine rolls, mostly of his own music, as well as his version of 'The Star-Spangled Banner'. Between 1919 and 1933 he made a total of thirty-five Ampico recordings. Soon after, he began sessions with Thomas Edison, maker of the first gramophone records. Recordings from this period include the C sharp minor Prelude (among other Rachmaninoff works), two Chopin waltzes and Liszt's Hungarian Rhapsody no. 2. This last, spread over three ten-inch records, featured Rachmaninoff's new and dazzling cadenza, which occurs before the hellish octaves of the coda. (On the score, Liszt invites the performer to play their own 'ad lib' cadenza.) This last is a remarkable aural document: both for displaying Rachmaninoff's pianistic brilliance, and for sounding as if the two composers have, for a moment, spectacularly forged their styles together.

For whatever reason, probably concerning disagreements over which take the pianist and the recording company preferred, Edison dallied too long in pinning down Rachmaninoff with a proper contract. That company was pipped by the Victor Talking Machine Company, with whom he signed a deal on 22 April 1920. The first contract stipulated twenty-five 'items' over five years, with a guaranteed annual advance against royalties of $15,000 (approximately $225,000 in today's money).[32] So began a long association with RCA, though Rachmaninoff was so fastidious and self-critical, as well as nervous in the studio, that the experience was not always happy. Little wonder, given his perfectionism, that he always refused to broadcast live on the radio.

He had been money-aware even when domiciled in Russia. In the States, as he adapted to life as a full-time soloist, his income soared. With a family to support, and a taste for comfort, this desire for income is understandable: more a reflection of anxiety than avarice. He had debts to pay, too, to those who had helped him leave Russia. As soon as he could (from the autumn of 1920), he would begin sending money regularly to his mother and the rest of his family, as well as his wife's, the Satins.

He also contributed to appeals to help his homeland, whenever possible sending funds, as he would for the rest of his life. The famine in Russia from 1921–2, caused by crop failure and civic chaos, had attracted worldwide attention. One of the largest peasant uprisings was in Rachmaninoff's home region of Tambov. It was quelled, brutally, by the Red Army, who marched in with guns and poison gas and murdered tens of thousands. In the summer of 1921 Lenin made a global appeal for 'bread and medicine'.[33] He was supported in this by Maxim Gorky (whose political allegiances changed many times). For Rachmaninoff to witness his old friend Gorky's embrace of Lenin and Communism cannot have been easy.

Rachmaninoff was generous to a fault. In April 1922, his benefit concert with the New York Symphony Orchestra at Carnegie Hall raised $7,100 (around $110,000 today): 'a vast sum when translated into Russian currency', as the *New York Times* reported, which would aid 'composers, artists and men of letters now destitute in the pianist's home country'.[34] It was distributed through the American Relief Administration (ARA), chaired by Herbert Hoover, then Secretary of Commerce. Rachmaninoff was soloist in both his Second and Third piano concertos and the conductor was Walter Damrosch, who with the same forces had given the premiere of the Third in 1909. (On that first New York tour Rachmaninoff had then played the concerto under the baton of Gustav Mahler. The composer-pianist was full of admiration for the composer-conductor's attention to detail. Their embryonic acquaintance was cut short by Mahler's early death.) Now, more than a decade later, the audience cheered the soloist until at last Rachmaninoff came out alone and played the notorious Prelude.

His largesse extended to almost anyone who asked. The Rachmaninoff archive in the Library of Congress, Washington, contains countless letters, from individuals and organisations, offering thanks for his bounty. At times a fundraising concert may simply have been an opportunity to play, to try out repertoire, to avoid sitting at home dwelling on the difficulties of his new life, and his failure to compose. In 1922, for example, the *New York Times* reported that 'a large assembly greeted Rachmaninoff' at his concert at the Waldorf-Astoria in aid of the Babies' Dairy Association.[35] A long list of women's names, there to support the cause, is given, but no record survives of the programme. Was he really a dedicated supporter of this particular cause?

One beneficiary was Nikolai Avierino, who had been a close associate of Tchaikovsky and Scriabin, and was friendly with Siloti and Chaliapin. The virtuoso violinist had played violin and piano duos with Rachmaninoff, and enjoyed a successful career in Moscow. Now he wrote from Athens where he was living in penurious exile, playing in a hotel orchestra. Rachmaninoff replied:

I am sending you 1500 drachmas today. Forgive me for sending so little! I can't manage more. [. . .] You ask about America? God keep you from trying to come here. There are ten candidates for every musical position. Besides, you'd never be given a visa with the recent ruling of this government, caused by an unprecedented flood of immigrants. Go to Paris, or London, or wherever you wish in Europe, but forget the 'Dollar Princess'.[36]

Undeterred, Avierino did eventually move to America in 1923, teaching and then, in the 1930s, playing viola in the Boston Symphony Orchestra.

After Rachmaninoff's second season in America, the family retreated to Goshen in Orange County, New York State, for the summer. Just as he had the previous year in Palo Alto, Rachmaninoff worked hard on learning new material – including some of *Children's Corner* by Debussy, a composer generally alien to him, as well as more Mozart, Beethoven, Chopin, Liszt, Schumann, Grieg, Daquin, Weber, Medtner. He knew well enough that he needed to expand his repertoire to nourish his busy recital schedule. His relaxation, as at Ivanovka, was to drive out for the day, in this instance, to the Shawangunk Ridge, part of the Appalachian Mountains, with his Russian chauffeur-mechanic. Perhaps he never forgot what he had written to Marietta Shaginian back in 1912, with some irony, at a time of creative difficulties: 'No wonder if I should after a while, make up my mind to abandon composition altogether and become, instead, a professional pianist, or a conductor, or a farmer, or even, perhaps, an automobilist . . .'[37]

Crossings, Meantime

Natalia Rachmaninoff's brother Vladimir Satin and his extended family had managed to leave Russia at the start of 1920, departing with other refugees from Yalta, landing at Constantinople. As Rachmaninoff's niece, Sophia Satin, recalled: 'Russian refugees were not popular in Turkey . . . there were placards everywhere stating "Russians and dogs are not welcome".'[38] The family eventually managed, via Greece and Venice, to reach Vienna, which was crowded with soldiers. Eventually they reached Dresden, where they soon reunited with the Rachmaninoffs on their European sojourn.

Rachmaninoff was concerned about Medtner, now a great friend (after the Shaginian years) and still in Russia. He persuaded Steinway's to invite Medtner to tour in America, thereby giving him a safe route out of Russia. The company requested an immediate reply. Medtner received neither the original telegram nor letter until the following February, which was too late. Instead he managed to go to Berlin. Germany did not welcome him. Rachmaninoff again urged him to come to the United States, with talk of possible contracts with Duo-Art, the piano roll company.[39] Rachmaninoff was a loyal cheerleader, but actually played little of Medtner's music, including only the short *Novellen* or one or two of the *Fairy Tales* in his recitals. Rachmaninoff was canny, and understood his audience. Broadening his material was one thing, which he did, assiduously. Introducing long works by unfamiliar composers, which he did not, was quite another.

He offered Medtner, out of his own pocket, fifty thousand marks, to help with various debts. Rachmaninoff also sympathised with the difficulties of life in Germany, saying he likewise felt the 'estrangement' of life in America, with few 'real and sincere' musicians around. Speaking, a few months earlier, to *Etude*, the celebrated pianist-composer presented a subtly different story. The upheaval in Russia prevented attempts at creative work. The US was the only place to be. 'I am in America at present for the reason that nowhere else in the world is there such music as there is here now. You have the finest orchestras, the most musically appreciative people, and I have more opportunity to hear fine orchestral works, and more opportunity to play.'[40]

The flood of migration from Russia continued apace. Prokofiev, in London on 28 May 1920, pondered in his diary on the whereabouts of friends and colleagues, several of them musicians. He had been to a show by the Russian artist Alexander Yakovlev:

The opening [was] attended by a large number of Russians, some of whom had recently arrived from Petrograd. I could not find anything out about Myaskovsky, Asafyev, Suvchinsky or Boris Verin. Benois and Siloti are in Finland. Medtner, Borovksy and Koussevitzky are safely in Moscow. Karatygin and Glazunov are still in Petrograd, and when last seen were not looking at all good. [. . .] The exhibition had made me tired, and when I left it I boarded a bus and went out to relax in Greenwich park to 'visit the meridian'.[41]

Man of a Hundred Faces

Siloti, as Prokofiev mentions, had managed to leave Russia, after a terrible ordeal. He and his wife and daughter had slept, fully dressed, in the unheated kitchen of their Petrograd apartment, where they were confined. The bedrooms and salon had been taken over by soldiers. Vera Siloti was the daughter of Pavel Tretyakov, the prominent banker, textile magnate and influential collector of Russian art. (The Tretyakov Gallery in Moscow today houses his bequest.) The politically liberal Siloti found himself in the line of fire due to his wide range of social associations.

Help came through the deliciously mysterious figure of an Englishman, Paul Dukes (1889–1967), the 'man of a hundred faces'. He deserves more than a footnote. Born in Somerset, trained at the St Petersburg Conservatory, he was skilled both as musician and linguist. In his musical guise, he coached singers at the Mariinsky Theatre as well as, for a period, acting as assistant conductor to Albert Coates (who, by 1919, was conductor of the London Symphony Orchestra, but would return to Soviet Russia to conduct, among other works, Rachmaninoff's *The Bells*).

Dukes had another, hidden existence. In addition to his public skills, he was deft at forgery and self-disguise, with a double life as a British MI6 officer and secret agent. Changing his name frequently, writing on tracing paper in almost illegibly tiny hand-writing, or blackening a tooth, was part of his complex spy-kit. With chameleon ability, he inveigled himself into Soviet life, into the Communist Party, the Red Army and the police (known as the *Cheka*). He was at the Finland Station for Lenin's famous arrival and at the same time had direct dealings with Winston Churchill. His main energies, working with a network of couriers, were spent smuggling people out of Russia via Finland to the west, including surviving members of the Romanov family (two nieces of Nicholas II), as well as the Silotis.

Knowing Siloti through musical connections, Dukes visited him at the Conservatory, as usual using a different name, only disclosing his identity – the whole episode, with its big reveal, is theatrical – after stripping off his false beard. He offered Siloti and his wife safe passage. They readily accepted, hiding in the back of a troika and leaving Petrograd in early 1920. Their daughter Kyriena Siloti remembers seeing a butcher wrap up meat in pages of her father's music, his library having been impounded by the Bolsheviks.

They made it to Germany, then Siloti went to London and performed with two star cellists. One was Pablo Casals, who lent him money – pitifully, given Vera's fabulous wealth until that point. The other was Guilhermina Suggia, immortalised in a portrait by Augustus John (now in Tate Britain). Then the family set sail for America on 17 December 1921, arriving at Ellis Island on Boxing Day. A circle of Russian musicians greeted them, and Siloti's old friend Coates, as clever at reinventing himself as Dukes and now established Stateside, gave him a date with the New York Symphony Orchestra in Philadelphia.

The selling point in the event's promotion was 'Siloti, pupil of Liszt . . .', while another headline, arguably more dispiriting for the pianist, announced him as 'Cousin of Rachmaninoff'.[42] The reviews were respectable but his American performing career never took off as he had hoped. He would enjoy a distinguished career teaching at the Juilliard School, keeping the Russian tradition of pianism alive, maintaining close ties with Rachmaninoff and, at the end of his life, enjoying lunches at his salon in the Ansonia Hotel or post-concert suppers at the Russian Tea Room with his old associate Stravinsky. He never enjoyed the creative influence which had been so central to Russian musical life in the old days.

As Stravinsky said to Kyriena Siloti: 'You know I am so grateful to your father. If it wasn't for him, we young people wouldn't [have known] modern music.'[43] Debussy and Ravel were rarely played in St Petersburg in the decade before *The Firebird*, 'but whatever performances did take place were due to the efforts of Alexander Siloti . . . It was Siloti who brought Schoenberg to conduct his *Pelleas und Melisande* in St Petersburg in 1912.'[44] As well as enabling the young Rachmaninoff's career at a critical moment, Siloti should be celebrated for another pivotal gesture of kindness: he introduced Stravinsky to Diaghilev, thereby acting as catalyst for one of the greatest artistic collaborations of the twentieth century.

Re-enter Nina Koshetz

In the continuing exodus from Russia, one eye-catching new arrival sailed into New York on the RMS *Pannonia*. Nina Koshetz had come, with her husband and eight-year-old daughter, via Constantinople. Prokofiev hurried to the harbour to meet her, his diary entry for 26 October 1920 telling us all we need to know:

When we arrived at the pier, we enquired where the first-class passengers were, to be told that on this ship there was only second class. Disembarkation began soon afterwards, and a steady stream of Greeks, Spaniards, Italians filed down the gangplank, bedraggled, grimy specimens of humanity laden with parcels done up with string – in a word a deeply dispiriting spectacle. All of a sudden there was Koshetz in her furs and diamonds flanked on one side by a clearly besotted Captain and on the other by his First Officer, behind them her husband, her daughter, her cousin, her secretary, an enormous doll, stewards, staggering under the weight of her trunks – the press representative [Mr Parmlee of Haensel's press agent] and I could only stare at one another with a wild surmise at this triumphant procession. The only thing I could possibly compare it with was the arrival of Babulenka in *The Gambler*. Koshetz, who had by the way become even lovelier than before, threw herself into my arms and called me the saviour of her and all her family.[45]

Prokofiev was halfway between disentangling himself from one affair, with a stage actress, Stella Adler, and entangling himself in a new one, with Lina, a singer, half-Spanish, half-Russian, who would become his wife. Beguiled by the elite circle of Russian artist exiles in New York, Lina had already encountered Rachmaninoff. Now she was in romantic thrall to his nemesis. She, like Koshetz, was the daughter of singers, but her talent was not in Koshetz's league. She greeted Nina's arrival with distrust, later telling Prokofiev that she had heard a good deal about this Koshetz woman, and that someone who knew her in Paris had labelled her a 'scoundrel' and an 'unbelievable show off' – polite in the circumstances.[46] Lina would have to tolerate Koshetz creating the role of Fata Morgana, the witch in Prokofiev's *Love for Three Oranges*, in Chicago the following year. She was going nowhere quietly.

However unreliable a witness he might be, Prokofiev could scarcely resist noting that relations between Koshetz and Rachmaninoff were cool. In a letter to Koshetz, Prokofiev had dismissively referred to Rachmaninoff's 'Polka concerts', belittling the latter's penchant for satisfying his audiences with popular bon-bons and salon pieces in his recitals. Now Prokofiev became more manipulative. Having settled the newly arrived Nina into her hotel – the fashionable Brevoort in Greenwich Village, where he himself was staying – Prokofiev 'told her of the truly intriguing correspondence that had occurred between Haensel and Rachmaninoff'.

According to Prokofiev, the agent Haensel, 'in the most courteous terms imaginable', had informed Rachmaninoff that Koshetz was coming to America. As she was not well known there, might Rachmaninoff help by introducing his compatriot to the Boston Symphony? Rachmaninoff responded by asking 'what sort of manager Haensel could be' not to be aware that orchestral concerts were fixed months earlier, 'in April, not October'. Prokofiev notes, in a barbed parenthesis, that Rachmaninoff seemed to have forgotten that he himself had arrived in November and was immediately offered engagements with all and sundry.

Haensel replied to Rachmaninoff. He had not 'expected a 'rude answer' to his 'polite letter', written, clearly mistakenly, as from one gentleman to another. Prokofiev reports: 'This information produced on Koshetz an effect like a thunderclap: as she said, when she had parted with Rachmaninoff three years ago, he had promised that whenever, or wherever, they met in future he would always do anything he could for her.' Dangerous words, if courteously offered.

Prokofiev continued plotting with Koshetz during her first days in New York. After taking her on a tour of the city 'from the top deck of an omnibus', he helped her draft a letter to Rachmaninoff. She was carrying letters from Russian friends to pass to him, so had a legitimate reason to be in contact. Prokofiev dismissed her first attempt and 'recommended she recast it according to my suggestions', concluding the letter: '"As I have never asked you for anything in the past, still less would it now have entered my head to ask you for anything." Koshetz was enraptured and called it a stroke of genius to end the letter in this way.'

The pair – that is, to be clear, Prokofiev and Koshetz – renewed their flirtations. A fortune-teller had predicted that her destiny was to be Prokofiev's lover. A day later (29 October 1920) Prokofiev noted with irritation that she still hadn't sent the letter to Rachmaninoff. In the midst of this ménage, her husband, Alexander von Schubert, an artist of modest talent, somehow managed to draw a portrait of Prokofiev, who commented: 'Although I sat patiently for him for two hours, I do not think it is a particularly good likeness.'[47] With her quick passions, apparently lax morals and grand diva behaviour, Koshetz was the wrong kind of person to be in Rachmaninoff's ordered life.

A Dusty Answer

Evidently she did send the letter concocted with Prokofiev. Rachmaninoff replied in stiff tones:

4 November 1920
New York

At some time in October (I don't recall the date as I did not keep the letter) I received a request from Haensel to secure an engagement for you in Boston with the Boston Orchestra, and for a week's tour with the orchestra. I replied that, as a manager, he should not only know me better, adding that by October all symphony organisations already have a full roster of artists. Privately, I considered that to make such an approach to me was strange and, in my experience, unprecedented. It has hitherto been my understanding that it is for *artists* to approach managers with requests to arrange concerts for them, but for a *manager* to approach artists with similar requests – this is the first time I have encountered such an occurrence. Furthermore, Haensel undoubtedly knows better than I do, that for an artist to secure an engagement in Boston without having previously appeared in America is practically an impossibility.

In response to my letter I received an 'abusive' one back from Haensel. I considered the incident closed . . . Great was therefore my astonishment to read in your letter to me that my response to Haensel's request, that is to say my brief and justifiable observation that by October orchestral managements already have their soloists lined up – this single observation! Nothing more! – 'would damage your first steps in America' and 'completely destroy your reputation and the belief in you not only of Haensel but of all his colleagues'?! I have specifically copied these turns of phrase to ask you, Nina Pavlovna, are you making fun of me? But you continue in the same tone, and ask me the 'inadmissible, dreadful, unanswerable' (and I would add, meaningless) question: 'Why??' I agree that it would be desirable to offer you some kind of reply.

I wish to state now, in order not to have to return to the subject later, that about ten days ago I had a letter from a lady unknown to me, Alice Preston, in which she writes that you are to appear in a concert under her auspices, and she would be glad if I would arrange another one. I replied that, unfortunately, arranging concerts is not what I do, but expressed my satisfaction that she does, and wished you all success. So far I have not received any abusive reply to my letter.

Then, last spring, another lady came to see me, wishing to know my opinion of your singing. I, of course, gave her the most glowing report. Also last spring, one of the Directors of the Metropolitan asked the same of my wife. She, naturally, answered in similarly positive vein. Finally, of another lady you mention, who is either planning to or already has visited me to ask about arranging engagements for you, I have no recollection.

That is the sum total of my felonious activities in regard to you. I regard the incident as now closed. In any case, I shall not reply to any possible future attempts to contact me with interrogatory or abusive correspondence.

I merely wish to tell you what has occurred, in what manner it occurred, and what has not . . .

With good wishes for your success and respect to you,

    S. Rachmaninoff[48]

Touché. Through her own network, Koshetz soon gave concerts in private homes of the rich, such as the Astors and Vanderbilts, introduced as the 'new Russian soprano'. The critic of the *New York Times*, Richard Aldrich, reviewed her song recital in March 1921 at Town Hall, where she sang works by Rimsky-Korsakov, Mussorgsky, Scriabin and Prokofiev ('many of them are dedicated to her') – but nothing by Rachmaninoff. Aldrich praised her Russian songs but scorned her Handel, 'for which her style and her technical equipment are not fitted'. He concluded that her voice 'is powerful but disappoints in its quality, especially in the upper tones', with a tendency to sing flat.[49]

Koshetz battled on undeterred, writing Prokofiev long letters full of gossip about New York life and her snub by Rachmaninoff. She took up residence at 610 Riverside Drive (at 138th Street) in the Russian area of Hamilton Heights, sufficiently far from Rachmaninoff's own five-storey residence at No 33 Riverside Drive. In one of her seances, 'the spirits told me' that she would be singing at the Metropolitan Opera in two months, that there would be a concert at Carnegie and 'I'll be in contact with Rachmaninoff in two weeks and he'll even be accompanying me this season'.[50] The spirits were not accurate. Soon Prokofiev, too, grew tired of her, and complained he would need bodyguards to quell her constant advances. They negotiated one another's tantrums in Chicago, where *Love for Three Oranges* received its premiere on 30 December 1921, to mixed reviews.

Eventually the opera reached New York. Aldrich, again in the *New York Times*, disliked it intensely, saying its confusion made *Alice in Wonderland* seem 'like a treatise on inductive logic'.[51] On the same page, a short column was devoted to a piano recital: 'Rachmaninoff's recital at Carnegie Hall the previous evening was full to overflowing on the same night that saw the only production here of an opera by his countryman, Sergei Prokofiev. The lucky audience, in a programme of Beethoven, Chopin, Liszt and some of the composer's own *Études-Tableaux* op. 39, had been rewarded with the C sharp minor Prelude.'

In Moscow, too, their names were yoked. The critic and composer Leonid Sabaneyev (1881–1968), surveying the 'anaemic' contemporary music scene in Soviet Russia, bemoaned the absence of new, post-Revolutionary voices and pitted 'modernists' against the 'conservatives', Prokofiev and Rachmaninoff, before discounting the pair altogether. He acknowledged Prokofiev's energy and sense of mischief but pitied his lack of psychological depth. Sabaneyev may have pulled his punches with Prokofiev, having once lambasted a new work of his when the performance was in fact cancelled (never a strong card for a critic). That said, in his influential *Modern Russian Composers* (1927), Sabaneyev condemned Rachmaninoff's First Symphony as being a melange of Russian ecclesiastical melodies. Had he been at the premiere or even seen the score? It seems unlikely, given firstly his youth at the time and secondly the comprehensive disappearance of the autograph manuscript and, at that stage, the orchestral parts too. He could scarcely conceal his disdain for Rachmaninoff: he is 'not even the yesterday of art. He is from some day last week. An interesting day admittedly, but a mournful one. We cannot really deal with him here for everything he wrote in the last few years was created in an American climate.'[52]

Escaping all this personal and professional unease, Rachmaninoff and the family beat a retreat for the summer. They were happy to be with their Russian friends abroad. This year they chose Locust Point, New Jersey, on the shores of the Atlantic Ocean, fifty miles from New York. Natalia's sister, Sofia Satina, one of the entourage, describes it:

Living next door were Rachmaninoff's close friends Yevgeny Somov, his wife and mother. Staying in a nearby Russian-run guest house were more Russians, with whom Rachmaninoff had frequent contact. [. . .] His chauffeur was a former Russian officer. Here, and for all the subsequent years he lived abroad, wherever and whenever it was possible to do so, Sergei Vasilievich invariably chose Russian people to look after him. Following the departure of Joe and his wife, the Rachmaninoffs always had Russian chauffeurs, chefs, cooks and domestic servants; the food at dinner was always Russian cuisine. In short, Sergei Vasilievich always opted for anyone or anything bearing a Russian stamp despite the inconveniences and complications this practice often incurred [. . .]

In the main, Sergei Vasilievich was treated by Russian doctors. Whenever he had time he would attend lectures and presentations given by Russians, and generally maintained a circle of acquaintances consisting for the most part of Russians. Only among such company could he feel himself unconstrained, free to laugh, joke and be relaxed in spirit.[53]

Burdens of Success

Fruitful personnel changes took place in Rachmaninoff's life around this time. Charles Foley took over from Charles Ellis as manager, on Ellis's retirement. Yevgeny Somov, a friend from Moscow days and a lifelong intimate of the family, became secretary, Dagmar Rybner having responded to the call of marriage (though she did maintain her music career, mainly teaching piano and voice). At Rachmaninoff's request, Somov wrote to Konstantin Balmont, the 'Silver Age' poet who had supplied a translation for *The Bells* and was now living in impecunious exile in France. Money had been despatched to Balmont from Rachmaninoff. Somov informed him of this on 15 March 1922:

Much respected Konstantin Dmitrievich,

Sergei Vasilievich Rachmaninoff has heard from mutual acquaintances of the straitened financial circumstances in which you presently find yourself. Since he is himself exceptionally preoccupied just now with his concert tours, he has not been able to write to you personally, and therefore commissioned me to arrange a telegraphic transfer to you of 500 francs from his account. This I have done today. I obtained your present address from the Morning newspaper, but since I am not completely certain of its accuracy would be grateful if you will confirm receipt of the money.

With greatest respect,

Ye. Somov

Konstantin Balmont bypassed Somov and wrote to Rachmaninoff in reply.

15 April 1922

43, Rue de le Tour, XVI Paris.

Thank you with all my heart for your goodness. I have received the 500 francs you sent me. It arrived at a most opportune time, and no matter how deep is my appreciation of this very real help to me in my present troubles, deeper still is my sense of the spiritual impulse by which you as a friend have been motivated to undertake such a beautiful and noble action. Ever since the days of my youth I have loved you as a supreme musical creator. I remember your first appearances in Moscow, I remember the first performance of your enchanting *Isle of the Dead*, the innumerable showers of ravishing sounds produced by your bewitching fingers, your transformation of 'Kolokolchiki and Kolokola' [his name for *The Bells*], and many other things that travel from soul to soul, from one artist to another. And now this act of kindness comes to me as a living embodiment of your voice from over the sea, a dazzling accumulation of sounds as they spill out from their creator's hands.

Tomorrow is Easter. Christ is risen. May heaven preserve you and may we meet one another again in Russia.

Your K. Balmont[54]

Rachmaninoff, soon to reach his fifties, may have been perceived by his friends, and by the many recipients of his charity such as Balmont, as rich and successful. He was, however, dealing with onerous seasons of sixty-six concerts (1921–2), then seventy-one (1922–3), which left him drained. Despite the usual plaudits, he was dissatisfied. Some of his more perceptive critics sensed it. In Boston, H. T. Parker (nicknamed 'Hard to Please') complained of Rachmaninoff's 'dry and dull mechanics'. In August 1922 Rachmaninoff described to Nikolai Medtner the daily electrical treatments he endured for aches in his head and hands. From London he wrote to Dagmar Rybner, saying that he was bored. He also admitted to her that, as a pessimist, he always chose sorrowful possibilities over joyous ones.

In a letter to his intimate friend Vladimir Vilshau, on 9 September 1922, he could barely conceal his feelings:

I dislike my occupation intensely. For this whole time I have not composed one line. I only play the piano and give a great many concerts. For four years now I practise, practise. I make some progress but actually the more I play, the more clearly do I see my inadequacies. If I ever learn this business thoroughly, it may be on the eve of my death. Materially I am quite secure. Bourgeois!

He adds that Natalia has changed little. 'She remains the same, though perhaps with a few more grey hairs.'[55]

Travels, Loss

Rachmaninoff was in London in spring 1922, playing two concerts at Queen's Hall (6 May and 20 May 1922). These were the first occasions on which Watson Lyle, who became the programme-note writer for Rachmaninoff's UK events, met his hero. He sympathised that Rachmaninoff, an avowed animal lover, could not keep large dogs in his New York apartment, 'which, as he pointed out to me, it would be sheer cruelty to attempt to keep there'. In summer, Lyle wrote, the Rachmaninoff family would 'go off to some country house, or farm. As far in the prairie country as possible, living the sort of life that attempted a kind of *rechauffage* of the previous summers at Ivanovka, "midst the illimitable plains of Southern Russia'.

Lyle's account, written and published in the early 1930s, has been dismissed for its chatty and admiring tone. It captures something, nevertheless, of Rachmaninoff's nature. He describes Rachmaninoff's 'characteristic' kindness, now his finances were more secure, in helping to 'rescue his wife's family, the Satins, from the hardships of their lot due to Bolshevik persecution'. He notes that Rachmaninoff had 'laid aside' composition since leaving Russia, but when someone enquired, 'he answered with one of his slow, amused smiles' that he had written something – 'a cadenza to the Second Hungarian Rhapsody of Liszt!' Lyle is not shy of putting himself in the picture too:

[Rachmaninoff] gave me a long and searching look, a look
that was almost wistful in its intensity. Long afterwards, when
I came to know of the nervous tension of these days for him,
I recalled that look, and understood its meaning. We have
since laughed over it. Despite my excellent credentials [. . .]
there remained the possibility that I might be an emissary of
the powers of evil – such was the undercurrent of dread in

the social life of distinguished Russian émigrés in those days. Apparently what he saw behind my homely features and my clear blue eyes passed muster, for he turned and indicated a very comfortable armchair near the Steinway . . .

Lyle was alarmed by Rachmaninoff's state of health: once again neuritis, or neuralgia, which had stopped him in his attempts to travel to Russia the previous year. (It is unlikely that, even in good health, he would have been allowed to return.) An unsuccessful operation the previous spring had not solved the problem. He found a cure only some years later, according to Lyle after treatment from a doctor in Harley Street. The more likely explanation is that a Russian dentist in Paris eventually diagnosed a tooth problem nearly a decade later.

There were other reasons for Rachmaninoff's poor state:

He bore still the marks of his mental tortures and anxieties of the last months in Russia, before his escape, though the general impression I had of the threatened disintegration of a great soul may have been temporarily more evident by the blow his affections had recently sustained in the death, by accident, of his friend Nikolai Struve in Paris.[56]

Two years earlier, the dedicatee of *The Isle of the Dead* had been fatally struck, mid-conversation, by an elevator. Struve it was who had accompanied the Rachmaninoffs out of Russia to Scandinavia in 1917. He had persuaded Rachmaninoff to orchestrate the final song of the Fourteen Romances, op. 34, the melancholy 'Vocalise' (1915). Rachmaninoff immediately did, adding a soprano voice to the orchestration (and prompting countless arrangements, by other hands and for multiple combinations of instruments, of this short piece). The families were close friends; the two men had taken long walks together in Dresden where they were parishioners of the city's Russian Orthodox Church of St Simeon Divnogorets. That church boasted a choir made up of members of the Dresden opera. Turgenev, Dostoyevsky and Bakunin had been members of the congregation. Rachmaninoff and Struve, their lives intertwined, were steeped in this close-knit, exiled community.

Riesemann comments on the quality of Rachmaninoff's friendship with Struve: 'No previous devotion was so warm; as a rule, Rachmaninoff was so restrained in expressing his feelings . . . that the slightest deviation from his custom should be considered an exception and a sign of special disposition.' When Struve died, Rachmaninoff wrote a letter of condolence to his son, which said: 'He was my faithful and, moreover, my only friend.' There is no evidence that this was quite the case, but the sentiment is heartfelt. He said that he, too, now felt like an orphan.[57]

Dark Eyes, Hot Nights

Over the next few summers, the Rachmaninoffs' get-away continued to be Locust Point, where he could swim and sail and socialise. Chaliapin and friends from the Moscow Art Theatre, which brought Rachmaninoff's early operatic success, *Aleko*, to New York in 1925, visited. Not that he had any wish to dwell on this Italianate student work, claiming he was ashamed by this 'nonsense'. Late parties were a feature, when Chaliapin, in expansive mode, would sing Russian gypsy songs, peasant songs, opera, accompanied by Rachmaninoff on the piano. 'Dark Eyes' (*Ochi chernye*) was a favourite of both accompanist and singer, who had recorded it, famously, with full chorus, sobbing balalaikas and his own histrionic sighs. The exiled Russian chemist Ivan

Ostromislensky, a specialist in the manufacture of rubber and part of New York's eclectic Russian diaspora, witnessed this spirited music-making into the small hours, and described it in *Novoe Russkoe Slovo* ('Russian Word', the Russian newspaper published in New York and widely read across the United States): 'On that hot July night at Rachmaninoff's house the small drawing room was divided in two, for the stage and the audience, the first row on the floor in Turkish style. With Sergei Vasilievich at the piano Chaliapin pranked and charmed us all night . . . Our party broke up only at 5 a.m.'

Next morning, Ostromislensky reports, Rachmaninoff had creases in his 'parchment-like' skin and exaggerated pouches under his eyes, as well he might, 'but his mood was cheerful'. If the previous concert season had wearied Rachmaninoff, these all-night parties prompted another kind of exhaustion. The heavy-eyed host asked his scientist guest which music had made the greatest impression, and without waiting for an answer said: 'I'm sure it was "Dark Eyes". I don't doubt it. How [Chaliapin] sighed, that villain, how he sobbed "you have ruined me!" – I couldn't sleep for thinking "How God endowed you beyond other men . . . Oh that sigh!"'[58]

That sigh is readily audible, some might say downright excessive, on Chaliapin's recording. The song had become an archetype of the romantic Russian gypsy ideal. In fact it was not a traditional romance at all but a setting of words from 1843 by the Ukrainian poet Yevhen Hrebinka to a waltz composed by a German, Florian Hermann. Over the next two decades it would become a nostalgic mainstay, with versions by Al Jolson (Russian-born), Chet Atkins and Django Reinhardt. It also made cartoon appearances, ranging from *Krazy Kat* to *Bugs Bunny*. Vernon Duke (1903–69), born in Kyiv as Vladimir Dukelsky, a friend of Prokofiev and of Nina Koshetz, had a particular association with the song.

As Dukelsky, he was a classical composer of concert music, working with Diaghilev and noticed by Aaron Copland and the young Elliott Carter. Reinvented as Duke, a collaborator with Gershwin, he was a deft spinner of Broadway songs ('April in Paris' among them). He made no attempt to unite his two musical styles, happily identifying his Dukelsky music as 'high genre' and his popular, jazzy side as 'low'. As he put it, quoted in an obituary, 'There's my Carnegie Hall self and my Lindy's self, my Russian heritage and my American influence.'[59] Rachmaninoff might have envied that easy-going acceptance of a divided, exile life, which he himself could never achieve. Duke's double personality is embedded, even so, in an arrangement he made in 1922, commissioned by Nina Koshetz, of Rachmaninoff's 'Vocalise', part of her attempt to win the composer over once again. The manuscript, held in the Morgan Library, New York, gives the title as: *Rachmaninoff's Vocalise, arranged by Vernon Duke: manuscript in the hand of the arranger, 1922.*

Koshetz's charm offensive continued when she performed a programme of Rachmaninoff at the Town Hall in 1923. A review noted that the 'large' audience included many Russians: 'Mr Rachmaninoff, for whom a box was reserved, was late in arriving, but two fellow composer-pianists present were Mr Siloti and the young Sergei Barsukov.'[60] Barsukov was the son of a Russian lieutenant, who had fought the Soviets and arrived in America penniless. He worked nights in a milk depot till he fell in with some Russians and launched a modest career, helped by his association with Koshetz. Did Rachmaninoff ever arrive at Town Hall that night, or was this a faint hope on Koshetz's part? Impossible to say.

Settled into his virtuoso-celebrity career, Rachmaninoff spoke to an interviewer about artistic inspiration. Nature, art, literature were important. He had a passion for Pushkin and, read in Russian, Shakespeare and Byron, but as for the female muse, here he was cautious:

A beautiful woman is certainly a source of perpetual inspiration, but you must run away from her and seek seclusion, otherwise you will compose nothing. Carry the inspiration in your heart and mind; think of her, but be all by yourself for creative work. Real inspiration must come from within.[61]

Technology, Flight, Money

Leaving mid-town Manhattan, we head an hour or two east out of New York City. The scene is a chicken farm on Long Island. The temperature is below freezing. Now being used as an open-air 'factory', the place looks ramshackle. Bent bed-frames and other bits of junkyard iron are being put to new use. A small group of labourers, working with hand tools for lack of proper machinery, has stopped work: it is too cold. The workforce is smaller than it was. Some have left the team. Money for the dream project to which they signed up is all but spent. They are no longer being paid.

The chicken farm's owner is Viktor Utgoff (1889–1930), a Russian noble and a much-decorated naval aviator in the Black Sea Fleet in World War I. The man in charge of the bed frames, junk iron and the labourers themselves, nearly all Russian immigrants, is Utgoff's fellow countryman, Igor Sikorsky (1889–1972), now living in America. Born into a family of doctors and Russian Orthodox priests, the aircraft pioneer made his first model flying machine at the age of twelve, in part inspired by his mother showing him the work of Leonardo da Vinci and Jules Verne. He never stopped inventing. Barely out of his teens, he attempted, unsuccessfully, to build a helicopter (the manufacture of which would later make the company's name). His fixed-wing aeroplanes, built for the Tsar, were used in World War I to defend Russia against Germany. He left Russia after the Revolution because the Bolsheviks threatened him with violence.

In New York in 1919, no one knew the newcomer. He taught high-school maths to earn cash. In March 1923 he set up the Sikorsky Aero Engineering Corporation on Long Island. He wanted, against the odds, to build a twin-engine, closed-cabin fourteen-passenger plane. The main structure of the fuselage was built with angle irons from discarded bedsteads. Turnbuckles, which were used to adjust wire tension, were found in a Woolworth's five-and-dime. Sikorsky's nephew, a ditch digger, was roped in, to dig space for the wheels and landing struts. The report on the Sikorsky website archive records a turning point in the company's early, troublesome history: 'One Sunday, a chauffeur-driven limousine drove up to the chicken house. A tall slender figure in a long black coat stepped out of the car and walked up to the airplane. In total silence, he inspected the aircraft.' Igor Sikorsky's son, Sergei, relates the story:

> Everyone on the farm got greatly excited. They all immediately recognised Sergei Rachmaninoff as their guest. My father went up to him and they began to talk. After about a half-hour visit, Rachmaninoff said: 'I believe in you and your plane and I want to help you.' The composer sat down and wrote a check for $5,000 [approx. $76,000 in 2022]. With a smile, he gave the cheque to the stunned Sikorsky and said, 'Pay me back when you can.'

Rachmaninoff wanted to help a fellow countryman follow through his visionary ideas. The financial contribution enabled Sikorsky to rent a hangar on Roosevelt Field, the Long Island runway from which Charles Lindbergh would take off for his historic solo transatlantic flight in 1927. The twin-engine, all metal, fourteen-passenger plane, S–29A (A for America) came into being. Only one such craft was made. It would be used by Howard

Hughes as a German plane in the film *Hell's Angels*, and crashed during filming. In thanks for his generous participation, Sikorsky invited Rachmaninoff to be the company's first vice-president. Rachmaninoff accepted. In 1929, Sikorsky was able to pay back the money, sending Rachmaninoff a cheque for $5,000 plus interest – with great pride, according to Sikorsky's son.

The two men visited each other regularly. Sikorsky was among the eminent Russians who attended Rachmaninoff's Carnegie Hall concerts. Rachmaninoff took his friend Josef Hofmann, pianist and inveterate inventor, to visit the Sikorsky plant at Stratford, Connecticut. One day they turned up, unannounced. Mrs Sikorsky had to make an impromptu lunch. Her son recalls:

> There were two or three reporters that were following
> Rachmaninoff to the factory and then to our house. My
> father had to walk out of the front door and ask the press.
> 'Gentlemen, please don't walk in our front yard or back yard.
> Please don't try to peek through the window and photograph,
> because it is very impolite. We are just here with friends.'[62]

The first profit the company made, fittingly, was by transporting two grand pianos from New York City to Washington, D.C.: one destined for a department store, the other for the wife of President Herbert Hoover, who had assisted Rachmaninoff in the business of sending food aid to Russia.

In 1939 all three men – Hoover, Rachmaninoff, Sikorsky – supported the establishment of the Tolstoy Foundation, a charity set up by Leo Tolstoy's youngest child, Alexandra Tolstoy, to assist Russian refugees in central Europe. Soon the charity, which had close links with the Russian Orthodox Church, New York, was bequeathed a farm, where a fond version of the Tolstoy family estate, Yasnaya Polyana, was created. Rachmaninoff would have enjoyed examining the livestock (four thousand chickens, thirteen hogs and six cattle). On Sundays grand feasts were served and visitors welcomed. Homegrown produce was turned into favourite Russian dishes, with cabbage and pickles for the borscht and sour cream (*smetana*) to go with it, followed by *kissel*. This berry dessert or drink, thickened with arrowroot, appears in Russian fairy tales as an epitome of plenty. A land of milk rivers and banks of *kissel* equates to paradise.

Jazz Notes, Jazz Jelly

Keen to disassociate himself from new American dance forms, Rachmaninoff insisted to friends back in Russia that rumours he had composed foxtrots were untrue. Curious about jazz, however, he was among the musicians invited to a one-off concert by Paul Whiteman and his Palais Royal Orchestra at Aeolian Hall, entitled 'An Experiment in Modern Music'. Whiteman and his orchestra had just released a cover version of the dance song 'Linger Awhile', which was now racing up the charts towards the No. 1 slot. His hordes of fans, dedicated or not, had no interest in experiments in modern music. Tickets were given away to 'paper' the concert on that midweek, midwinter's afternoon of Tuesday 12 February 1924. In the end the hall was full, but for Whiteman it was a financial disaster: he lost some $7,000 of his own money.

Stravinsky, Damrosch, Kreisler and the bandleader John Philip Sousa were in the crowd too. The programme consisted of more than two dozen items, by Jerome Kern, Irving Berlin and others, ending curiously with Elgar's *Pomp and Circumstance* March no. 1 (1901). The *New York Times* critic Olin Downes, judging that the event would have 'curdled the blood of a Stokowski or a Mengelberg', noted that the brass section included 'frying pans, large tin utensils and a speaking trumpet, later stuck into the end of a trombone'. One player blew into a bathtub. Another wore a squashed top hat. Whiteman, unlike Mengelberg or Stokowski, 'does not conduct. He trembles, wobbles, quivers – a piece of jazz jelly.'[63]

The concert was historic, one of the West Forty-Third Street venue's most famous events, a defining moment of the Jazz Age, and in some opinions, the quintessence of the entire Roaring Twenties. The reason was one work in particular. Whiteman had commissioned George Gershwin's *Rhapsody in Blue*, asking for an extended jazz concerto with the composer as soloist. As the Rhapsody was the penultimate event on the long programme, many people missed this vital world premiere, having already left to make snowbound journeys home.

The arrangement for smallish ensemble, complete with tenor banjo, was by Ferde Grofé, but the signature glissando which opens the work was an impromptu 'jazzy' touch that day by Whiteman's clarinettist, Ross Gorman. That languid upward slide became an indelible feature of the score. The audience (those who had stuck it out) loved the piece, the critics were cool, but the catchphrase soon used repeatedly was that Gershwin 'had made an honest woman out of jazz'. Downes, while slating Gershwin for his immaturity and technical incompetence, agreed that this was an exciting new work, a reinvention of that faded form, the classic piano concerto. He reported that the applause was 'tumultuous'. Above all, it was no 'mere dance-tune set'. Rachmaninoff had a friendly admiration for Gershwin, after his early death praising him as one of America's musical geniuses. He was always keen, however, to quell any idea that he himself had written any of the jazz and rag versions of his infernal C sharp minor Prelude.

Europe and a Wedding

The family, jazzed out and jaded, headed to Europe for a rest, arriving in Italy in time for Easter in Florence. As so often, Rachmaninoff had sundry health problems and was feeling unwell, which he attributed vaguely to 'old age, I suppose'. The Medtners were there; Rachmaninoff was still trying to help his friend launch an American career. Not for the first time, and perhaps defensively, Medtner asked Rachmaninoff why he no longer composed.

> He smiled and in return asked 'How can I compose without melody?' The melody had gone from his life, and until it returned he would not be able to defile his art, nor would he strain the power which he believed to be natural and spontaneous.[64]

He put on weight, considered healthy for his ever-angular frame. The blossoms were out, he wrote on a postcard to Dagmar Rybner, with whom he loyally kept in touch. As usual, he found a Russian 'colony', telling the Somovs they had discovered it 'when we attended the Russian Orthodox church for the bringing out of Christ's effigy on Good Friday, and for the midnight service. And these Russians, mostly titled, turn out to be nice, affable and amiable . . .' – one of many confirmations that Rachmaninoff, throughout his life, had the liturgical milestones of the Orthodox year deep in his psyche and routines, however passive or active his religious faith.

From Italy they all went to Zurich, and on to Germany, staying in Dresden, so fruitful for him in earlier years. At the end of May 1924, the Medtners went to Paris, which smelt of 'tar and petrol' and where they attended an all-Stravinsky concert conducted by Koussevitzky and including the premiere of the Concerto for

Piano and Wind.[65] It distressed them so much, Medtner complained to Rachmaninoff, that they left in the middle of *The Rite of Spring*, the last work on the programme. (A few years later, after hearing Richard Strauss's *Ein Heldenleben*, the sensitive and ultra-conservative Medtner had to walk round Central Park to recover.)

While the family was in Dresden, Prince Pyotr Volkonsky and Rachmaninoff's older daughter, Irina, became engaged. Volkonsky, in his mid-twenties, was from a noble and sprawling St Petersburg family. He was working to become a painter and sculptor. After the quickest of engagements, the pair were married weeks later on 24 September 1924. In a letter to his friend Vilshau, Rachmaninoff described the new liaison as 'unexpected', requiring a sudden change in travel plans. The day after the wedding the bride's parents would leave for concerts in London – 'but there are only three of us now (Irina and her husband will spend the winter in Munich)'[66] – and from there, in mid-October, return to America. Chaliapin sent him a warm letter of congratulations on the forthcoming marriage and, prematurely, his 'grandfatherhood'.

In America, Rachmaninoff continued to listen to Paul Whiteman, attending another of his concerts and praising this as 'authentic American music, for it can be heard nowhere else that I know of'. Paradoxically, given his musical reputation, Rachmaninoff praised above all the power of the new in Whiteman's work:

> The charm and interest of this orchestra for the musician is that it is undoubtedly new. That is to say, it expands and develops its material in a characteristic and novel fashion which to me is absolutely fascinating. This may certainly be called authentic American music, for it can be heard nowhere else that I know of.[67]

He told a newspaper reporter: 'Each month I send to my daughter in Europe the records made by this remarkable organisation.'[68] He also complimented Whiteman's narrative powers, saying his pieces are stories, 'Excellent, pointed anecdotes, crisply told, with all the human breeziness and snap that are so characteristic of the American people'. Rachmaninoff's own preludes for solo piano, each one a self-contained musical drama, could be said to do the same: a reminder of his insistence to Marietta Shaginian that a work, and its performance, must have a 'point' or it was nothing. Shape, purpose, drama, denouement: all were part of a composition's power and distinction. As Gorky had once noted of the op. 23 set, 'How well he hears the silence.'[69]

Tragedy

Irina, the 'daughter in Europe', was expecting her first child, her parents' first grandchild. On 12 August 1925, three weeks before the child's birth, and less than a year after the couple's marriage, Pyotr Volkonsky died suddenly. Three weeks later, on 4 September, his widow gave birth to Sophie Petrovna Volkonsky. Rachmaninoff's letters from this time, sparse but emotional, show his grief at his child's fate.

One letter is to Nadezhda Korotneva, an amateur mezzo-soprano with whom Rachmaninoff often corresponded during this period. In replies to her, he invariably apologised for not writing more frequently. (Eventually, in 1936, his impatience was evident. He ended his letter with: 'I send you my most cordial greetings and beg you to forgive me for my silence both in the past and in the future . . .') This extract from his letter of 25 August 1925, sent from Château de Corbeville, Orsay, shows his stress:

You lie heavy on my conscience, the more so as I very much value your friendly disposition towards me. But please do not be angry that, try as I may, I cannot promise to write to you more often. I have too many commitments, work and worries. Where I am at the moment I have been hoping for peace and quiet, but so far have not succeeded in finding any. The way life has turned out makes it impossible. I spent the month of June in Germany, where my younger daughter and I stayed in a Sanatorium until the 10th July. The idea was for me to recover my health, but somehow I failed to do so. In mid-July we came here to join the rest of my family and have been here for about a month and a half. On the surface it is pleasant here, but my inner peace has entirely disintegrated. Ten days ago my son-in-law Volkonsky, whom I loved as if he were my own son, died suddenly; his wife, my poor daughter, is due to give birth if not today then tomorrow.

On the 17th October I will return to America, to resume my work. I had intended to travel with my wife, leaving our children in Paris. But whether we shall be able to leave them I now cannot say. Everything has been turned upside down and all our previously made arrangements no longer work.

At present we are seeing nobody here, and I am trying to work as much as I can.

How are you? And how is your life progressing?

Good-bye! S R

The next letter was to his sister-in-law, Sofia Satina.

Château de Corbeville, 2 September 1925

Please pass on this letter to the Somovs: I'm writing to all three of you as I can't manage separate letters. It is now ten o'clock in the morning, and at three o'clock a.m. earlier today Irinochka went into labour. We got the news by telephone at nine o'clock because the telephone doesn't work until then. The new mother went to Paris, while Tanya and I are staying here waiting for Natasha to ring from the hospital. If all goes well the baby will be born this evening. In this connection a strange synchronicity of days keeps coming into my head: today is a Wednesday; it was on a Wednesday that Pyotrik [Volkonsky] proposed to Irina; their civil marriage took place in Germany on a Wednesday; the church marriage ceremony was on a Wednesday; and finally Pyotrik died on Wednesday. I draw absolutely no conclusions from this, but it would not surprise me if Irinochka were to attribute some special significance to it. My poor, poor Irinochka!

The birth is very late. Even if everything is as it should be, she will not be able to come to us in the countryside before 15th September. Popov [the doctor] warned us that he will insist on twelve days' rest. It means that she can only be with us for about a month, since on 17th October I, or Natasha and I if she can come with me, must leave for New York. So far we haven't succeeded in finding an apartment for the girls, despite the most energetic efforts and the help of two agents and offices. Cursed city!

I have to interrupt this letter now. A baby girl was born at twelve o'clock. She is to be called Sophie in honour of Pyotrik's mother and in honour of the sister of her grandpa, i.e. me. Perhaps she will be as beautiful as her great-aunt. At half past two Tanya and I left by train for Paris, and by about four o'clock we were with Irina. She did so well! And looks wonderful, immediately more lovely than before. The look in her eyes is amazing. The birth lasted altogether nine hours.

Although Popov had promised chloroform, he deceived her and when he put on the mask it had no chloroform in it. The instant Sonechka appeared in the world she began to cry in the loudest imaginable voice and kept it up without a pause until we arrived, so that as we were coming up in the lift we could hear her. Our presence had a beneficial effect on her; she stopped crying and behaved impeccably for the hour we spent with them. I made the sign of the cross over her and kissed her several times, because I have already fallen in love with her. She has long black hair, like mine when I don't crop it short, and it sticks up just like mine does. The length of her hair caused a sensation in the hospital, and all the nurses crowded in to look at it. The midwife combed it with Irina's comb. The whole time I was sitting by Irina's bed, Natasha stood near the baby and never took her eyes off her. I fear she is going to be really spoilt by her grandma.

We were chased out after an hour, and went home. As for a full description of Sonechka, I think it better if Natasha writes it.

Good-bye. Greetings to one and all. S R

Natasha's addition, handwritten at the end of her husband's letter, is as full of pain as his own, making for essential reading. Sonechka is the new baby, Sophie, Petya is Prince Volkonsky, Boolya is Irina.

Sonechka is lovely, and to my mind will take after Petya. Unfortunately, she has not yet opened her eyes so I cannot tell you what colour they are. Her hair is truly remarkable, I've never seen the like [even] on a year-old child. Her head is completely covered with hair, you could almost plait it. Her hands are incredible, with beautiful little fingers and nails.

111

She cries lustily, and I fear poor Irina is not going to get much sleep. I already love [the baby] terribly. Lord, if only everything can now turn out for the best. The doctor said that if the next twelve days go well, there will be no need to worry any longer. We'll be going in to see her again, our poor Boolya, tomorrow. It is such a shame that we don't seem able to find an apartment for her. That is a real punishment in Paris. Good-bye now, I kiss you all.

Natasha

The suddenness of Volkonsky's death was passed over. Some light is thrown in a letter Medtner wrote to Alexander Goldenweiser, another of the Taneyev–Arensky class at Moscow Conservatory.

17 September 1925

It is certainly the case that young Volkonsky was an extremely nervous person, but otherwise appeared to be in generally good health. However, Sergei Vasilievich told me that he [Volkonsky] was mentally disturbed about what he saw as the death of religion, as a result of which the doctors considered that he needed treatment for religious mania.[70]

Aftermath

This disruption in the family's life explains much about why Rachmaninoff, for the remainder of his days, never stopped working; why he, the family's sole earner, felt the need to secure large sums of money, and why in 1925 he set up Tair, the small, Paris-based publishing house. Its name an amalgam of those of his daughters, Tair published Russian-language books as well as Russian music, including Rachmaninoff's own. The intention was to give Tatiana and Irina stability and income, as well as occupation. For a short time, it did. The last book published under the imprint was Medtner's *The Muse and the Fashion* (1935), an attack on the 'stifling, exploding ideology' of modernism. Largely ignored, it had a few qualities Rachmaninoff admired. When Medtner sent him a copy he called it witty, interesting and profound, but kept a distance from its most extreme, conservative conclusions.

Rachmaninoff tackled his new and unforeseen responsibilities with quiet dedication. He was the closest his granddaughter would have to a father. He took on the role without ever much referring to it, though to Vilshau, he spoke of the picture of baby Sophie, aged six months, which he kept above his bed, her smiling face making him smile too. To Mrs Cornelius Rybner, mother of Dagmar, he wrote: 'I only want to tell you that I have a granddaughter, Sophie, who is an exact likeness of her father.' He says how very much he likes her, visits her every day, and looks forward to wheeling her around in her carriage.[71]

Photographs and home movies of him playing with Sophie, as a toddler and small child, give insight into his close involvement with his family. Irina never married again and lived mostly near her parents for the rest of their lives. Biographies mostly skim over the Volkonsky episode and even the Russian editor of Rachmaninoff's letters and associated writings, Z. A. Apetian – usually reliable in providing detailed footnotes – merely says: 'the cause of P. G. Volkonsky's sudden demise is not known to us.' One of the few to shed light is Rachmaninoff's niece, Sophia Satin, in her short, personable memoir.

She recalls that 'Uncle' had helped her family buy a plot of land in Dresden. Next door was Count Oblonsky and his family: 'Visits from one house to the other were frequent and friendly. The

Oblonskys had a lodger, a young man who was studying art and wanted to be a painter: Prince Peter Volkonsky. He was a very kind young man, very good-looking.' As a nine-year-old child, Sophia Satin writes, she was 'not aware that a courtship had started in our garden.' The young couple had walked in the orchard every evening, and a marriage proposal ensued.

'The wedding took place in our lovely church in Dresden . . . the wedding dress was ordered from the most fabulous couturier in Dresden, Hirsch and Co.' – the dress was even displayed in the window, without the name of the bride being disclosed. Several months later, sad news arrived: Prince Volkonsky had died in a clinic. 'Much later I understood that he had committed suicide being in a confused state of mind. But the older members of the family kept quiet. It was like a conspiracy not to let the outside world know the full truth.'[72]

In *Rachmaninoff and the Symphonies*, David Butler Cannata, having investigated local documents, records that Volkonsky died at 1.30 a.m. on 12 August 1925 at the Sanatorium de la Malmaison, Rueil, Seine et Oise.[73] Two days later, without evidence of a church ceremony, he was buried at the Batignolles cemetery in Paris, a preferred burial ground at the time for members of the exiled Russian Orthodox community. Prince Pierre Volkonsky's grave remained unmarked until 27 March 1940. A simple Russian Orthodox cross was erected. Today, the cemetery is partially covered by the Paris ring-road, the Boulevard Périphérique.

On the Road Again

Rachmaninoff carried on working as usual. Under the headline 'Tallest Man on Stage', Ohio's *Canton Daily News* [1 Nov 1925] reported his imminent concert appearance:

Rachmaninoff has been preparing his programs and working out in the open during the summer on his farm in the Catskills where he finds the quiet, healthful, simple life which he loves. Here he prefers to live his own life – away from disturbance. He scoured the country for a place where there would be plenty of room and where he would, Russian-like, find himself close to the soil. Every fine day of the summer he is out in his garden or his fields, a workman in overalls.

The other members of his family, including his daughters, one of whom spent a year at Bryn Mawr, each have their own garden for which they care. In his studio, Rachmaninoff is inaccessible; no one disturbs him. In the evening there are books in many languages, Russian tobacco and good talk. All this has made for a much-needed rest, fresh enthusiasm for the winter's work and reservoirs of physical strength which is an absolute requisite, even for a physical giant like Rachmaninoff, for he is possibly the tallest artist appearing in concert halls.

Through the winter of 1925–6, not his usual season for composition, if anything could be called usual since his departure from Russia, he battled on with the Fourth Piano Concerto. He kept the matter, mostly, to himself. Aided by his new agent, Foley, he had made this a sabbatical year from concerts, after the pressures of the last seven seasons. The previous season alone he had given sixty-nine concerts, fifty-seven of them recitals. Judging from references and sketches, Rachmaninoff had begun the new concerto in Russia, but put it aside unfinished, probably in the summer of 1914. Now he returned to it, working first in West End Avenue, where New York musical society banged on his door, metaphorically or literally, too often for sustained concentration.

The *New Yorker* of 9 January 1926 carried a melancholy article about Rachmaninoff, describing him as 'austere, solitary, aristocratic, morosely sensitive and simple', left spiritually homeless by his wrench with Russia:

> If one or two or three years ago you were one who had the pleasant habit of taking long, fast-paced walks at dusk on Riverside Drive, you must have met Rachmaninoff. And if you are addicted to driving a car madly over the Westchester roads at night you very likely have passed him. This is all there is to his hobbies and diversions. He is still out seeking, alone and constant, among such moods, wherein for him, comes music.
>
> The walks are put in the past tense, because in the past year, the Rachmaninoff home at 33 Riverside Drive has been sold. A story was connected with this that did not get into the papers. His elder daughter, Irina, married a Russian prince, and the family went to France and bought a farm, planning a new life on the old continent again. But the son-in-law died, and Rachmaninoff came back with his family last month a grandfather.
>
> The house of the Rachmaninoffs at Riverside Drive will long remain in the memory of those who have visited there. It was white without, and it had a shadowed quietude within. While waiting for the appearance of one of his daughters, who were always his emissaries, the caller became conscious of a suzerainty of order, of punctilious nobility, of a fair, natural elegance that livened into magnificent and to tender gloom as the sunlight eddied in and withdrew through the heavy plated windows. The house was not Russian in furnishings or atmosphere, but something else was there that Rachmaninoff wanted – it was the old order in its tempo and mood. A blonde

and child-like Russian servant girl beamed wanly as if suddenly roused, and then one waited and had the rare pleasure of seeing Tatiana or Irina walk measuredly down the arched stairways, beautiful girls walking carelessly and elegantly.

He managed to work more on the composition in Europe, travelling that summer to Paris, to see his daughters, and on to Dresden. The family then went to Cannes, renting a villa belonging to the Rothschilds with 'a price to match', as he put it, and a piano, as well as great heat, and battalions of mosquitos.

On 30 August 1926, he wrote to Dagmar Rybner about his usual concerns – car, health – with vital news in the PS.

My dear Miss Rybner

Thank you for your kind letter.

Tomorrow Irina and I are leaving for Nice by automobile where we expect to stay till the first of November.

There is lots of work ahead of me. I have not touched the piano for eight months so that not only my second finger but all the others are lazy.

With best regards to your parents, Mr Barclay and to yourself.

Yours sincerely

PS I finished a new piano concerto a few days ago.[74]

This new concerto, so long in gestation, would have a painful birth. For now, let us put it aside, it its pristine state of unplayed optimism.

A New Friend

Since his arrival in America, Rachmaninoff had been courted by Steinway & Sons, who made their pianos – 'The Instrument of the Immortals' – available to him wherever he performed. The history of the company, and the pianos on offer in its famous Basement on West Fifty-Seventh Street, is inextricable from the world of émigré New York. Its important story, only touched on here, has fascinating twists.[75] The company was established in 1853 by a German, Heinrich Engelhard Steinweg. He changed his name to Steinway and began manufacturing pianos from a loft behind 85 Varick Street, on the Lower West Side. A turning point for the public profile of the company had occurred in 1872 when Anton Rubinstein, Rachmaninoff's pianistic idol, agreed to play Steinway pianos on his American tour (215 concerts in 239 days!). Rachmaninoff might also have enjoyed the association, at the turn of the century, between Steinway and G. Daimler of Mercedes, with Steinway aiding in the manufacture of car parts and marine engines. Pro-German feelings ran high, a mark of seriousness and quality, and a reflection on the economic value of the millions of German-Americans contributing to the nation's economy. That attitude changed after the Great War. 'Cancel culture', as we might now call it, went mad. The Metropolitan Opera pulled its German opera repertoire. The Pittsburgh Orchestra Association announced a ban on 'all music written by any German composer, and all music composed by a subject of any of Germany's allies.' Alas poor Bach and Beethoven, Schumann and Brahms.

Steinway had to act, fast. German accents were silenced. The American character of the company was emphasised: one of the firm's additional responsibilities was to help co-ordinate music at the White House and provide pianos for state occasions. This could not be jeopardised. A new international relationship was formed. The Russian Alexander 'Sasha' Greiner, soon to become a great friend of the Rachmaninoffs, was hired by Steinway & Sons in 1926. Greiner had studied at the Moscow Conservatory. He left Russia at the time of the Revolution, apparently in great danger, though the story has an element of mystery. He travelled mostly on foot and for a time worked for the Red Cross before reaching New York. At Steinway he proved immediately invaluable, as manager of the artists and concert department and in his ability to make close friendships with leading Steinway artists, aiding communications with the Russian influx, among whom was Vladimir Horowitz.

Through Greiner, Rachmaninoff and Horowitz met in 1928, the day after Horowitz's arrival in New York – at Rachmaninoff's invitation. He had heard from Fritz Kreisler that the young Russian, Koshetz's one-time duo partner, was a wizard performer of Rachmaninoff's Piano Concerto no. 3. Their first encounter was in the basement of Steinway Hall. With Rachmaninoff playing the orchestral part on one piano, Horowitz the solo part on another, they played through the Third Piano Concerto, a work forever linked with Horowitz.

'He swallowed it whole,' an impressed Rachmaninoff is said to have remarked.[76] It is a pity he did not live to hear the American pianist Van Cliburn win the Tchaikovsky Piano Competition in 1958, not only an American triumphing in Moscow at the height of the Cold War, but playing this work in its full, uncut version, with a lyricism and tenderness entirely different from Horowitz's fiery intensity. Van Cliburn's massive hands make light work of the big chords in the first movement cadenza. The grainy film version (on YouTube), despite its sound quality, captures all the passion and brilliance, of work and player. (Somewhere it has to be mentioned that the 1996 film *Shine*, directed by Scott Hicks,

fictionalised the endeavours of the Australian pianist David Helf-
gott to perform Rachmaninoff's Piano Concerto no. 3. This is as
good a place as any.)

In a compilation of home movies of Rachmaninoff and his
family, Greiner is narrator, and includes a vivid description of his
friend Sergei Vasilievich, also praising his exactitude and fabled
promptness as a timekeeper. Greiner revered him, his affection
irrepressible in these touching scraps of film:

> Behind an austere, perhaps even severe, countenance there
> was a most warm-hearted lovable man with a wonderful sense
> of humour. Yes, a wonderful sense of humour. Rachmaninoff
> thoroughly enjoyed a good story, and no one who hasn't seen
> him laugh with the tears running down his cheeks would
> believe it possible.[77]

'Rocky' and Mr Hupfer

Thanks to Greiner, Rachmaninoff acquired his own piano
mechanic who travelled with him on tour, from 1928 for the next
thirteen years. For a pianist to tour with a piano and a tuner was
standard for top-level virtuosos, but to gain a constant technical
companion, as Rachmaninoff did, was invaluable. His name was
William Hupfer. He was born in the Bronx in 1896, the son of a
piano factory worker, and had assisted star pianists such as Myra
Hess and Josef Hofmann, yet Rachmaninoff – or 'Rocky' as Hupfer
called him – was apprehensive. 'Give him a try,' Greiner urged.
'You don't have to marry him.'

Hupfer had keyboard skills of a different kind, having played
in a high-school dance band. All his career, even after 1946 when,

as 'chief toner', he was responsible for approving every piano Steinway's New York factory produced, he feigned ignorance about concert music. How tempting it must have been to proffer opinions to the artists he met, but he played down his expertise, calling himself a technician. His priority was not tuning the piano strings, but 'voicing' the instrument: modulating, regulating, gradating the tone, aligning the keys, working with the eighty-eight hammer felts, filing, rubbing, sanding, renewing. After their first encounter, Hupfer found 'Rocky' inscrutable, and had no idea whether his handiwork was admired or despised. Rachmaninoff, however, claimed not to have Hupfer's sensibilities or sharp ears ('Highly ordinary-looking ears', as an in-depth profile in the *New Yorker* of 9 May 1953 describes them. That article, drawn on here, is a rare source of detailed information about Hupfer.)

Thereafter Rachmaninoff, despite not knowing quite what this agreeable man, tinkering inside the piano, was doing, trusted his work completely. On tour, one of Hupfer's tasks was to request a Steinway practice piano for Rachmaninoff's hotel room, a factor which added immeasurably to the instrument's value, further enlarged by the pianist's willingness to autograph any piano he played. (All he needed was a chance to loosen up his fingers, he said, not to play a fine instrument.) This also explains why, at one time, as many pianos were described as Rachmaninoff's 'own' as John the Baptist allegedly had heads.

The responsibilities of Hupfer's job were both nerve-wracking and tedious: the worst of combinations which he weathered, always reliable, his work impeccable. By noon he would have gone to the concert hall and adjusted the piano as required. His duty was done. Then he was free until the evening performance. 'I never knew what to do with myself. I ate lunch as slowly as I could. I went to the movies whenever there was one I hadn't already seen. I read every newspaper and magazine I could find, and I'm only sorry now that I didn't have a taste for books . . . It was a dreadful life for a young man. I had to fight temptation every afternoon.'

Under the 'Knout'

After dining with Rachmaninoff, and Natalia who now accompanied him on his tours, Hupfer's duty was to call a taxi and all three would go to the concert hall. During the performance, he always stood in the wings with Natalia until the end, in case anything went wrong. Hupfer said of this habit:

> It was a pretty funny idea. I figure old Rocky must have picked it up somewhere in Europe, where a piano might need retuning during the intermission or break a hammer, or something of the sort. But these old babies of ours are built to last, so nothing like that ever happened. I was always standing here ready, for all those years, and I never had a thing to do except listen.

It is hard to pity him his unique access to this particular virtuoso.

Press reports of Rachmaninoff's concert 'habits', which Hupfer witnessed hundreds of times, always mention certain traits: his wife's constant presence, his need to warm his hands on an electric muff, his excessive punctuality, his taste for sipping a cherry malted milk float after a concert unless he had to rush for yet another train. (His experiment, in the 1920s, with renting a train, equipped with piano and obviating the need for hotels, proved unworkable and was short-lived.) Rachmaninoff, in private, gave a different account, writing to Vilshau in Moscow that the touring schedule left him exhausted. That letter dates from a decade later (15 April 1936) but his complaints would have applied to any one of his punishing American seasons. As he wrote to Vilshau in that particular, fairly typical year, he gave sixty-one concerts: thirty-five in America, fourteen in England, three in Switzerland, three in Paris, two in Warsaw and one in each of Vienna, Budapest, 'etc.', all in a period of six months. At the end of every season, he 'had to go under the knout' [in Imperial Russia, a whip for flogging]:

Next season is already being put together. It will start on 16th October and finish on 6th April. By the end of every concert season, I find myself 'under the knout', so exhausted that during the interval I resort to the port wine! Not that it helps much, I must admit! Perhaps a bit towards imagination, nothing else! Life is very oddly arranged. When you are young and strong, all you can think about is getting engagements, which refuse to materialise. When you get old and feeble, you don't know what to do with the mass of invitations! I cannot satisfy half of the demands, so have to turn them down.[78]

His repertoire consisted mainly of well-known Bach, Beethoven, Schubert, Chopin and, at the end, some Liszt, with a piece or two of his own. 'I do not play the works of modern composers,' he said, as if he himself was outside that constituent group. He joked frequently about his familiarity with railway carriages, being known to remark to the Pullman porter stowing his luggage, 'Well, home again!' He added his gratitude to Natalia for travelling with him, helping him 'take care of his things' in the hurried few hours he might spend in a town before moving on to the next. He might have added that by now she took care not only of his things but of the man himself, protecting him from prying journalists or fawning public, nurturing his spirits and his health. She, like their daughters, shunned the limelight. If she had the unhappy role of gatekeeper, she attracted no negative press, always referred to passingly but generously.

The way Rachmaninoff describes life on the road removes all mystery about his inability to work on compositions. 'When composing I am a slave. Beginning at nine in the morning, I allow myself no respite until after eleven at night.' During such times, he cannot touch the piano, and can concentrate on only one thing. The same is true, in reverse, on a concert tour:

> I devote all my day to the concert I am to give. Usually I arrive
> in the morning of the day of my concert, going to my hotel.
> I concentrate upon the performance – other artists might be
> able to enjoy an afternoon tea, or a lawn party, I am not that
> fortunate. I must relax so that I may give to my public all that
> is within me during my concert.[79]

Tobacco was a constant prop: on one foreign trip he asked Somov to send him a thousand cigarettes.

Hupfer, travelling all those untold miles across America for weeks on end, leaving his young wife behind, maintained that he would really have preferred being stationary in Manhattan. Apart from anything else, there were no temptations. (Their exact nature can only be imagined: he does not specify.) In the Basement, the piano numbered CD–15 – one of many played by Rachmaninoff – acquired an aura, much to Hupfer's impatience. In his view, a piano's magic rested entirely on its component parts and their precise assemblage, not on whose hands had touched the keys. If you switched the labels round, he said, no one but he would know which instrument was which. A top piano is a top piano. He used to joke that customers assumed the CD–15 could play Rocky's C sharp minor Prelude by itself.

Piano Coda

The Steinway Rachmaninoff preferred playing in the UK, on all his tours between 1929 and 1938, is now in the Holburne Museum, Bath, and still used in recitals. He told Somov, 'the Steinway is quite satisfactory in its melodiousness and its *piano* is even better than the American make. The only thing it lacks is the American power.'[80] The piano, on long-term loan to the museum, was left to the University of Bath by the widow of Eric Hodges, a tutor in music at University College, Cardiff, in 1977. After many invitations to visit the city, Rachmaninoff finally played in Bath, at the Pavilion, in March 1934: Beethoven's 'Moonlight' Sonata, some Debussy, Chopin and Liszt, and his own *Études-Tableaux*, opp. 33 and 39. The *Bath Chronicle and Weekly Gazette* of 17 March 1934 noted: 'A Steinway Grand Pianoforte was used.' The C sharp minor Prelude was the popular encore.

On the same day, the paper's 'Notes by the way' columnist reported that he had challenged the great composer on the hidden meaning of the famous prelude. Is it true, the intrepid journalist asked, that it depicts someone waking up and finding he has been buried alive? No, came the terse reply. It is just a composition. With the rest of a column to fill and a celebrity in his midst, the reporter revealed that the Russian pianist enjoyed a cup of tea after the manner of his fellow countrymen. Nothing escaped the eyes of this sleuth. 'After the performance I noted that he was sipping his tea without milk, but with the addition of a slice of lemon.'

A few years later, an American reviewer explained the 'true' meaning of the Prelude. Frustrated that Rachmaninoff had refused to play it as an encore (in Madison, Georgia, 31 October 1941), thereby ruining 'our whole evening' by his ungracious and brutish behaviour, the writer concludes: 'The Prelude, as you know, is a music-picture of Napoleon's storming and final capture of Moscow. Although Rachmaninoff is a WHITE Russian, he couldn't be exactly happy over the plight of his homeland. 'Scuse us Mr Sergei. We're always shooting off our mouth like THAT.' The comments were squeezed into a down-page corner, out of the way. The main space was given to a review of the 'magnificent' new *Citizen Kane*, which introduced Orson Welles to the motion-picture public: a technical masterpiece and a 'throbbing, living story'.[81] That was the kind of journalistic punishment meted out when Rachmaninoff failed to play the Prelude.

Powder and Paint

In the febrile atmosphere of Russian New York, Rachmaninoff composed the *Trois Chansons Russes*, op. 41 (1926). This group of folk-song arrangements, rarely performed, was his last work for chorus and large orchestra, following the tradition of *Spring*, op. 20, and the work he particularly treasured, *The Bells*, op. 35. In the custom of aristocratic Russians of his era, he spoke good French (his English remained faltering) and gave several works French titles. Written for low voices on subjects ranging from a duck and a drake to a husband who takes a silken whip to his unfaithful wife, these songs embrace and exude the Russian folk idiom. One song may have come to Rachmaninoff via the Moscow Art Theatre's recent tour, a second was known through Chaliapin.

The last – in English, 'My Fairness, my Rosy Cheeks' – he also recorded, in a high-spirited version for voice and piano, with Nadezhda Plevitskaya. (The song is also known as 'Powder and Paint'.[82] The MS is in the Glinka State Central Museum of Musical Culture, one of the few post-1917 autographs in Russia, given by Somov in 1945.) Plevitskaya, a popular folk singer from

Kursk, had long been a household name in Russia, and gave concerts in Manhattan in 1926. A photograph of the mezzo-soprano in traditional dress, giving a come-hither sideways glance, is inscribed: 'To esteemed Sergei Vasilievich Rachmaninoff from N. Plevitskaya who is caressed, deeply touched, by his grand Russian soul. New York, 15 March 1926.'[83] We can be sure that had she indeed been caressed she would not have needed to write it on the photo.

Not long after, having failed to make the anticipated fortune, Plevitskaya became a Soviet agent, to be seen draped in furs and jewels, nails lacquered, and travelling in an official Soviet embassy Cadillac, until her arrest, imprisonment and death in 1940. Vladimir Nabokov immortalised her (under a different name) in one of his short stories, 'The Assistant Producer'. He describes the rhythmic stamping of her booted feet, and her popular 'hodgepodge' of artificial folklore, military melodrama and official patriotism, mixed in with a dash of authentic *tzigane* and peasant stock. Chaliapin makes an appearance in his story:

In Fyodor Chaliapin's dressing room there hung a photograph of her: Russian headgear with pearls, hand propping cheek, dazzling teeth between fleshy lips, and a great clumsy scrawl right across: 'For you, Fedyusha.'[84]

Rachmaninoff's *Trois Chansons* were dedicated to Leopold Stokowski and first performed by him with the Philadelphia Orchestra on 18 March 1927. According to the memory of one young singer who took part, local Russian Orthodox priests had to be drafted in to enrich the deeper-than-deep *profondo* bass line.

Fourth Concerto Debacle

In the same concert as the *Trois Chansons*, Rachmaninoff gave the premiere of the Fourth Piano Concerto, in G minor, op. 40. The new concerto was long and difficult, he wrote to Medtner, to whom it was dedicated. He joked that, owing to its *Ring*-like length, it would have to be performed over several evenings. His anxiety was clear, despite the humour. He also wondered whether it should be called a concerto for orchestra and piano instead of a piano concerto, given the orchestra's weighty presence. And was the theme in the second movement a replica of the opening movement of Schumann's Piano Concerto, an unwitting plagiarism? (One critic noted the similarity.) He worried away at all this, expecting Medtner to come up with reassuring answers. His friend dutifully tried: he had just completed his own Piano Concerto no. 2, and dedicated it to Rachmaninoff (who could have helped its chances by playing it, but never did). That other close musician friend, Josef Hofmann, examined the score and made polite noises, while adding that it looked frankly difficult to play, with its metric complexities.

The problems were all too apparent to the Philadelphia critic after the premiere, conducted by Stokowski with the composer as soloist:

The opening attack was made with a new concerto; Rachmaninoff came reeling back from the charge in disorder and defeat. But like Napoleon at Marengo, yesterday evening he turned the most disastrous rout of his career into decisive victory. After the intermission a chorus of twenty proceeded to redeem the catastrophe with his three latest settings for voice and orchestra of Russian folk-songs.[85]

After Philadelphia he played the concerto in New York, Washington and Baltimore, remaining dissatisfied. The reviews could hardly have been worse, calling it, variously – some critics carried away with the verbal brilliance of their own insults – tawdry, orotund, weepily sentimental, old fashioned, the kind of thing Mme Cécile Chaminade might have 'perpetrated' on her third glass of vodka (the writer making the lowest of insults: comparison of Rachmaninoff to a 'lady' composer).[86]

Rachmaninoff made two more versions of the work: one in 1928; a third in 1941 – heavily shorn, it is now the most commonly performed. As with the First Concerto, as with the Second Sonata, he could not yield up these precious musical children, as if the connection of these works, with their roots in a lost Russia, somehow epitomised his whole artistic life in exile.

Man, Mouse

The concerto's narrative is dense, its history tangled. The Rachmaninoff Estate authorised Boosey & Hawkes to publish the original 1926 score, aided by the Rachmaninoff scholar-pianist Robert Threlfall, and the pianist Leslie Howard. In *Rachmaninoff: Life, Works, Recordings*, Max Harrison makes a strong case both for the modernity and authority of that first version, the score for which was not released until 2000. Vladimir Ashkenazy, among the most wholehearted and exhaustive of modern Rachmaninoff interpreters, immersed himself as pianist and conductor in all three versions, and likewise prefers the original manuscript. The pianist Stephen Hough, a Rachmaninoff devotee of the highest order, admires the final 1941 version, calling it as 'tight as a drum' and a unique, original twentieth-century masterpiece, 'a musical *Waste Land* [1922], an evocation of alienation equivalent in some ways to T. S. Eliot's poem'.[87]

Rachmaninoff took the concerto to Europe, beginning in London in November 1929, by which time Tair, the family firm, had published the revised version. Then he abandoned it until 1941, performing the last version in America and recording it with RCA Victor at the end of that year. Troubled by this concerto to the last, Rachmaninoff was working on a two-piano version at the time of his death. Performers must find their own preferences and take audiences with them. The upset of the First Symphony and its aftermath left indelible scars on Rachmaninoff. At times it seems that as much as he wanted to return to composition, he may have preferred to have the excuse of a punishing performing career to prevent him. He was in thrall to his own self-doubt, ever retreating from one precipice and piloting himself straight towards another.

To add to his low spirits, news had arrived of his mother's death in Novgorod. Having remained in Russia, she had not seen her son since his emigration twelve years earlier. By his own account, they were not close, but he had supported her financially, and behaved honourably from afar. A blood link with his homeland had been broken. The chronic condition he called 'neuralgia' was playing up. In Paris he visited a dentist and a hypnotist and gained some relief. Professionally he was under pressure, yet again, about allowing radio companies to broadcast his concerts. Despite the prospect of generous rewards – 'how much should I ask?' he asked Foley, speculatively – he still declined.[88] His British schedule was heavy, with fifteen concerts, including the Fourth Concerto with Albert Coates conducting (to tepid reviews), and *The Bells* in Manchester. To his own surprise, Rachmaninoff found the 'barn' acoustic of the Royal Albert Hall, where he gave a solo recital, not merely not as bad as he had feared, but very good indeed.[89] He admitted to the Somovs that he was, for once, pleased with himself. The joy was short-lived. His neuralgia returned with new fire, the pain nearly jeopardising a second Albert Hall concert. Cancelling his last two concerts in England, he hastened to Paris for another dose of medical attention.

The year provided at least one fillip. Rachmaninoff had the distraction of his own Hollywood moment. In *The Opry House* (1929), the second ever *Mickey Mouse* film, the small rodent plays the Prelude in C sharp Minor, in combat with a recalcitrant piano, prompting Rachmaninoff's much quoted comment to Disney himself: 'I have heard my inescapable piece done marvellously by some of the best pianists, and murdered cruelly by amateurs, but I was never more stirred than by the performance of Maestro Mouse.' When the film reached the UK the following year, the British critic and diarist James Agate compressed a dose of sour prejudice into his round-up film review for *The Tatler* (21 May 1930):

There was also a *Mickey Mouse* cartoon which demonstrated the proper treatment to be meted out today to Rachmaninoff's awful Prelude and Liszt's abominable Second Rhapsody. I shall never forget how the piano reeled under the first and collapsed under the second, recovering sufficiently to come on by itself and make an unaided bow, after which the ivories detached themselves, doubled themselves up, and snapped defiance at the audience in imitation of that dental masterpiece which nightly reposes in a tumbler of cold water, solaced by a teaspoonful of Milton.

High Seas, Floating Palaces

In his touring career Rachmaninoff spent long periods of every year aboard ocean liners, sailing from America to Europe, back and forth. Those great ships shaped a new style of living and dreaming:

a glamorous mix of imperial grandeur and 'streamline moderne'. Le Corbusier credited liners as giving us freedom, 'a liberation from the cursed enslavement of the past'.[90] (The workforce who toiled below deck in the furnace and coal-dust of the stoking room may have had other views.) What did Rachmaninoff do on those blank days at sea? He had the choice of whiling away hours in the gracious palm court or tea garden, of dancing in the grand ball-room, or exercising in the gymnasium. Did he bestride the open decks, buffeted by gales, breathing salt air into his tobacco-tarred lungs? Play deck tennis or golf? Or did he retire to his first-class suite to practise the piano installed for his use or, on one voyage when preparing the Third Piano Concerto, a 'dumb piano' (as he described it to Riesemann)?

In the last days of 1929, he sailed back from Europe on the RMS *Berengaria*, the large and luxurious liner featured by F. Scott Fitzgerald in *The Beautiful and the Damned*. With accommodation for some 2,300 passengers (seven hundred first class) and crew of a thousand, the ship was originally built as a symbol of German might and given to Britain as war reparation for the loss of the *Lusitania*. After her maiden voyage, with the *Titanic* too recent a memory, the ornate marble bathrooms in first class had to be removed for fear of causing the ship to sink.

The first vessel aboard which public wireless telephone calls could be made at sea, the *Berengaria* was packed with precisely the kind of gadgetry to satisfy Rachmaninoff: electricity, call bells and a form of air conditioning. Elevators connected the five decks. A state-of-the-art swimming bath, for first-class passengers, was modelled on the Pompeii-inspired pool at London's Royal Automobile Club, with fluted pillars, tiles and marble, mosaics, bronze fittings, a glass roof to the height of three decks and a continuous cascade of water tumbling down at one end.

The *Berengaria*'s updating coincided with stringent restrictions by the United States on immigration numbers. What had once been steerage, in the bow – the lowest-cost passengers crammed together in inhumane conditions – was upgraded to 'Tourist Third Cabin'. No traveller wanted to be thought poor. The spirit of this new budget class described its appeal as being to the 'educational or otherwise intellectual type'. Rachmaninoff was both those things but he was also by now extremely rich and travelled in elite luxury.

Sailing over Christmas, from 24 to 31 December 1929, he found himself in illustrious company. Bertensson and Leyda tell how the composer, seeing a crowd of photographers 'bearing down on him' as he boarded, assumed the worst and prepared himself for the paparazzi onslaught.[91] They rushed straight past him in pursuit of their real target: the huge Italian prizefighter Primo Carnera, nicknamed the 'Ambling Alp'. Years later, Rachmaninoff could not relate this episode without laughing.

A gaggle of Russian-born musicians was also on board: the violinists Mischa Elman and Jascha Brodsky and the pianists Mischa Levitsky and Alexander Brailowsky. A veritable *boîte à musique*, in the words of another passenger, Sergei Prokofiev. He had been in Europe enjoying some success with *The Prodigal Son*, his last ballet for Diaghilev, choreographed by Balanchine. That autumn Prokofiev had heard music by Poulenc which was not 'egregiously bad', and the premiere of Stravinsky's *Capriccio*, which he thought good in parts. He had also attended a concert by Rachmaninoff, complaining it was 'very much a gala occasion, we had to pay 300 francs for a pair of tickets'.

Despite the other three thousand crew and passengers milling around on deck, they must have found it hard to avoid each other. As it happened, the pair had met in Paris a few days earlier, at 'the publishers' [Éditions Russes], when Rachmaninoff came in with his daughter Tatiana, described by the ever-constant diarist as 'a young lady of twenty-three or thereabouts' who did her best to 'keep the conversation going'. Rachmaninoff looked 'old and worn out'.

> I tried to be gentle and affectionate [. . .] He was not in form for his recital, playing less well than last year. Still I was going to go backstage to shake his hand until as his last item he played his new paraphrase of some appalling piece of vulgarity by Kreisler (and the paraphrase was mediocre too).

The work was a transcription of Kreisler's *Liebesfreud*, for violin and piano. As Prokofiev intimates, this salon piece has plenty of schmaltz, but Rachmaninoff's own recording of the piece, graceful, controlled but bursting with wit, suggests he was having fun.

Prokofiev gives a fine description of the *Berengaria*: 'an unbeliev-able colossus of a ship with seven decks, all illuminated'. It rolled at first but by the third day, he writes, the sea was calm. The food was top class: caviar and so on.

> Rachmaninoff had the most luxurious suite imaginable. He did not show himself much, walking round the empty decks on his own, looking bored. Seeing that I was disposed to be friendly, he invited me to his state-room in the evenings and I went there almost every night to play patience – a touching idyll.[92]

In his *Old Friends and New Music*, Nicolas Nabokov, composer and writer, and cousin of Vladimir Nabokov, maintained that Prokofiev and Rachmaninoff had played chess, and had patched up an ancient argument about Rachmaninoff's Scriabin season years earlier.[93] The amity only went so far. A charity concert was organised on board the *Berengaria*, and an unsuccessful attempt made to engage the distinguished Russian *boîte à musique* to join in. 'After suggesting a duet with the great "violinist" Rachmaninoff, I more seriously recommended Brodsky, who was in second class.'

The *Berengaria* eventually sailed into New York harbour, twenty-four hours late, on New Year's Eve. 'The only person there to meet us', Prokofiev grumbled, 'was a representative from Steinway, a Russian called Greiner.' Greiner was there partly to greet Prokofiev on his American tour, but primarily to welcome home his dear friend, Steinway's most illustrious client, Rachmaninoff.

A Foreign Language

When he was alive, and since his death, the assumption has been that Rachmaninoff was a conservative, his music rooted in the nineteenth century. Rachmaninoff let the image persist, in conversations with friends and in press interviews. He had a way of closing the subject by feigning bafflement about so-called modernity, putting the blame on himself. Phrases such as 'I am organically incapable of understanding' or 'the language is foreign to me' occur repeatedly. Such remarks leave no chink for further enquiry: the shutters are down. In Belgium in 1933, an interviewer dared ask why he included no 'modern' music in his own recital programmes. (Clearly the composer himself was not placed in that category.) The matter was simple, Rachmaninoff replied: 'I understand nothing of modern music of today.' He did admit, as if giving a sop to his endless scrutineers, to liking Poulenc's *Toccata*, because of its 'spontaneous inspiration'. Regarding his own work, he insisted he had not given up. He returned to composition in summer breaks and had worked recently on several transcriptions.[94]

How far do his spoken statements square with the music he

wrote, or the life he led? His embrace of the contemporary world was in so many respects absolute: the house he would soon build in Switzerland was the height of modernity in look and function; his passion for automobiles, motorboats, aviation, gadgets of every kind and, before he left Russia, all the latest farming machinery, show his fascination with the new, in aesthetic style and technological function. In recent reassessments of his music, vigorous attempts have been made to claim for him, if not radical then at least modernist tendencies: leaner lines, greater dissonance and chromaticism are noted in the few works he wrote in America.

This may be true, but equally can be seen as a natural progress towards his mature style. A more concise mode of expression, honing the motifs that make a creative voice distinctive, is a recognised artistic path. For Rachmaninoff, the *Dies irae* obsessed him from his earliest compositions to his last, in some works a dominant presence, in others a mere suggestion, like an elusive scent.[95] Capturing this plainchant in whatever varied musical attire was as vital as Cézanne revisiting Mont Sainte-Victoire or Monet repainting waterlilies in various conditions. Rachmaninoff cared primarily about expressing his own musical truth. He grappled with the question of tradition in an interview in 1910, at the time of his first American tour. The concrete had not yet set on the critical assumption that he was a relic of the nineteenth century. He certainly did not hold that view, stating that artists should respect tradition but not be bound by it: 'Iconoclasm is the law of artistic progress. All great composers and performers have built on the ruins of conventions they themselves have destroyed.'[96]

In the eyes of self-declared modernists, Rachmaninoff's failing was to have found a musical voice in his youth, a popular one at that, and stuck with it. In this he was not alone among his contemporaries. Ralph Vaughan Williams (1872–1958) was similarly accused, and suffered accordingly after his death, redemption coming later. Richard Strauss (1864–1949) somehow escaped wholesale critical contempt but, after the wild expressionism of *Salome* and *Elektra*, was dismissed as conservative. Jean Sibelius (1865–1957) was called 'the worst composer in the world' by René Leibowitz, the Polish-French disciple of the avant-garde Second Viennese School,[97] while Virgil Thomson, the composer-critic, called the same composer's Second Symphony 'vulgar, self-indulgent and provincial'.[98]

Thomson, a one-time student of Nadia Boulanger and Parisian show-off of the 1920s, held spiteful sway when he returned home to America. His attitudes prevailed particularly in the years immediately after Rachmaninoff's death. When Victor Seroff published his biography of the composer in 1950, he invited Thomson to write the preface. Thomson came to bury, not praise. Rachmaninoff's talent was not in question, he conceded, but the Russian's music was a pillow, a sedative, a retreat from battle. As for the man himself, he was gloomy and suffered an 'opulence of discontent'; 'rich wells of blackness' gushed forth constantly; as a young modernist in Russia he 'suffered defeat' at the hands of Scriabin, and was bitter about the success of Stravinsky.[99] Thomson's crushing assessment was that Rachmaninoff would have liked to be popular, conservative and advanced all at the same. The question is why Seroff asked Thomson to write the preface at all. Did he feel that presenting a contrarian view would give credence to the enterprise, given that his subject was so deeply out of fashion?

An Unlikely Pupil

No artistic progress happens in isolation. The history of music is leavened and enriched with chance encounters and unlikely friendships. The composer, pioneer and inventor Henry Cowell

(1897–1965), described by his pupil John Cage as 'the open sesame for new music in America', was a crusader for ultra-modernism.[100] Born and raised in California, Cowell had no obvious kinship with Rachmaninoff except, perhaps, an anguished childhood. Despite an upbringing shattered by the San Francisco earthquake, his parents' divorce and his mother's early death, Cowell managed to become a fine musician. He was never interested in orthodoxy. The first of his *Ings* pieces, 'Fleeting' (1917), a dreamy, pianistic miniature, requires none of the full-arm keyboard thumps and tone-clusters that would become his hallmarks.

Cowell had first met Rachmaninoff in the summer of 1919, aged twenty-two, when Rachmaninoff and his family spent the summer in Menlo Park. One of his daughters took a course at nearby Stanford University with the English professor Samuel Seward, unofficial guardian to the young Cowell.

And so I went to his home and, being inexperienced, took with me several hundred compositions, and was of course asked to select one. I selected a small piece, a two-page work for piano 'Fleeting' and Rachmaninoff kindly took this piece and examined it through an eyeglass for just two hours without saying anything whatsoever. Then he got out a small red pencil, and he put a tiny red circle around forty-one notes in these two pages, and he handed it to me with a smile and great courtesy, and said, 'There are forty-one wrong notes in your composition.' So then I said, 'What makes you think they are wrong?' and he said, 'They are not within the rules of harmony.' 'But', I said, 'do you really think that people now, in composing, should follow the rules of harmony?' He said, 'Oh yes. These are divine rules, the rules of harmony.' Very kindly he said, 'I too, when I was a boy, sometimes wrote wrong notes.'[101]

The lesson was not helpful but they parted on friendly terms, and subsequently met in New York, Chicago and elsewhere. Rachmaninoff 'always remembered me . . . He always singled me out for a warm conversation, because I had been the first musician that he met after he came to this country.'[102]

This last statement was not quite true. Rachmaninoff had met many musicians. He may have had a sympathy for Cowell, given the shared circumstance of a fragmented childhood and a determined spirit. Cowell visited the USSR in 1929, which could have been an additional source of discussion for the unlikely couple. His biographer, Sachs, adds an important corrective to that early encounter:

Although the story shows signs of embroidery, Rachmaninoff's reaction must not be dismissed as hopelessly conservative. Showing him 'Fleeting' rather than a cluster piece probably was a mistake. While Rachmaninoff would have thought using arms and elbows was absurd, 'Fleeting' could have been even more puzzling.[103]

Cowell's life drifted far beyond the boundaries of Rachmaninoff's familial landscape. When he spent four years in San Quentin prison [1936–40], sentenced for engaging in the illegal practice of oral sex, Cowell's visitors included leading figures in American musical life: the composers Lou Harrison, William Grant Still and Edgard Varèse (who described Cowell to another composer, Milton Babbitt, as 'that fucking pederast').[104] Charles Ives cut off all communication. Did Rachmaninoff visit? His friendships are characterised by enduring loyalty, with no sign of moral judgement. Cowell was not allowed to keep the list of his visitors when he left San Quentin, so we cannot know.

Slow Notes: How to Practise

In 1931 Harpo Marx was staying in the Garden of Allah Hotel, a peaceful but celebrated retreat on Hollywood's Sunset Boulevard with twenty-five villas spread around its grounds, founded by the Russian actress-director Alla Nazimova. Born in Yalta, Crimea, she was admired for her Chekhov and Ibsen and was part of Stanislavsky's Moscow Art Theatre, but her film *Salomé* (1923), now judged one of early cinema's feminist landmarks, made her name. Among her friends was Chaliapin, who reportedly visited after his performances in the mid-1920s, eating two big steaks, drinking half a bottle of vodka, and telling lewd stories until morning. (Parties at the Garden of Allah at that time were noted, among other features, for their sexual liberty.) Nazimova's hotelier skills were lacking, and the Garden of Allah had changed hands by the time Marx stayed. The comedian and musician, second oldest of the Marx Brothers, planned to do some serious harp practice, 'until a piano player moved into a bungalow across from mine and shattered the peace'. The playing grew louder and more insistent. Marx made an official complaint. 'The new guest, whose playing was driving me nuts, was Sergei Rachmaninoff. They were not about to ask him to move.'

Marx found his own mean solution:

I opened the door and all the windows in my place and began to play the first four bars of Rachmaninoff's Prelude in C sharp Minor, over and over, fortissimo. Two hours later my fingers were getting numb. But I didn't let up, not until I heard a thunderous crash of notes from across the way, like the keyboard had been attacked with a pair of sledgehammers. Then there was silence. This time it was Rachmaninoff who went to complain. He asked to be moved to another bungalow immediately, the farthest possible from that dreadful silence. Peace returned to the Garden.[105]

Marx included a 'performance' of the Prelude in *A Day at the Races* (1937), in which he pummels the piano so hard it falls apart – an even more extreme effort than Mickey Mouse's attempt with a collapsing keyboard in *The Opry House*.

Everyone, it seemed, who came into contact with Rachmaninoff had views on his practice habits. In his witty memoirs, Herman Finck (1872–1939) relates one typical encounter. As a leading musical-theatre conductor at the Theatre Royal, Drury Lane, and a composer (his popular song, 'The Shadows', was among the last pieces of music played on the *Titanic*, guaranteeing him enduring fame), he moved in eclectic musical circles. One of his friends was Benno Moiseiwitsch, with whom he regularly shared a bottle of champagne over a game of cards or dominoes. He does not, however, seem to have known Benno's friend Rachmaninoff:

When I was on tour with *Merrie England* in Glasgow, I went upstairs to dress for dinner, and was surprised to hear brilliant pianoforte playing. Someone was playing Chopin, then dropping into [Mendelssohn's] *Midsummer Night's Dream* scherzo. A part of the scherzo would be played very slowly, them more Chopin would follow.

I was so fascinated by the playing that I began to undress in the corridor, outside my bedroom, to listen.

'Who is that playing' I asked the chambermaid.

'Oh I can't pronounce his name,' she replied.

'Rachmaninoff?' I asked.

'Yes that's it.'

Rachmaninoff was giving a recital in Glasgow that night, but as

I stood in the corridor, wrestling with a white tie, I could not for the life of me think why he should be playing Mendelssohn at that dirge-like tempo.

Months later I heard that Rachmaninoff had prepared an elaborate pianoforte arrangement of the scherzo. So I was the first person to hear it; he had been going through it slowly that night in Glasgow.[106]

This was Rachmaninoff's usual method. The English musician Arthur Hirst heard him from another room playing so slowly that the work in question, by Liszt and known to Hirst, was unrecognisable. A guest at Villers-sur-Mers in the summer of 1928, the pianist-teacher Olga Conus, was enthralled by hearing him practise, every morning for at least half an hour, the trill and arpeggio in Czerny's Étude op. 740, and nothing but. She noted that the arpeggios were impeccably clear and light as a bird. Boris Chaliapin, painting him while he was practising, in the summer of 1940, had a different, and more exciting, experience: his sitter (by default) started very slowly then eventually speeded up, covering the whole keyboard in rapid scales, then working at particular passages, sometimes fast, at others, slow. He used a metronome, adjusting it faster or slower accordingly.

All his logic in practising, as a composer bringing creativity and colour to everything he played, whether his own music or not, comes back to comments he made years earlier to Marietta Shaginian. He had to understand the mechanics of a piece. He peered into every corner, taking out every screw, so that it could be put together, properly, as a whole. Above all he wanted to grasp the culminating 'point' of a work, otherwise he had failed. He shared that view with his friend Chaliapin. Each variously complained, on occasion, of having missed, or slipped the 'point'.

Time and Motion Studies

These 'overheard practising' stories amount to more than anecdotes. They reveal much about Rachmaninoff's dedication, as well as his approach: his insistence on dismantling every work he played in order to understand it, and then to reassemble it in performance. The habit went on until late in life. In December 1941, in Beverly Hills, the Rachmaninoffs had a visit from Abram Chasins, an American composer and pianist. He recalled the occasion in a sleeve-note to recordings of the piano and orchestral works made between 1934 and 1941 with Ormandy, Stokowski and the Philadelphia Orchestra. Knowing Rachmaninoff's famed exactitude as a timekeeper, Chasins arrived early.

He stood outside the house, the sound of a piano audible. Eventually he identified the slow procession of notes as Chopin's Étude in G sharp minor, op. 25 no. 6, also called the 'double-thirds étude' because of the rapid trilling of thirds at the start. He calculated that every bar took Rachmaninoff twenty seconds to play, his pace for nearly an hour. Chasins was 'riveted to the spot' and could not bring himself to ring the doorbell.

Rachmaninoff had no patience with colleagues who considered practice a matter of running through a programme before a concert. Russians have a proverb, a version of slow and steady wins the race but without the same urgency of competition. In this case the metaphor relates to horses: ride slower and you'll get further. As an experienced equestrian, owning around a hundred horses in his Ivanovka days, Rachmaninoff would have understood the expression.

After lunch that day, having eventually rung the doorbell, Chasins had an idea:

Knowing Rachmaninoff's enthusiasm for motoring, I suggested late that afternoon an automobile drive in an

143

Isotta-Fraschini – one of those fantastic Italian cars loaned to
me by my California host for this auspicious pilgrimage. He
accepted eagerly and kept exclaiming excitedly over the car's
performance. When we got to Santa Monica, he couldn't hold
out any longer and asked if he could drive it. At the wheel,
he displayed from the first moment the same precisional
coordination and rhythmic rightness of his piano mastery.[107]

As Gloria Swanson's character, Norma Desmond, says of her
own 1929 Isotta-Fraschini in *Sunset Boulevard* (1950): 'we have a
car. Not one of those cheap things made of chromium and spit but
Isotta Fraschini. Have you ever heard of Isotta Fraschini? All hand-
made. It cost me twenty-eight thousand dollars.' Rachmaninoff did
not purchase one, but by now he had abandoned his Ford Lincoln
in favour of a faster and more luxurious Packard.

An article in American *Vogue* in April 1943, published soon after
his death, described the three things he liked about America. Firstly,
the respect the country showed for a human being, 'for what he is
and for what he does, and it does not matter where he came from'.
Secondly, the quality of American orchestras:

He cupped his hands behind his ears and closed his eyes.
'I can hear how the Philadelphia Orchestra sounds or the
Boston Orchestra. Just to go and hear them play is the greatest
pleasure. Naturally, I love to play with them.'
    Third and last? Cars.
    He sighs when he speaks of them, and there is an expression
in his eyes like that of a young girl swallowing ice-cream. 'They
are the best in the world.' He smiled suddenly. 'If one must
have a hobby – American cars might be mine.'

1930-1939

France, Switzerland, Second Exile

Le Pavillon, France

After more than a decade in exile, the yearning for Europe and the need for a summer retreat grew pressing. Rachmaninoff rented in France, close to his daughters, a house named 'Le Pavillon', an hour's drive south-west of Paris, in the village of Clairefontaine. Riesemann draws a bucolic picture of this rural hideaway in the Île-de-France:

> As one enters the village there rises a high wall with a high gate, but this only opens to the pull of a bell, which must be a century old. Through the wrought iron gate one can see the corner of an unpretentious manor house . . . Before the house stretches the broad *pelouse*, surrounded by magnificent old chestnut and lime-trees, through which one gets a glimpse of the tennis court, while immediately behind the lawn an arrow-straight avenue, flanked by the grey beech trunks and silver birches of the park, seems to dwindle into infinite distance. There are ponds close by bordered by lush meadows and soaring woods – loud with the croaking of frogs. 'I would not exchange this concert for the most beautiful chorus of nightingales,' says the Composer. For the rest there is silence.[1]

After time in Paris attending concerts by Toscanini, as well as two Russian evenings, with readings from Turgenev and Gogol, Rachmaninoff retreated to 'Le Pavillon'. Visitors were frequent, including young friends of Tatiana and Irina who came at weekends from Paris, turning it into 'Babel', as their father wrote to a friend.

On 12 May 1930, in merry mood, he urged their close friends, Katherine and Alfred Swan, to come:

Dear Alfred Alfredovich,

    Our hearty greetings to the Swans. Yesterday, we moved here into the country. The tennis court is being lengthened and widened. The surface is being rolled and improved. I have bought new rackets. New balls. I am bankrupt. When will you come?[2]

The Swans, remembering their friendship with Rachmaninoff after his death, painted their own lively sketch of the chateau. Set back from the street, hidden away, it 'lent itself well to this Russian life on a large scale, which rolled on comfortably in the cheerful rooms, just big enough to remain liveable'. They describe the sandy avenues flanked with tall, old trees, the tennis court 'tucked away among shrubs'. They also mention a Russian maid.

The whole arrangement was very much like that of a Russian estate. The park of the Pavillon adjoined the summer residence of the President of France. A small gate opened into its vast hunting grounds: pinewood with innumerable rabbits. Rachmaninoff loved to sit under the pine-trees and watch the games and pranks of the rabbits. In the morning the big table in the dining-room was set for breakfast. As in the country in Russia, tea was served and with it cream, ham, cheese, hard-boiled eggs.

Mushroom hunting was a favourite activity with Rachmaninoff, always an early riser, gathering them before anyone else was up. On one occasion, he teased everyone by 'replanting' his harvest not in the woods where he found them but amid moss and grass, enjoying their surprise discoveries by his perplexed household. Life was relaxed, but with an unspoken routine, as recorded by Swan:

After tea, no matter how many guests there were, the big house would plunge into silence. Quietly and very inconspicuously, Rachmaninoff closed the doors of the drawing room and sat down at the piano. He did not practise in the strict sense of the word; he played something through, went with his fingers over the keyboard meditatively, and then suddenly the loud and victorious sounds of Beethoven's 'Les Adieux' would be heard. Then he would again appear in the garden or the dining room . . .

Did Rachmaninoff choose Beethoven's middle-period Sonata no. 26 in E flat for the digital workout it provided, or was it an ironic indication that his practice time was over? He would introduce 'Les Adieux' into the following season, together with the *Oriental Sketch* he had written in Russia in 1917, and more Brahms, Chopin and Liszt. (Another work, not yet written, would be added too, perhaps to the composer's own surprise.)

Swan's fond account includes noisy games of poker 'in which Medtner was the principal loser' – Medtner, ever the underdog – followed by singing round the piano with Rachmaninoff playing popular Russian songs, one in particular, at the request of his daughters:

'Bublichki', known in both Yiddish and Russian, about the bubliks, or doughnut-like pastries shaped like bagels and sold by street vendors. Sergei and Natalia also played his *Italian Polka* – the *secondo* part loud and thumping, the *primo* rapid and trifling. Rachmaninoff would jest, not forgetting that Natalia was a skilled pianist herself, that 'This is the only thing Nataschenchka knows . . .'

Next morning Medtner, characteristically earnest, found Rachmaninoff at the piano, and hoped to engage him in a discussion about music in general, composition in particular. Medtner told Swan:

> All my life has passed parallel to his, but with no one have I talked so little about music as with him. Once I even told him how I wanted to discuss with him the subject of harmony. Immediately his face became very distant and he said, 'Yes, yes, we must sometime.'[3]

They never did.

Bricks and Mortar

Now Rachmaninoff wanted his own property. The shock to the world economy of the New York stock-market crash in October 1929, the subsequent collapse of the banking system and the Great Depression intensified his desire to act. He was nearly sixty. He needed to invest his hard-earned wealth in bricks and mortar. Back in 1902 he and Natalia had spent part of their honeymoon in Lucerne. In 1930 he visited Riesemann, who lived in the area. One of Rachmaninoff's aims that summer was to rework his Second Piano Sonata. He thought it too protracted and thickly written. He would eventually cut it substantially, by around 120 bars, and thin out its textures. The revision, almost a different sonata, less virtuosic, less monumental, would take on some of the lean qualities of an entirely new composition for piano and, not for the first time in his output, leave performers in dispute about which version to perform.

Amid all this, Rachmaninoff attended a concert in Switzerland by the twenty-seven-year-old Nathan Milstein. In his memoir *From*

Russia to the West, the Odesa-born violinist tells an insightful story about the particular way in which the usually patient Rachmaninoff was provoked. He entertained Rachmaninoff with tales of his triumphs at blackjack, roulette and a roulette spin-off, caramel, encouraging the older man to have a lucky win at the casino in Lucerne. Milstein had just played a concert which included Bach's solo E major Partita. Rachmaninoff was impressed and decided to make a piano transcription of the Prelude, Gavotte and Fugue.

In a long account, Milstein describes his own pride at, in due course, being invited to Rachmaninoff's first performance of the new work, in Paris. He listened closely and dared tell the composer he thought one part had not sounded idiomatically 'Bachian'. Milstein writes: 'Rachmaninoff interrupted angrily, "Go to hell." Oh boy, I thought, this is coming to a bad end for me. Of course, going to hell was not obligatory, but staying around Rachmaninoff was uncomfortable.' A dinner was being held by his daughter Tatiana. Seeing Milstein's unhappiness, 'his wife, Natalia Alexandrovna, saw me still at the theatre, clearly in despair, and came over to me. "Do come with us. Sergei Vasilievich didn't mean to offend you. He was just nervous after performing." I went, feeling I were headed for questioning by the Soviet *cheka*.'[4]

As Milstein tells it, amusingly, all Rachmaninoff's composer friends were there – Glazunov, Medtner, Grechaninov, Julius Conus (father of Tatiana's husband, Boris). None, when quizzed by their agitated host, had spotted any infelicity, or admitted to hearing any problem. Milstein began to doubt his ears. Had they been listening? Worse still, had he? Both he and Rachmaninoff were staying at the Hotel Majestic on avenue Kléber in the sixteenth arrondissement. Later that night, he was summoned via the concierge to go to Rachmaninoff's room. Milstein was of modest height. Bearing that in mind, the picture he paints has additional humour. 'I was afraid. What if he cursed me again? I meekly opened the door to his suite – just a tiny bit, not daring to enter – and he shouted, "Come in, come in. You were right!" I was ecstatic!'[5]

This *volte-face* is typical of Rachmaninoff – a quick burst of anger, then in every case an equally rapid climbdown, except with Prokofiev where the about-face never really occurred. The rest of Milstein's recollections are about the brilliance of Rachmaninoff's musicianship and his sense of fun: the frequent visits to see him in Switzerland, his delight at Horowitz's parodies of fellow pianists – Paderewski, Artur Schnabel, Walter Gieseking – though he took offence at the gloomy, feet-dragging, face-rubbing figure that was a witty portrayal of himself. 'And that was funny too!' Milstein chuckled. The pattern is clear: Rachmaninoff struggled, at least momentarily, when he was the butt of humour or criticism.

In this period, the early 1930s, with factual input from his sister-in-law Sofia Satina, Rachmaninoff agreed to work with Riesemann on the conversations which would result in *Rachmaninoff's Recollections, told to Oskar von Riesemann* (1934). According to Satina, Riesemann wrote nothing down, didn't even carry a pencil, and Rachmaninoff was uncomfortable about the results, requested revisions and then dismissed its accuracy. As anyone who has ever interviewed anyone knows, 'writing things down' is no guarantee of pleasing the subject, who will certainly say, on seeing their words in print, that they never said anything of the kind. They may also give a significantly different version to another interviewer on another day. Riesemann's book is lively, sympathetic and readable. It aligns with the man we know from letters and other accounts, in spirit if not always in fact. Riesemann's eye-witness observations have fed many subsequent studies. We should be glad of his efforts.

Rachmaninoff may not have thanked Riesemann for the book, but he had another reason for gratitude. It was he who, on

Rachmaninoff's behalf in 1930, posted an advertisement with a box number seeking a property in Lucerne. They received a response from the newly widowed owner (Susanna Olga Schmidt-Vogt) of a lakeside estate offering, for rent or purchase: country house with eleven rooms, park 1.5 hectares, 150 metres of lake front with quay, boat/bathhouse. Rachmaninoff's response was immediate. Hardly pausing, he bought the lakeside property on 13 September 1930.

Lucerne, Switzerland

Of the myths and mysteries associated with Lake Lucerne – witches, dragons, the legendary Swiss hero, William Tell – its shape is its greatest enigma. With four bent arms, each fed by a different river, this majestic lake twists from south to north, west to east, dominated by the mountain massif Pilatus at one end, a ring of Alpine peaks to the other. On a summer morning, from the vantage point of a paddlewheel steamer sailing away from the town itself, lake and mountain merge into a misty, light-filled distance. Behind, receding, are the railway station, churches and bell-towers, and palatial tourist hotels built in the years before World War I. Grandest, to this day, is the Hotel Montana (1910), set against the hillside, with its own electric funicular railway to carry guests to its lobby. On an opposite, projecting headland stands the villa Tribschen, with its own waterfront. This was where the exiled Richard Wagner lived in unwedded bliss with Cosima von Bülow (née Liszt) for six productive years. Inside on the stairs, his *Siegfried Idyll* was first performed on Christmas morning 1870. It was at Tribschen that he finished *Die Meistersinger von Nürnberg* and *Siegfried* and began *Götterdämmerung*.

Rachmaninoff's land was across the lake on the northern shore. Whereas an impecunious Wagner was helped by 'Mad King

Ludwig', Ludwig II of Bavaria, Rachmaninoff required no patron, wealthy or mad: he was by now one of the highest-earning performers in the world. In 1927, Prokofiev noted in his diary that Rachmaninoff's wealth was estimated at $1.5 million, and that he earned $3,000 per concert, adding pointedly, and without much proof: 'Nevertheless he is as bored as the devil.'[6] By 1942 *Time* magazine (21 September) reported that he had earned $2.4 million during his American career.

In Lucerne, on the quiet promontory of Hertenstein, he had chosen a place remote from the 'boundless ocean', the endless fields of wheat, rye and oats, of Ivanovka. Here instead was a landscape of alpine grandeur, closer to Edmund Burke's ideal of the sublime, dominated by Mount Pilatus. The existing house, a Swiss-style chalet, dated from 1910, with farm buildings, a spice 'factory' to process spices grown by the lake, and a boathouse. Initially Rachmaninoff hired a Swiss architect, Emil Felix, to add a separate studio. Within days that plan was scrapped. They would build a new house from scratch, keeping Felix's idea of a flat roof 'so the family can spend time there in fine weather'.[7]

Grand Designs

Less than a month later, the Lucerne architects Möri & Krebs bid for the contract. It was they who had built the famous Hotel Montana, with its pioneering funicular: precisely Rachmaninoff's kind of modernity. He would have to find ways to pay for it. On 25 October 1930, he embarked on a European tour of twenty-two concerts, starting in Oslo and ending, on 10 December, in Zurich. Two days later in that city, at the Hotel Baur au Lac, he met Alfred Möri to discuss plans. This was no ordinary hotel but one of Zurich's most lavish, numbering tsarinas, emperors and empresses

FRANCE, SWITZERLAND, SECOND EXILE

among its guests. It was here that Wagner gave a performance of Act I of *Die Walküre*, for his father-in-law Liszt's forty-fifth birthday. Wagner sang Siegmund and Hunding with Liszt on the piano: an event too enthralling to picture.

By the end of the meeting with Möri, all was fixed. Existing buildings would be demolished. Five metres of rocky outcrop by the lake would be removed, reutilised to create walls and paths, the entire terrain landscaped. Work would start immediately on the gardener's house and garage. Rachmaninoff was clear about his needs: large study, salon, hallway, dining room, kitchen, two rooms with a bath for staff, cellar, laundry, four bedrooms with three bathrooms. He also specified: 'The best room should be the study, with large windows 3.5 to 4 metres high looking out over Lake Lucerne.'[8]

The family returned to New York. Möri sent plans. His client replied by return. No wallpaper, he instructed, but smoothly plastered rooms, colour to be decided. Could the gardener's house be less meagre, less of a plain box (but without excess costs)? How about a balcony or loggia to match the 'big' house? An Art Deco dream villa, crouching in green grass like an ocean liner in blue sea, was about to be realised.

Rachmaninoff had a heavy schedule for his next American season, with a spring tour from the East Coast to the West, taking in Canada. Reviews were poor. He was puzzled and grumpy. 'I played well and I'm pleased with myself. But the critics are sour. What does it mean?' he wrote to his secretary, Somov. The critic of the *Kalamazoo College Index*, on 1 January 1931, expressed awe at the flawless pianism, but commented: 'Not only did he maintain an aloofness which completely set him on a different plane from his audience, but even his face seemed an expressionless mask, coldly composed.'

Tagore Troubles

Having kept himself away from public controversy concerning the Soviet Union since he left Russia, Rachmaninoff found himself in a political cauldron. The cause was a letter dated 12 January 1931, published three days later in the *New York Times*, condemning Rabindranath Tagore, the Bengali poet, for his benign views on the Soviet Union. Tagore had visited the country recently, and given enthusiastic interviews to the press, notably about Soviet education. Rachmaninoff's two co-signatories were Ivan Ostromislensky, his Russian chemist friend, and Count Ilya L. Tolstoy, second son of Leo Tolstoy, now living in the United States. Writing as from the 'Circle of Russian Culture', the aim of which 'is to foster intellectual intercourse among the Russian immigrants in New York', they questioned Tagore's views: 'Strangely, not a word did he utter on the horrors perpetrated by the Soviet Government, and the OGPU [secret police] in particular.'

The letter points out that at the time of Tagore's visit, 'forty-six Russian professors and engineers were executed' without any pretence of trial. Millions of labourers and workers had been exiled to the frozen far north, starved and tortured. 'At no time, and in no country, has there ever existed a government responsible for so many cruelties, wholesale murders and common law crimes in general as those perpetrated by the Bolsheviki.'

Rachmaninoff soon felt the weight of Soviet cultural ire. The Russian Association of Proletarian Musicians slated his work as 'reactionary, reflecting a decadent mood of the petit bourgeoisie' as well as 'harmful in the bitter conditions of class struggle'. This campaign against Rachmaninoff led to some performances of his work in the Soviet Union being cancelled, but no edict was issued to proscribe his music, which, in the shifting sands of political and cultural opinion, remained part of the canon.

Those performances that did take place provoked well-co-ordinated attacks. On 5 and 6 March 1931 Albert Coates, born in Russia to British parents, conducted *The Bells* (alongside Holst's *The Planets*). The combination of Coates on the podium, verses by the symbolist poet Balmont (in Poe's translation) and music by Rachmaninoff fuelled the sharp-tongued Nikolai Vygodsky, organist and pianist at the Moscow Conservatory. He was a key proponent of music for the masses, which *The Bells* decidedly was not, as a reflection of Soviet ideology. Vygodsky attacked Holst too, calling him a 'glorifier of the contemporary imperialist bourgeoisie of Europe and America' and absurdly complaining that his capital-ist and 'deeply political' *Planets* had omitted Earth in its line-up.

Vygodsky's first targets, though, were Rachmaninoff, *The Bells and all connected with the work*. To have these 'demigods of the deca-dent pre-Revolutionary intelligentsia of the bourgeois salons, now turned White émigrés', together with a conductor fashionable in Europe 'who left Russia in 1917', merely heaped suspicion on sus-picion. Rachmaninoff and the poet Balmont were dubbed enemies of the working class and 'pillars' of the past. The complaints were limitless: the work is gloomy and pessimistic, full of cold and deathly horror. The music, rampant with individualism and psychological instability, intoxicates (not a compliment), clouding the consciousness and weakening the will. All this to the accom-paniment, the horror, of church bells. 'Just where are we supposed to be? Is this a funeral service, a black mass, a spiritualist seance or a sacred concert? Where does all this horror and the mysticism spring from?'[9]

Ongoing Ding-Dong

The ripple effect was felt on both sides of the world. In the *Syracuse Herald* of 21 March 1931, a diary column lampooned the Soviet response:

> A boycott is declared by Moscow and Leningrad conservatories on the works of Sergei Rachmaninoff, Russian composer. The Rachmaninoff compositions are attacked as 'reactionary' and particularly dangerous to conditions in the acute class struggle on the musical front. This establishes the world's record for asininity. Next the Bolsheviki will boycott the sun because it continues to shine on Piłsudski, Briand, Churchill and the Pope.

On the same day the Washington *Evening Star* carried a report from a journalist who had 'doorstepped' Rachmaninoff after his concert:

> Wrestling with a pair of rubbers, a woollen scarf and an overcoat, Sergei Rachmaninoff, the great Russian pianist and composer, flung out a brief 'Proud of it' when questioned on what he thought of having his compositions banned . . . and thereupon beat a hasty retreat from his dressing room after a brilliant recital at Constitution Hall. 'Why shouldn't I be?' he added.

Asked, in immemorial journalistic fashion, whether Rachmaninoff had anything to add, he called 'No!', having 'run partway down the hall'. The previous day Rachmaninoff had admitted to being surprised by the 'ban', only hearing about it after reading the newspapers. Far from shrinking from the compositions which 'had aroused such wrath in his native land' he played some as encores, including 'the famous Prelude in C sharp minor'. Then after countless more encores, a man walked out on the stage and closed the piano.

The furore over the Tagore letter made Rachmaninoff cautious, and in public, non-committal. Asked about the Russian situation a few months later he 'frankly declared' that he did not concern himself with politics: 'The last I saw of Russia was when I left it in 1918 [*sic*]. I do not know whether the Soviet plan is really improving conditions and I cannot express sympathy nor can I utter scorn.' The article concluded that he would go to Europe for concerts the next year and 'probably' visit his homeland. He did not, and never would.

On this occasion, as on several others, he stated his preference for playing to a live concert audience. 'Will I ever present concerts over radio or on the sound screen? No – I think not. The radio is very nice but I can do my best when I perform on a platform in front of an audience, where the tone of the music is true and real.'[10]

Villa Senar

By the end of July 1931, Rachmaninoff had purchased another 2,563 square metres of adjoining land at Hertenstein and the smaller house was ready.[11] First the family spent one last period at 'Le Pavillon'. Rachmaninoff protested that 'guests, guests and guests' came all week, not just weekends. At the same time work kept him from guests. He was working 'a lot', he wrote to Somov, adding: 'The latest political events have swooped down on us like a thunderstorm. It's no longer good to be living on this earth! And it seems to me that the worst times are still ahead.'[12] In his home-land, Stalinism was on the rise, the drive for rapid industrialisation causing shockwaves. In February that year, Stalin had addressed 'industrial managers' about fighting the backwardness which had dogged 'old Russia':

> She was beaten by the Mongol khans. She was beaten by the
> Turkish beys. She was beaten by the Swedish feudal lords.
> She was beaten by the Polish and Lithuanian gentry. She
> was beaten by the British and French capitalists. She was
> beaten by the Japanese barons. All beat her because of her
> backwardness, military backwardness, cultural backwardness,
> political backwardness, industrial backwardness, agricultural
> backwardness [. . .] But now that we have overthrown
> capitalism and power is in our hands, in the hands of
> the people, we have a fatherland, and we will defend its
> independence . . .[13]

As ever, Rachmaninoff gathered Russian friends around him. One was Michael Chekhov, nephew of Anton Chekhov and an influential actor and theatre practitioner. A disciple of Stanislavsky, he would eventually, using his own teaching methods, tutor Marilyn Monroe,[14] Gregory Peck, Clint Eastwood, Yul Brynner and other Hollywood stars. He was also connected with the early days of Dartington Hall, Devon as a cultural centre, rebuilt by Dorothy and Leonard Elmhirst from 1925: he almost persuaded Rachmaninoff's secretary, Somov, to work at his theatre school there, a plan that fizzled out when Chekhov moved to America.

Chekhov, like others, recalled the particular and distinctive way his host practised: he worked through scales every morning, emerging with a long face. Then he would walk to the tennis court, watch the game in progress, light another cigarette and relax. (The record producer O'Connell was fascinated by the smoking: 'I often wondered how he managed, without painful accidents, to insert between his lips the cigarette butts he smoked continuously.'[15]) Chekhov also delighted in the effect Chaliapin had on Rachmaninoff, who would always beam at the sight of him.

> He loved Fyodor Ivanovich dearly. They walked through the garden, both tall and graceful (each in his own way), and talked: F. I. the louder, S. V. the softer. S. V. would lift his right eyebrow slyly, look askance at his friend, then laugh heartily . . .
>
> Rachmaninoff would want Chaliapin to sing. Chaliapin would refuse, then eventually yield.
>
> At the piano S. V. touched a few chords; and then, as Fedya sang, S. V. looked so joyful, so young, now and then glancing at us as if successfully performing a trick. The singing ended. S. V. laughed and patted Fedya's powerful shoulder, and I noticed tears in his eyes.[16]

Corelli Variations

Despite the jovial interludes with Chaliapin, that summer Rachmaninoff wrote one of his most introverted and sombre works. The difficulties of the year, the bad reviews, the accusations of weariness and lassitude of spirit, as one critic put it, dragged him down, yet he produced a masterpiece. *Variations on a Theme of Corelli*, op. 42, was his only solo piano piece since leaving Russia. It was also the last work he wrote that was – predominantly, and with some radical harmonic departures en route – in his favoured key of D minor: the key of his Symphony no. 1, Piano Sonata no. 1 and Piano Concerto no. 3.

The 'Corelli theme', *La Folia*, was a traditional Portuguese dance melody: rather dull, an ideal blank canvas for invention, and not by Corelli at all. It had been used by composers before – and by others since – but Rachmaninoff stuck to his title. His source was Corelli's Violin Sonata, op. 5 no. 12, also in D minor. The tune had a story attached: of a shepherd whose love was not returned and who, in his anguish, threw himself off a rock to his death. Rachmaninoff's work occupies a less dramatic landscape. Sadness and poignancy, with erratic, rapid interruptions, colour the mood. He told Alfred Swan that the work had not come easily, 'not as in former years'. He also complained that he had burst blood-vessels on his fingertips, which interfered with his playing, but that even so, a life without concerts would 'be the end of me'.[17]

Rachmaninoff gave the *Corelli Variations*' premiere in Montreal at the start of the 1931–2 season, to the kind of mixed reception becoming a habit with his new works. He confessed to friends that he dropped some of the variations at whim, according to the level of coughing in the audience. On one notably raucous occasion he played only ten variations. In Queen's Hall, London, he omitted two, no. 12 (*L'istesso tempo*) and no. 19 (*Più mosso, Agitato*).[18] He remained ambivalent about the piece and, after the 1933–4 season, stopped playing it; he never recorded it.

The dedicatee was Kreisler – who had written his own variations, and whose famous insouciance and openness were as far from Rachmaninoff's personality, or that of his *Corelli Variations*, as it was possible to be. Having met first in Kreisler's home city of Vienna in 1903, they shared a manager in Charles Foley. They appear to have played rarely if at all in public together, but they made recordings, Kreisler usually content with the first endeavour, Rachmaninoff always gloomily insisting on many retakes until the performance was perfect. A story still circulating among New York musicians pinpoints the contrasting musical intelligence of these two dazzling virtuosi: the violinist all warmth, generous vibrato, abundant expression, the pianist disciplined, precise, crystalline.

First, the reader must know that a *Nachschlag* (literally, an 'after-beat') is a type of ornament, not easy to define, in some musical situations considered *de trop*. The tale is best told in the present tense: the pair are rehearsing Beethoven's last violin sonata, op. 96 in G major, which opens with a trill in the violin, followed by a responding trill in the piano. Kreisler plays his with a *Nachschlag*. Rachmaninoff comes in, playing his without. So Rachmaninoff stops and says, 'Let's try that again'. Once again Kreisler plays it with a *Nachschlag*, Rachmaninoff without. So Rachmaninoff turns to Kreisler and says, 'Let's not play this piece!'.[19]

Koussevitzky's Gamble

The effects of the Wall Street Crash continued to filter through to cultural life. Bookings and concert attendances were down. Rachmaninoff, after spending liberally at Senar in the summer of 1932 – a large motorboat, the installation of a Marconi wireless gramophone – momentarily wobbled financially. In January 1933 he sent a telegram to Switzerland asking for construction work to be postponed. Within weeks he had changed his mind, and the building process, with all mod cons requested, began again. He had given fewer recitals the previous year but redressed his losses with a heavy 1932–3 season. His appearances with orchestras remained a draw. Ormandy in Minneapolis and Frederick Stock in Chicago conducted him as soloist in Piano Concertos nos 2 and 3 respectively, to rave reviews.

Less successfully, Koussevitzky had commissioned the Italian composer Ottorino Respighi to orchestrate five of Rachmaninoff's piano *Études-Tableaux* (one from op. 33, four from op. 39). The entrepreneurial Koussevitzky was hoping for the same success he had had with another high-profile orchestration: Ravel's glittering version of Mussorgsky's *Pictures at An Exhibition*. No luck alas, second time round. This new orchestration never caught on but it winkled out of the usually reluctant Rachmaninoff a 'programme' for each of the five *Études* in question – notably the association of op. 39 no. 6, a frenzy of chromatic rumbles, sudden silences, scurrying responses, with Little Red Riding Hood and the Wolf – a bid for approachability perhaps.

Much store has been set by these pictorial explanations, yet they feel out of place in relation to the original piano pieces. The distinction of op. 39 is the way these short pieces conjure dark, complex but essentially abstract moods, without specific meaning. As Rachmaninoff always said, listeners should paint for themselves what the music most suggests. In any case Respighi's effort was a failure, and remains a concert-hall rarity.

Before sailing once again to Europe, Rachmaninoff reminded a *New York Times* interviewer that he thought his best works were *The Bells* and the *All-Night Vigil*, the latter still almost unknown. In March 1932 he was in London to play his Third Concerto conducted by Henry Wood. He was awarded the Royal Philharmonic Society's highest honour, the Gold Medal, following in the wake not only of Wood, but of composers he admired: Gustav Holst and Ralph Vaughan Williams (both in 1930), and in 1931, Arnold Bax. (Bax was not so keen on Rachmaninoff. A collection of his letters that came up for sale at Sotheby's revealed complaints that Rachmaninoff showed 'too much of the Romantic-Russian self-pity'.)[20]

That summer Rachmaninoff's younger daughter, Tatiana, married Boris Conus, son of her parents' old friend from Russia, the violinist Julius Conus. There were reservations about the match. A terse paragraph from Sophia Satin's memoir, *A 20th Century Life*, describes their wedding:

My favourite cousin, Tatiana Rachmaninoff, married Boris Conus. My mother was asked by Tanya to attend. Only my aunt was there since Uncle Sergei did not approve of Tatiana's choice and was absent. I could never understand Tanya. Why, of all her admirers, did she choose him? I always considered him not very clever and he loved to talk in a silly way.[21]

If her account is accurate, it is remarkable that so dedicated a father as Rachmaninoff should choose not to attend his daughter's wedding.

Around this time Rachmaninoff received an appeal from Vladimir Nabokov, exiled in Europe and living in Berlin. The writer had left Russia, having lost the family estate. He was writing, in Russian, under the pen-name Vladimir Sirin. Rachmaninoff was a keen reader of 'Sirin'.

Nabokov knew all about Rachmaninoff's new life, and even the name of his (former) powerful agent, Charles Ellis. Robert Roper, in *Nabokov in America*, writes:

Nabokov cared little for music, classical or any other kind, but he knew this story [of Rachmaninoff's success in America] (as did everyone else in the emigration) and may be said to have traced a writerly version of Rachmaninoff's trajectory, although his own progress was more halting [. . .] like [Nabokov] Rachmaninoff was of a contemplative but adventurous temperament – a gleeful speeder in powerful cars, for instance.[22]

Their connection was closer than this suggests. In 1932 Nabokov met 'Mme [Mlle?] Rachmaninoff' – probably Tatiana – in Paris when she was running Tair. He describes how she she gave him a lift home when they were both at tea with the journalist Lollii Lvov (working on the Paris paper *Russia and Slavdom*), a friend of Nabokov and a literary consultant at Tair. One of the main aims of the family firm was to make available to the émigré community new books which Russian authors had difficulty in getting published. They discussed the possibility of publishing Nabokov's *Glory*, and the author would later approach Rachmaninoff about publishing *The Gift*. Neither came to fruition in the course of Tair's brief existence, though the conversations went on even after the company had folded.

Champs-Elysées *à la Russe*

Loyalty was one of Rachmaninoff's most attractive qualities. Given the birth agonies of that First Symphony in St Petersburg nearly forty years earlier, he might have been expected to sever contact with Glazunov, a target of blame. Rightly or not, his association with the work has become a sorry part of musical history. Instead, the two men retained a fond contact, if now with a degree of pathos. Glazunov had stayed in the Soviet Union. A conservative but respected presence, he was still director of the renamed Leningrad Conservatory, escaping the worst Bolshevik strictures. When Prokofiev visited him on a trip to Leningrad in 1927, he was living, elderly and unwell, in a cavernous but dilapidated apartment within the grand building built by his merchant forebears in better days.

Under the guise of health reasons, he left Leningrad the next year and went to Paris, a city thronging with Russian cultural life in exile. Glazunov arrived in time to attend Rachmaninoff's first Paris concert in 1928. Prokofiev was there too, naturally noting that Paris had so far taken little interest in Rachmaninoff, nor he in it. A celebrity crowd turned out to listen to the great virtuoso, including Diaghilev, as well as the fashionable Paris milliner

Fatma Hanum (a friend of Prokofiev's, she begged him not to let his spiky comments upset her relationship with her affluent new clients, Tatiana and Irina Rachmaninoff). Prokofiev did not care for the concert. He regretted that Rachmaninoff had not played Beethoven, disliked his Chopin, thought he played his own music badly but still could not help finding him a 'formidably interesting' personality. 'The way he walks on to the stage is incredible: a sort of sidelong, hesitating shuffle that makes you wonder if he is ever going to make it to the piano.' We can only be grateful to Prokofiev for his unstinting bitchiness: his comments may be unkind but they have a terrible, vivid authenticity.

Nor does the unstoppable chronicler always paint the kindest picture of himself. Sheltering from the rain at his barber's on the Champs-Elysées, Prokofiev spotted Glazunov stumbling slowly along without an umbrella. Thinking to avoid him, instead he greeted him with – he admits – embarrassment. The great Glazunov had shrunk to a piteous, shambling figure. Later that day, Prokofiev bumped into Stravinsky at the publishers – Paris bristled with such luminous encounters – and told him about his meeting. Stravinsky replied that, days before, he visited Glazunov in the artists' room following the latter's concert. He did not recognise Stravinsky who cried, 'Look it's me, Stravinsky!' At which Glazunov coldly shook his hand and turned away.[23]

Read in full, in the context of Prokofiev's *Diaries*, spite is detectable from both composers towards Glazunov. It fell to Rachmaninoff to offer support and friendship.

The correspondence between the two, written in the intimate *tu* form of Russian (rare for Rachmaninoff, outside family and closest friends), rather than the usual *vous*, shows a gentle intimacy. As so often with ageing mentor and golden student, the balance of friendship, and power, had shifted. According to the biographer

Seroff, Rachmaninoff presented Glazunov with the score of his Fourth Concerto.[24] Whether by design or error, Glazunov left it in a taxi.

There was an insatiable fascination with contemporary life in the 'grands boulevards' and their environs. Under the headline 'This is Paris: Folk and Famous Folks', a Paris-based gossip columnist for the *Winona Republican Herald* of 27 June 1930 paints an irresistible picture:

> The reason celebrities love Paris is because nobody pays any particular attention to them in their spare time. Rachmaninoff felt so safe when he went to the opening concert of the New York Philharmonic Symphony Orchestra at the opera that he took his peanuts along – or so his neighbours of the evening said.

The writer offers helpful tips on star-gazing:

> If you know your notables and love to pick them out, the spot to do it is the short stretch of boulevard between the Opéra and the Madeleine on a balmy spring night. Select yourself a front-row chair at a sidewalk cafe on the right-hand side of the street going towards the Madeleine . . . One week's span saw these people treading Paris pavements: Willa Cather, Edna Ferber, Anita Loos, Rosa Ponselle, Gigli, Rachmaninoff, Heifetz and Kreisler; General Pershing, Giovanni Martinelli and Yehudi Menuhin. The three writing ladies all were on their way elsewhere with a short stopover for shopping. Rosa Ponselle and Gigli gave Paris concerts. So did Heifetz and Kreisler. Yehudi Menuhin's mother went with him wherever the boy violinist appeared.

Top left: Rachmaninoff, aged ten

Top right: Rachmaninoff, aged twenty-six, with his dog Levko.
Pictured on the Khopyor river, 1899

Bottom: Rachmaninoff with the Skalon sisters at the Ignatov estate, 1897

Top left: Natalia Satina Rachmaninoff, c.1900

Top right: First cousins – Rachmaninoff with his wife Natalia,
sister-in-law Sofia Satina and brother-in-law Vladimir Satin, 1899

Bottom: Rachmaninoff and Natalia, London, 1932

Top left: Marietta Shaginian, c. 1920s
Top right: Nina Koshetz, 1916
Bottom: Rachmaninoff and Nina Koshetz, summer 1916

Top: Rachmaninoff's daughter Irina,
with her husband Prince Volkonsky, c. 1924

Bottom: Rachmaninoff with his granddaughter,
Sophie Volkonsky, in New York, 1927

Top: Sergei Prokofiev at his desk in New York, 1918

Bottom: Rachmaninoff at his desk in
Villa Senar, Lucerne, Switzerland, 1930s

Top: Rachmmaninoff and latest automobile. Switzerland, early 1930s.

Bottom: (left to right) Baron Solovieff, Sergei Rachmaninoff and Igor Sikorsky in front of the S-29-A aircraft, Roosevelt Field, Long Island, NY, in 1924.

Top: 11 January 1925, Steinway Hall, 109 East 14th Street, New York City: [left to right] Igor Stravinsky, Nikolai Medtner, Wilhelm Furtwängler, George Engles, Alexander Siloti, Frederick Steinway, Fritz Kreisler, Sergei Rachmaninoff, Josef Hofmann, Pierre Monteux

Bottom: Rachmaninoff in rehearsal with Eugene Ormandy at the Academy of Music, Philadelphia, 1939

Top: Rachmaninoff with his grandchildren,
Alexander Conus and Sophie Volkonsky, in 1936

Bottom: The extended family at Villa Senar, c. 1936.
Rachmaninoff's wife Natalia is on the extreme left

Her visits included a foray to the china department of a boulevard store where the journalist evidently snooped after them, reporting that the young Menuhin picked out china salt-shakers shaped as rabbits and cats 'with dark roving eyes'. Glazunov, never mentioned, no celebrity, escaped these unwelcome paparazzi attentions.

Glazunov's Demise

Given his impecunious circumstances, he might have been better off selling Rachmaninoff's gift instead of leaving it in *le taxi*. Glazunov's letters, requesting money, are a sad record of failing health in a foreign land, but his insights remain pertinent and alive. He discusses his own use of the saxophone (which Rachmaninoff would try out nearly a decade later); Rachmaninoff's damaged hand and recovery; and his colleague's 1932–3 season of concerts in honour of his fortieth anniversary as a pianist and his sixtieth birthday. Glazunov's account of Ravel's *Pictures at an Exhibition* orchestration stands as a perceptive analysis. This sample of his letters tells us much about the writer, the recipient, and their occupations.[25]

20 September 1932
9, Rue Lemoine, Boulogne sur Seine, Tel. Molitor 1138

Dear Sergei Vasilievich,
I well remember our unexpected encounter in the Bois de Boulogne in the spring of this year, when in answer to your enquiry as to my health, I was complaining of a malady in my right leg. At the time I did not expect the condition to develop such complications or to turn out to be so protracted. The entire summer was lost as far as my work was concerned, since I had to spend most of the time in bed, quite unable

to think about music. Now, I am beginning to detect some signs of improvement: I am recovering some of my energy along with my appetite, and my temperature is returning to somewhere like normal. But the constant pains in my joints from rheumatism and gout stop me sleeping, affect my nerves and generally knock me off track.

On two occasions during the five years I have been living abroad you have been so kind and solicitous as to ask me if I needed any money. In thanking you most warmly, I told you that, at least for the time being, I had enough to get by. Now, however, in consequence of my debilitating illness, I must confess that I am in need. Relying, therefore, on those generous suggestions from you in the past, I have concluded that I should turn to you for help by asking you to lend me for a time a certain sum. Since you yourself will be fully cognisant of the circumstances of life today, I should be extremely obliged if you could lend me at least twenty thousand francs.

Please be as completely frank with me as I with you and forgive my temerity in appealing to you. I trust that all our discussions may remain entirely between ourselves. It is regrettable that I am prevented from coming to see you personally.

In expectation of your answer, I remain your deeply respectful and devoted

Glazunov

27 September 1932

9, Rue Lemoine, Boulogne sur Seine, Tel. Molitor 1138

Dear Sergei Vasilievich,

Yesterday I received from you 5,000 francs, for which please accept my most sincere and friendly gratitude. [. . .]

As for my new composition, the Quartet for Four Saxophones, I am extremely grateful for your advice to seek out an American publisher.*

In consequence of my ill health I have so far had no opportunity to listen to my new piece played on saxophones. [. . .]

I send you my best wishes for indestructible health, good spirits and whole-hearted happiness.

Your devoted

A. Glazunov

17 November 1932

11, Rue de Transwaal, Boulogne s/Seine

Dear Sergei Vasilievich,

I am, as before, living in Boulogne, not going out and isolated from the world outside. I get my news from the newspapers and from friends and acquaintances who visit me. [. . .]

We have moved from our former apartment on Rue Lemoine with its stone floor and abundance of draughty cracks to a better constructed and more hygienic one in the same area.

My health is extremely variable. [. . .]

I shall hope to receive the remaining 5,000 francs as promised by you, on which I am counting because only in January shall I receive my royalties from the Société des Auteurs, Compositeurs, etc.

I guarantee to repay my debt to you as soon as my health improves, from the above-mentioned source.

Your devoted and unceasingly grateful

A. Glazunov

* It was eventually published by M. P. Belaïev, Bonn, in 1959.

19 December 1932
14 Rue de la France Mutualiste, Boulogne s/Seine

Dear Sergei Vasilievich,

I received your kind letter and enclosed cheque on 17 December, finding it hard adequately to express my thanks to you for this assistance. The day before yesterday, on learning from a colleague now living in New York of the celebrations honouring your four decades of creative artistry, I immediately despatched a congratulatory telegram to the editors of *New Russian Word*. With all my heart I wish you good health and creative power.

Yesterday morning, in accordance with your advice, I took advantage of the warm sunshine to go for a long walk in the Bois de Boulogne. Of course, I had to stop and rest frequently, so that my actual walking will not have been more than three quarters of an hour.

But that was not all: after lunch I attended an afternoon concert by the Pasdeloup orchestra, at which I heard for the first time Ravel's orchestration of Mussorgsky's *Pictures from an Exhibition by Hartmann*. I have to confess to you that I am not particularly enamoured of this work. Its reputation has been so terribly inflated in Europe and America, while as long ago as the start of my own musical activities in the 1880s I did not often hear such admiring comments even from people formerly closely connected with the composer, like the Rimsky-Korsakovs, and others. Bowing to the mastery of Ravel, I nevertheless find his orchestration somewhat mannered [. . .]

I take the opportunity on behalf of myself and my wife of sending to my dear friends yourself and your wife all good wishes for the coming New Year celebrations. What will the

172

new year bring? For myself, I can say no more than that there has never been a worse year than 1932!

Your devoted

A. Glazunov

22 December 1933

14 Rue de la France Mutualiste, Boulogne s/Seine

Dear Sergei Vasilievich,

First of all, may I congratulate you and dear Natalia Alexandrovna on the coming New Year . . .

May I please, as I have done before, ask you for some friendly advice?

I have been informed that following the formal recognition of Soviet Russia by the United States, we shall be able to claim copyright compensation. This could greatly benefit me financially, and also allow me to liquidate my indebtedness. I do not know what steps I ought to take, but I have no desire to apply to our Embassy here for information. I should be extremely grateful if you would ask your secretary to make some enquiries and apprise me of the results. Should my hopes come to fruition, I would need to be informed about the technical details of the actual application process.

My general state of health is better than it was last year. [. . .]

My Saxophone Quartet was recently performed at the Russian Conservatoire on the Avenue Tokio.

Composition is proceeding very sluggishly, I somehow do not seem to be in the mood.

Of late I have been walking a lot in the frost, and greatly missing the snow.

Once again I send you all best wishes.
Your devoted
A. Glazunov

28 January 1936
14 Rue de la France-Mutualiste, Boulogne s/Seine

Dear Sergei Vasilievich,
    These last few days I have again been feeling unwell,
suffering from gastric and intestinal upsets and insomnia;
nevertheless, since Monday I have returned to work. I very
much hope not to relapse again, and that Sunday can still be
a fixture for us.

The loans were never repaid. Rachmaninoff made his own
handwritten annotation on the letter: 'Last letter from Glazunov.'
Glazunov died in Paris on 21 March 1936.

Pravda and the Prodigy Problem

As Glazunov noted, in November 1933 President Franklin Roosevelt had ended sixteen years of non-recognition of the Soviet Union
following negotiations with the Soviet commissar for Foreign
Affairs, Maxim Litvinov. During this temporary easing of relations,
Rachmaninoff heard from both Vladimir Vilshau and Albert Coates
that his music was again being played in Moscow. Soon, however,
Stalin's own involvement in artistic matters soured the pleasure.
Shostakovich's *Lady Macbeth of the Mtsensk District* was a hit after
its 1934 premiere, but once Stalin saw it, in 1936, it was vilified.
Pravda carried its infamous 'Muddle not Music' article. Shostako-
vich would not hear his opera performed again in the Soviet Union

until 1962, and was toppled from his position as the leading role model for Soviet musicians. In his place, the exiled, hitherto lampooned Rachmaninoff was now held up as a nationalistic exemplar, his *Trois Chansons Russes* admired for having drawn on old Russian folk roots. This, according to Soviet ideology, was the acceptable face of modernism. The irony was lost on no one.

Two constants in Rachmaninoff's life were his refusal to teach and his near abhorrence of the premature promotion of child prodigies. In Kyiv he had failed to turn up to hear the twelve-year-old Vladimir Horowitz (1903–89) for that very reason. In spring 1934, these twin dislikes came together, publicly, in the press interviews that preceded his annual departure for Europe. Nine-year-old Ruth Slenczynska from Berkeley was contracted to earn $75,000 dollars that year: thirty concerts at $2,500 each. Behind 'the miracle child' was a pushy father. A violinist wounded in World War I, Josef Slenczynsky had dreamt of having a musically gifted child, even before she was born. That child would have the career he had lost. Rachmaninoff spoke out to journalists about the dangers of allowing a child such public exposure, and urged her parents to cancel her tour. Eventually, after the young girl had replaced him in a concert when he was ill, they met, and he gave her musical advice, by all accounts (hers, in subsequent interviews) kindly and gently. His instinct was right. By 1940, when she was fourteen, her career appeared to be over.

'Whatever happened to Ruth Slenczynska, child prodigy?' speculated various newspapers in 1958, wondering whether readers remembered 'the fat little girl' who at eight made her American debut and was hailed as another Mozart.[26] Revolt followed. She eloped, aged nineteen, and was reported to be 'learning to do housework' and making flapjacks. After a brief marriage, various jobs and, as she informed her interviewer, a weight-loss diet of cottage-cheese, she relaunched her career, making recordings in the 1950s and 1960s and publishing her autobiography, *Forbidden Childhood*, in 1957. Then she retreated from the concert platform, pursuing a long and distinguished teaching career, until in 2022, aged ninety-seven, she made headlines again. Decca released a new recording, heralding her as 'Rachmaninoff's last pupil', thereby giving her the celebrity in extreme old age she had enjoyed (or her father had, vicariously) in extreme youth.

Girls, Women, Cars

In London Rachmaninoff returned to Queen's Hall for a Saturday matinee recital. His programme for the 1933–4 season featured Beethoven's 'Moonlight' Sonata and Debussy's 'Golliwog's Cakewalk' together with Liszt's *Petrarch Sonnet 123*, some Chopin and the composer's own C sharp minor Prelude: repertory which 'might have been selected from a schoolgirl's satchel', and nothing 'likely to go over the heads of the audience, mainly women', as Neville Cardus noted in the *Manchester Guardian* on 12 March 1934. His attitude to Rachmaninoff echoes Prokofiev's: he finds much to sniff at, in this case the popular nature of the programme, yet he cannot help finding Rachmaninoff an astonishing pianist, 'and what a fascinating personality! He puts us under a spell.' Then follows the usual description of his chilly manner, his stiff walk, his mask-like face, but Cardus is in rhapsodies over Rachmaninoff's use of the pedal in the 'Moonlight' Sonata: 'cloud and sunshine over the valley is not more soft and changeful than Rachmaninoff's light and shade, achieved by sensitive pedalling.' Unfortunately Cardus disliked the Chopin, which he dismisses as Rachmaninoff being, 'for all his versatility of style', a Russian. In conclusion, this was a 'perfect concert', but nothing more than that, and certainly not what Matthew Arnold called the 'criticism of life'.

Before his UK tour of 1934 ended, Rachmaninoff had other, speed-related matters to think about. He wrote to the Somovs, from London, on 14 March:

> Only two concerts still to do, after which we have decided to 'fly off' to Paris, partly influenced by my two managers, Foley and Ibbs. I'm talking about an aeroplane. My Natashechka is not opposed to this, and her reason is the same as mine: if we go by train it will be late by the time we arrive, and we won't be able to catch the grandchildren until they are too tired. By air we can leave at noon and be in Paris by 2 o'clock, with all afternoon at our disposal.[27]

Once in France, something more urgent and pleasurable lay in store:

> To Greiner from Paris, 28 March 1934
> We will stay here until approximately the 8th April. Tomorrow I'm going with Foley to Le Havre to collect my new Lincoln. Now we shall really be rolling!

> To Sofia Satina from Paris, 2 April 1934
> The day before yesterday I got my car. It is in perfect order and excites the curiosity and admiration of all who see it. As before, passers-by on the street stop and gape in astonishment which, as before, gives me great satisfaction.

> To the Somovs from Senar, 11 April 1934
> We left Paris for Hertenstein the day before yesterday at a quarter to seven in the morning. [. . .] Because the road surfaces in France were slippery I was not able as planned to put the

Lincoln thoroughly through its paces. And once one gets into Switzerland one cannot go fast because of the many twists and turns of the road. We arrived at the gates of Senar at eight o'clock in the evening. It was already dark.[28]

Arriving at his new house by night, Rachmaninoff went through the garden and, in the dark, examined the progress of the trees. Senar, with echoes of Tair, its name a union of the first letters of Sergei and Natalia Rachmaninoff, was ready. Soon after their arrival, a new grand piano, a gift from Steinway for his sixtieth birthday, also arrived. It was destined for the studio, the room at the far corner of the house, at a lower level down three steps and somewhat separate, or out of earshot, from the rest of the house. The piano, still there today, faced into the room: better both for light and concentration for the pianist to have his back to the large windows with their inviting views. On 12 April he wrote gratefully to Greiner.

We arrived here three days ago. And today my new piano was delivered. It is already installed in my studio, wrapped and tied up in paper. Since the house is not yet ready and most of the furniture has not yet come, I don't want to open the instrument. All I did was stealthily lift up the veil and quietly play a few notes. The piano seems to me to be a magnificent specimen.

I should have liked to send a telegram immediately to Steinway in New York to express my delight and deep gratitude for a gift far in excess of anything I could have dreamed of. Only my disgraceful ignorance of the English language prevented me from doing so. All I can do is write in Russian to my daughters in Paris and ask them to translate it and send it to the right address.[29]

Somov provided an unusual house-warming gift, a reflection on the new owner's desire for peace and quiet. He wrote from Senar on 17 May:

Now for something else. We have now been living in the big house for ten days, although one or two things still need to be done. There are clearly visible reminders of you: first, in three different positions around my property, the No Entry signs kindly donated by you have been put up; secondly, my bookcase is now adorned, in addition to many portraits, by your caricature of me in which I am dreaming of an automobile.

Paganini Rhapsody

At the end of the 1933–4 season, Rachmaninoff told Vilshau he felt like a squeezed lemon, not nice to be around, and more exhausted with every passing year. Even so, he had agreed to increase the number of concerts in his next season to sixty-five, wondering to his friend whether he would be able to bear it. With Vilshau and Somov, closest of friends, he shared frustrations, anxieties, frailties: he was at his most emotionally unbuttoned.

After a minor operation in May (with his wife staying in an adjoining room in the hospital) and convalescence in Monte Carlo and Lake Como, Rachmaninoff returned to Senar, looking forward to gardening and tending the flowers. Instead, or given the strictness of his routines, perhaps in addition, he worked intensively – night and day – on a major new work for piano and orchestra: more variations, this time twenty-four on an original theme from Paganini's Caprice in A minor for solo violin (also used by Liszt, Brahms and others since). He was already certain that it would be completed in time to perform in Philadelphia and Chicago the next season. The family, with both his daughters and his two grandchildren, Sophie, aged eight, and Tatiana's son Alexander, still a baby, were there. Rachmaninoff was at peace. He gave frequent updates on each new variation to Horowitz, who was staying at the Palace Hotel, Lucerne that summer. He was pleased to be at work, properly, in the new house – especially having spent such a fortune building it. In a matter of weeks he had completed the new variations. Grouped into three sections, the work's shape and scale are close to a concerto, but the ideas are concise and episodic. The score is dated 3 July to 16 August 1934.

The seventh variation presented the *Dies irae* theme. Years earlier he had discussed a ballet with Mikhail Fokine (1880–1942), who as choreographer with Diaghilev and the Ballets Russes was responsible for Stravinsky's ballets *The Firebird* and *Petrushka*. Now a new collaboration was planned: the *Rhapsody* as a ballet, Rachmaninoff explained, would tell the story of Paganini, his pact with the Devil, and his doomed love for a woman. The *Dies irae*, every time it occurred, was linked to the evil spirit; the voluptuous, tender (and now universally popular) Variation 18 was a love episode. He claimed that Variation 18, an inversion of the main theme, was there to please his manager, and guarantee the work's success: a not inaccurate prediction. (Speaking to the author in 2022, the American pianist Gary Graffman verified the story. He was told it by Horowitz who was in Senar when the work had just been completed. It's a good remark. No doubt Rachmaninoff made the wry comment to many apart from Horowitz.) The *Rhapsody* concludes with a menacing parody of the *Dies irae* for full orchestra but ends, brilliantly, unexpectedly, with a surreptitious wink at the main theme from the piano solo. (Fokine did turn the work into a ballet, amending Rachmaninoff's synopsis. It was performed at the Royal Opera House, Covent Garden, London in 1939, and in New York in 1940.)

By this time, Tair had ceased to operate as an independent enterprise. Rachmaninoff assigned publishing rights of the *Rhapsody on a Theme of Paganini* to Charles Foley, his manager since 1923, three years later giving Foley all publishing rights to his work. Unquestionably Foley exercised considerable influence; some commentators have implied that Rachmaninoff was putty in his hands. This is to ignore the evidence, from letters and comments from those who knew both men, of a sincere and affectionate friendship between them.

That Rachmaninoff wanted to pass the burden of his business affairs to someone he trusted is more likely to have been the case. They were a team. Foley's personality is hard to grasp, but we glean some insight from Nathan Milstein, who had no qualms in saying anything about anyone. In the same paragraph as describing Kreisler's wife Harriet as abrasive and, in her own words, something of a 'bitch', he calls Foley 'a hospitable man and a real gentleman'.[30] Charles O'Connell praised Foley as 'an Irishman' of great acumen:

Rachmaninoff knew the power of money, and was acutely aware of a dollar's value, yet I think that he required money more as a tribute to his eminence as a pianist and composer than because of any acquisitiveness for money per se [. . .]. Mr Rachmaninoff's affairs were invariably handled by the lovable Charlie, who drove a hard bargain. The artist himself never, ostensibly at least, entered into such matters.

He continues, sagely, that Rachmaninoff's was the will 'which dictated his affairs in the minutest detail', and those dealings were 'invariably fair'.[31]

On 7 November 1934, at the Lyric Opera House, Baltimore,

the *Rhapsody* was given its premiere in a concert with Stravinsky's *Firebird* suite, with Stokowski conducting the Philadelphia Orchestra and the composer as soloist. 'Pianist is Heard with Orchestra', ran the local headline, guardedly. A new work by Mary Howe, a student of Nadia Boulanger and founder with Amy Beach of the Association of American Women Composers, got barely a mention.

The same forces recorded the *Rhapsody* for RCA, in New Jersey, on Christmas Eve. Bruno Walter conducted it at a Philharmonic-Symphony Society concert at Carnegie Hall: the work was launched. The critic from the *Brooklyn Times Union* was not impressed by the appearance of the 'long and melancholy figure' of Rachmaninoff, or, despite its brilliance and ingenuity, his 'thin, brittle' new creation.[32] All reports agreed that the applause was thunderous. Rachmaninoff was sceptical that the success could be so instant, telling the Somovs he thought it looked 'suspicious'. He was not easily reassured.

Health, Wealth

Travel, to which Rachmaninoff was at once addicted and resistant, took its toll on health, energy and any possible repose for composition. His schedule in the British Isles included the usual Queen's Hall date, a first trip to Ireland, a Beethoven concerto and the UK premiere of the new *Rhapsody* on 7 March 1935 at Manchester Free Trade Hall under the Russian, Nikolai Malko (briefly chief conductor of the short-lived Yorkshire Symphony Orchestra). That was the occasion on which Rachmaninoff was paid a princely sum of £157.10s (nearly £15,000 in 2022 prices): more than the conductor, and more than the whole orchestra combined.

A recital on the south coast, according to the *Hastings and St Leonards Observer* (30 March 1935) 'proved not quite a success'.

Rachmaninoff appeared out of sorts, and his 'playing of the C sharp minor Prelude appeared almost as a challenge to galvanise the audience into some greater show of appreciation'. The writer attributes the subdued mood, of performer and audience alike, to the large number of empty seats. 'One can only assume that the management's idea of charging London prices was just too much for the pockets of Hastings music lovers.'

Rachmaninoff's spirits were indeed low. He was worried about money, with the growing realisation that his irrepressible generosity was becoming a problem. When a planned tour to Latin America was abandoned, he admitted his concerns to Somov:

Cancelling South America is a blow to me financially. My finances are generally in a deplorable state. It is a long time since I was in such a bad position. My children need money, and the thought that they might be in need is the hardest and bitterest of all to me. I cannot get out of my mind that I have given too much to others and failed to secure the needs of my own flesh and blood. Please God let this thought not enter their minds as well.

He was exhausted, took up the matter with Foley, and reported all to Natalia's sister Sofia Satina in a letter dated 22 April 1935:

When we returned to Paris, at the urging of my children, I had a heart-to-heart discussion with Foley, and he relieved me of my promise to travel to South America. I cannot describe to you my relief, although my financial affairs will suffer. They are not brilliant. The day before yesterday Foley left by Zeppelin at 10 o'clock American time, having risen from his sick bed only the previous day. To do so was crazy. I and everyone else told him so. But the chief actor in all this was Fritz [Kreisler].

Although he had been making pompous statements to all the newspapers about how concerned he was at his 'friend's' illness and had flown to Paris expressly to see him, in fact, reassured by the doctor's declaration that there was 'no risk to life', he agreed to Charlie's departure. [. . .] He looks absolutely dreadful, and we are all extremely worried about him.[33]

As well as his finances, Rachmaninoff was expanding his usual list of chronic medical worries, necessitating the habitual summer cures. In 1935 he spent time at Baden-Baden, urged by his doctor, taking 'pine-electrical baths', massage and rest.

Friends Like These

That summer and the next Rachmaninoff worked hard on the Symphony no. 3, op. 44. His early biographer Victor Seroff, a figure not short of turncoat tendencies, called the work so thoroughly Russian (having called the *Rhapsody* thoroughly un-Russian) 'that one might call the symphony "My memories of Russia"'. He heard in the work echoes of Tchaikovsky, Rimsky-Korsakov and Borodin but was otherwise dismissive, concluding that Rachmaninoff had already said, many times, what he had to say: he was out of date, irrelevant except as a virtuoso pianist. The voices of the future were Stravinsky and his younger contemporaries, Prokofiev and Shostakovich, who 'tell their fantastic story' more interestingly.[34] Seroff's view was that Rachmaninoff gave up conducting because he disliked the competition of other composers' works, knowing that in his pianism he had no rival. This seems both a miscalculation and an insult, but Seroff was unsubtle in his opinions.

By the end of the summer there were other issues to consider. As usual, Rachmaninoff passed the burden to Somov, writing from Senar on 1 September: 'I completely forgot about my driving licence, which expired on 31st May. I enclose two necessary documents and ask you kindly to get it renewed without delay.' Dogged, as so often, by thoughts of old age, and still at Senar, he wrote to Vilshau on 26 September 1935:

> My health is rotten. I'm rapidly falling to pieces. When I had
> my health, I distinguished myself by exceptional laziness;
> now that it is showing signs of failing, I can think of nothing
> but work. It is a sign that I do not belong in the ranks of the
> truly talented, for I believe that alongside the gifts of the truly
> talented one must, from the very first day of recognising those
> gifts, also possess the willingness and capacity to work hard.
> From the days of my youth I did everything I possibly could to
> suppress them.
>
> Old age is hardly the time to expect a renaissance! The result
> is that it is now difficult for me to increase the output from my
> activities; my health simply does not permit it. Consequently,
> I have not achieved all that I could have in my life, and the
> awareness of that fact deprives my remaining days of happiness.
>
> I won't go on about it. Forgive the minor mode.[35]

He pushed on with the Third Symphony, finishing it the following summer and writing 'Finished, I thank God. 30 June 1936, Senar' on the bottom of the score. (That manuscript is in the Library of Congress, Washington. A facsimile is kept at Senar.) The next day he and Natalia drove to Aix-les-Bains and both embarked on treatment, his chiefly for the arthritis which was impeding his playing. He found the process boring and expressed his scepticism to the Somovs, sharing the usual inordinate detail about his motley medical conditions.

Before the new symphony's premiere in Philadelphia, due in November, he had another engagement. His annual presence in Britain was always a central feature of touring life. In October 1936, *The Bells* was performed at the Sheffield Festival – long overdue, the work had been originally scheduled for the 1914 festival before it was cancelled due to World War I. It was sung in English by a chorus of four hundred, with the London Philharmonic, and conducted by Henry Wood, who had given its eventual UK premiere in Liverpool in 1921. (Several amiable and reverential letters survive from Wood to Rachmaninoff, typed by the conductor himself and sharing news of the new Lady [Jessie] Wood and their dog, Michael.) Rachmaninoff was pleased with the performance but called the City Hall the 'deadest' acoustic he had ever encountered. It was cold too: the soloists, who included the leading Scottish soprano Isobel Baillie, were muffled in overcoats, with only the energetic Wood daring to remove his outer layers. *The Times* enthused about the entrancing sound of a huge orchestra and chorus, and observed that English bells had no equivalent to the Russian Orthodox sound but, with a final sting, wondered if in all this pealing and tolling there was not a risk of bathos.

The composer was back home in America for the premiere of the Third Symphony, conducted by Stokowski, played by the orchestra for which it was written, on 6 November 1936 and, hard now to believe, loved by few. The bad reviews weighed down most of that season. When asked, at a press reception, where he now made his home, he answered "'On the train, in the Pullman car," proving the stern pianist really had a sense of humour.'[36] Many were of the view that Rachmaninoff had given up the compositional struggle. The press reports, from all over that year, make dismal reading. Despite his own attempts, and those of his interviewers, to make this 'sallow, lank Russian' sound genial, he comes across as merely grumpy: irritated about speaking to the press, especially before breakfast, fed up with the C sharp minor Prelude, pessimistic about modern music, unsure whether he is primarily a composer, conductor or pianist.

His London trip that spring was only averagely successful, Ibbs keeping some of the negative reviews from him. In Europe even the weather was bad. In Senar, his finger hurt, the wind rattled around the house and he was restless. Early cherry blossom, and plans for the bare garden, provided some much-needed cheer. The Medtners visited, and Horowitz, which also lifted the spirits, and gave an opportunity for playing piano four-hands. He assured Vilshau that he believed in the new symphony, but he was stung, once again, by the scorn it received. It had one, dedicated champion: Sir Henry Wood, who took up the cause with enthusiasm, and a promise of performances in Liverpool and London in the new year.

Not Great, But Very Good

In spring 1938 Rachmaninoff embarked on a crammed European tour of Scandinavia, Holland, Hungary and France, as well as Austria and the UK. A concert in Vienna had to be cancelled – the Rachmaninoffs heard pro-Nazi shouts beneath their window – and a second cancellation followed (a planned performance of *The Bells*). Now German troops marched into Graz, leading to the *Anschluss*: the annexation of Austria to Germany with thousands of arrests and growing anti-Semitism.

On 10 March 1938, the *Daily Herald*, a left-wing British daily paper, published in London from 1912 to 1964, carried the following article by Stuart Fletcher:

Composer Hears a Piano and is Glum

Gaunt, tired-eyed, world-weary, 65-year-old Sergei Rachmaninoff came to town yesterday.

The famous Russian composer and pianist is playing at Queen's Hall on Saturday afternoon before setting out on a tour of the British Isles.

Yesterday morning he sat in a heavily furnished hotel sitting-room overlooking Piccadilly, staring glumly at the sombre red carpet, restlessly tearing used matches into fragments, while twenty Pressmen asked him questions.

And all the time in the room above another pianist practised.

Thump-thump-trickle-trickle-bang . . .

Rachmaninoff is tall, angular, mournfully-clothed.

His voice is deep and crackles drily like the snapping dead wood. His eyes are dark and far-away. He seems like a sardonic ghost from a past generation.

Look of Protest

'Do you, M. Rachmaninoff,' someone asks, 'play any other instrument beside the piano?' 'No,' comes the mournful answer, and a moment later, drily, 'Sorry!'

Tinkle – tinkle – pom pom-pom – pom – thump!

Rachmaninoff looks protestingly at the ceiling, then answers another question. 'No,' he says, 'I do not like modern music – I do not understand it.

'Myself, I am not modern enough to enjoy my own music. I think some of it is good, but only some . . .'

Tiddle – tiddle – pompetty – pompetty-pompetty-bang!

'I remember,' Rachmaninoff goes on, 'Tchaikovsky attending a performance of *Eugene Onegin*, his most popular opera.

He did not come into his box until the second act. Then he wriggled and fidgeted, and at last ran out of the theatre. He could not bear it.

Suffering Eyes

'It was the same when his ambition to have a piece of his music put on to pianola roll came true. He had always wanted this. But when he heard it was a piece from *Eugene Onegin* – he was miserable. But perhaps he was wrong.'

There is silence while Rachmaninoff continues to split dead matches into tiny splinters – except for the piano upstairs.

BANG – BANG – tinkle-tinkle-poppetty-poppetty-THUMP!

The suffering eyes look with an infinite weariness up to the ceiling.

'Whew!' says Rachmaninoff.

'Gentlemen,' he pleads, 'is it not enough?'

And the Press reception breaks up.

This press conference, as with any such event, produced several versions of the same story, though none provided the same 'pompetty-bang' insights, useful additions to any music critic's lexicon. They made no bones about Rachmaninoff's hastening decrepitude, noting that, at sixty-five, he looked as if he had worked himself hard. *The Belfast News Letter* (10 March 1938) reported that 'the eminent pianist and conductor', despite travelling all over the world and traversing the Atlantic several times a year, was nervous about crossing the Irish Sea for the first time as it 'is apt to be somewhat rough at this time of year'. During his tours he practises for three hours every day. 'I compose in the summertime,' he said, 'when I have no telephone calls to answer and no interviews to give' – a sad half-truth.

The correspondent of the *Staffordshire Sentinel* (18 March 1938) was not prepared to be over-impressed, picking him up on a few wrong notes and comparing him unfavourably with Horowitz for 'sheer brilliance of execution'. The writer also considered the obligatory C sharp minor Prelude the cause of Mr Rachmaninoff's 'depressed, world-weary air', believed to be so typical of Russian melancholy. 'He is not, I think, a great composer, but he is a very good one.'

Despite his mood the UK tour was a success financially. As promised Henry Wood conducted the Symphony no. 3 in Liverpool, repeating it a few days later for BBC radio broadcast. In between performances, Rachmaninoff helped Wood to prepare the score. He went to Wood's home and played it through on the piano, 'two hours chock full' of intensive study, as Wood recalled in his memoir, *About Conducting*.[37] He was a lonely fan of the work, and thought it would gain Rachmaninoff the same popularity as Tchaikovsky's Fifth: alas not; it remains the least played of the three symphonies, with the Second an easy winner.

A concert with Thomas Beecham took place at the Queen's Hall. Rachmaninoff was soloist in Beethoven's C major Piano Concerto, and in his own *Paganini Rhapsody*. The orchestra was the London Philharmonic, which Beecham had founded, with Malcolm Sargent, six years earlier in 1932. (They were helped by the industrialist Samuel Courtauld, who, in the same year founded the art institute in London named after him.) The *Illustrated London News* (9 April 1938) gave a rave review of the encounter between Beecham and Rachmaninoff, while making a timely point about box office driving artistic decisions:

The collaboration of great musical virtuosos in a concert
is rarely to be heard nowadays, and the reasons are almost

exclusively commercial, since it is clear that if one celebrity can fill the Queen's Hall, it is superfluous, from the financial point of view, to add another. Therefore, we never witness such a conjunction as Toscanini and Schnabel or Kreisler and Rachmaninoff, but each of these stars revolves in a lonely orbit. This is, no doubt, a loss to music, especially when the reason for such isolation is exclusively one of the box-office.

'The Chaliapin Era is Over'

Still in London, Rachmaninoff received news from Paris. Chaliapin was mortally ill. Rachmaninoff rushed to his bedside, visiting him twice a day, joking with him a little just as in old times. On 20 April 1938, eight days after his friend's death, he wrote to Sofia Satina:

We have now been back in Senar for eight days, and it is eight days since Fedya [Chaliapin] died. He was dying as we were en route. I went to see him in Paris twice a day, the last day was the 10th April. As before, I managed to cheer him up a little, and just before I left he began to tell me how, once he was better, he wanted to write another book for artists, the theme of which would be the art of scenography. Of course, he could only speak very, very slowly, gasping for breath. His heart was scarcely working. I let him get to the end of what he wanted to tell me, and then as I got up to go, said that I also had plans: that as soon as I could stop performing I would write a book, the subject of which would be Chaliapin. He gave me a smile and stroked my hand. Then we parted. For ever! The next day, 11th April, I waited until the evening to visit again. They had given him a morphine injection and he was unconscious so I didn't see him. I told his wife that we had to go away on the morrow but that I would come back again in ten days' time. I felt then that he would not last that long. She felt the same. And then for the first time, having all that time, all those long days, kept up heroically, she broke down and wept as we said goodbye to one another. I hurried to leave. Next morning, 12th April, at six o'clock we left for Senar, and got there at half past five in the evening. He died at a quarter past five. I expect you get *Latest News* [Russian-language newspaper in America] don't you? It is all laid out in detail there. The Chaliapin era is over! We never saw the like before and never will again.[38]

Rachmaninoff was affected by the loss. He could not work but spent the days reading, walking and lying on the balcony. Later that month, he told Somov, he had 'sclerosis' of mind and body, a combination of exhaustion and grief. He was forgetting Russian words; losing his power of visual judgement (having scraped the precious car) and his hearing was going. Natasha busied herself 'with the flowers' all day, a dedication he found exceptionally touching. (Whether she was outside planting them or inside arranging them is not clear.) He was asked to contribute an article about Chaliapin for a newspaper. He quoted the proverb, 'Only he who is forgotten is dead,' before concluding 'If this is true, then Chaliapin will never die.'[39]

Potions from Dr Dahl

Letter from Sofia Satina from Cold Spring Harbour to Dr Nikolai Dahl, 15 April 1938

Dear Nikolai Vladimirovich,

I don't know if you remember me, but I am one of many, many people whose health at one time or another you have unselfishly helped to restore, and who, thanks to you, is now full of energy, confidence and strength despite the horrors all around us. At the present time I am contacting you to ask a great favour on behalf of my sister Natalia Rachmaninova. She has written to me explaining that Sergei Vasilievich is extremely distressed at having inexplicably lost, while he was in England recently, the talisman you sent to him two or three years ago.

It was very important to him, he guarded it with great care and was never without it. My sister in an effort to console him promised to ask you if you could find some way of sending him another version to replace the one he has lost. As she did not know your address she asked me to write to you about the talisman. From the end of April to the middle of September they will be at this address: Herr S. Rachmaninoff, Hertenstein, bei Luzern, Villa Senar, Switzerland. Please forgive me for troubling you, and thank you once again for your past kindnesses. With my best wishes,

S. Satina

From Dr Nikolai Dahl to SVR, 2 May 1938

Dear Sergei Vasilievich,

I have received a letter from Sofia Alexandrovna Satina informing me that while you were in England you inadvertently lost the talisman, and are upset about it. Don't be upset! From the occult perspective there is no such thing as chance; the chain of cause and effect is not interrupted and what we call chance is no more than the consequence of our limited understanding causing some of the links in the chain to slip out from our field of vision. The talisman was lost because it was necessary for you to lose it. For what reason? That I cannot say, but perhaps because it might prompt me to send you another, more powerful one that I have already recently acquired; and perhaps because it would impel me to be in touch with you to tell you that I have had the good fortune to develop a cure for facial trigeminal neuralgia, which has hitherto been considered incurable.

From the enclosed description of the condition, written by the sufferer herself at my request, you will be able to judge whether or not it conforms to your own complaint. If it does, try my treatment. It is very simple: a tincture of red geranium distilled in alcohol – a flower that can be found growing everywhere. The preparation is also extremely simple: take flowers, leaves and stems (young seedlings) and infuse them in alcohol for a week, after which the mixture will have amalgamated. Dilute with water and take a teaspoonful two or three times a day. When the painful attacks cease you can stop taking the tincture. There are no side-effects and you can keep up the dosage indefinitely if needed. Do try this remedy if you have not yet succeeded in ridding yourself of the neuralgia; I should be so happy if it brings you relief. Please pass on to your wife my greetings and gratitude for having afforded me this opportunity be in touch with you. Best wishes to you, and stay well. Yours, N. Dahl.

PS I take the opportunity of sending you my most recent article, which was published in an occult compilation entitled 'Occultism and Yoga'.

Rachmaninoff had no plans for anything new, which would require a cheerfulness of mood rather than his current gloom, as he wrote to the devoted Somov. He could not face making the necessary changes to the last movement of the Fourth Piano Concerto, a work that was still bothering him. He preoccupied himself with an enquiry from Vladimir Nabokov regarding his novel *The Gift*, his last Russian work, written (as Sirin) in Berlin between 1935 and 1937, exploring the close-knit circle of Russian émigré life in Germany. So far only episodes had been published. On 28 May 1938 Rachmaninoff wrote to Nabokov, regretting the novelist's state of 'ghastly destitution' (Nabokov's words) and sending $2,500 by telegram, to be repaid only when or if the period of 'ghastly destitution' was past. And were this not soon, it 'doesn't matter'. He concludes by saying that publication of *The Gift* by Tair would have to be delayed for now (it was not published in full until 1952).

In July Rachmaninoff wrote yet again to the Somovs:

I have also been making corrections to my latest [Third] Symphony. There are not many of them, and they are all minor, but thinking about them has occupied me for the past two weeks. I have now given everything to the copyist so that it can be integrated into the orchestral parts: the symphony is going to be performed again in London in August by Henry

Wood. I think I wrote to you in the spring that he very much likes the Symphony. This enables me now to count on three fingers of my right hand the people who like it. The second is the violinist Busch, and the third (forgive me!) is myself. When I run out of fingers on both hands, I shall give up counting. But when will that be? [. . .]

PS A new record. From Paris to Senar is 610 kilometres. This trajectory we accomplished, with two stops for food, one stop for petrol and one stop at the border, in ten hours and ten minutes. Quite a car, the Packard! The chauffeur drove for two hours, I drove the rest of the time.

Rockin' the Boat

One of the duties of Rachmaninoff's London agent, R. Leigh Ibbs, in the usual manner of concert managers and artists' agents, was to occupy his star visitor on nights off. Rachmaninoff scarcely knew what to do when not working (unless a fast car or a motorboat was on hand), and often asked for extra concerts to be scheduled. In a pause between concerts he and Natalia went to the cinema with Ibbs, and saw the box-office hit of the moment, *The Life of Emile Zola*. ('Wonderful picture,' Rachmaninoff noted. The 1937 film, which had a score by Max Steiner, was widely praised though Graham Greene, one-time film critic, was less rhapsodic. To make a film about the Dreyfus Affair without mentioning attitudes towards Dreyfus's Jewish identity, he complained, was a mixed achievement.)

Rachmaninoff, all his sensitivities on red alert, had a heightened response to movies. His wife recalled:

Sergei Vasilievich liked going sometimes to the cinema, but could not tolerate vulgarity and usually went home immediately if the picture was not to his taste. Once we went together to see the film of *Frankenstein* [starring Boris Karloff, born William Pratt in south-east London]. Right at the beginning we are shown a grave and a cross. The moment he saw it I heard him say, 'You stay if you like, but I'm going home.' I think best of all he liked comic action, for instance he would laugh until he cried at Charlie Chaplin impersonating a man trying on skates for the first time.[40]

The relative safety of a good film may have suited Ibbs better than a spin in a boat, as when they had all been in Senar a couple of years earlier. Rachmaninoff, on a beautiful afternoon, announced his intention to take the boat out on the lake, as he did every day, always himself at the wheel. Swan, in the perceptive reminiscences he wrote with his wife, observed: 'He got up quietly. He did everything quietly and firmly; hesitation was alien to his nature.' The Swans were to join him. Ibbs, 'a corpulent man with a round, ruddy face', asked to come too. This led to near-disaster. Ibbs's determination to try his hand at steering sent the boat spinning and tilting, the screw 'thumping loudly in the air', the boat close to capsizing.

Swan's account catches the atmosphere, the three of them crouched on the back seat watching in dead silence, Ibbs turning 'as red as a beetroot'. Calmly, quietly, politely, Rachmaninoff shoved Ibbs aside and, in the nick of time, set the boat back on course, 'and we glided back to the embankment of the Villa Senar. Nobody said a word.' As they walked back up the steep, sweeping path to the house, Rachmaninoff, frowning and tapping his head, said only: 'Don't say anything to Natasha. She won't let me go boating any more.'[41]

Toscanini at Tribschen

After a quiet time together, the Rachmaninoffs grew more sociable, holding a populous dinner with Toscanini and friends, described by Sophia Satin (their niece), one of the many visitors:

> During my stay in Hertenstein I was lucky to hear Toscanini conduct in Lucerne. That very year they had an interesting music festival at Tribschen to commemorate Wagner's stay there . . . as the Toscaninis were acquainted with the Rachmaninovs, Aunt Natalie invited them to Senar for dinner. It was quite an occasion as about twenty people had to be looked after. Mr and Mrs Toscanini, their daughter and her Italian husband were the guests of honour.[42]

This must refer to Wally Toscanini, who married an Italian count. The Toscaninis' second daughter, Wanda, married Horowitz in 1933.

The outdoor concert on the sloping lawns of Wagner's lakeside home, which took place on 25 August 1938 between four and seven o'clock, was a significant event in cultural history, a prelude to a new, international Lucerne Festival, later reported in detail in the *New York Times* (2 October 1938). The writer compared the lake to a watery version of Broadway and Forty-Second Street, or Piccadilly Circus. Countless policemen in helmets, looking like a flock of London 'bobbies', 'stood in equally innumerable rowboats, motor launches and other craft' regulating the traffic. Lake steamers were prevented from hooting and asked to muffle their paddle wheels, and for the duration of the concert 'no hen should cackle, no cock should crow and no grazing cow ring its bell or utter a bovine lament'. Luminaries came from 'all points of the compass', including Princess Maria of Italy, Rachmaninoff, Horowitz, Huberman, Bruno Walter, Ernest Schelling, Daniela Thode [von Bülow Liszt], daughter of Cosima, 'who romped on those same grounds in Wagner's sight nearly seventy years ago'.[43] What would Wagner have made, the reporter pondered, of a couple of thousand 'bustling strangers' thronging his beloved Tribschen, a place prized for its seclusion. Rachmaninoff would surely have recognised the sentiment.

Satin, in her comic account, noted the diminutive stature of the Toscaninis, 'who wore shoes with cork soles to make them look taller'. Her uncle (who, as she liked to point out, was also her second cousin) and Maestro Toscanini went for a walk in the garden: 'It was a remarkable duo. Uncle tall and slender. Toscanini short and slightly chubby . . . Uncle trying not to walk too fast.' The next day Toscanini conducted a concert including music by Mendelssohn, at that time banned in Germany because he was Jewish. She describes, too, the fine weather and the chance to swim in the lake, entering the water from the steps and stone terrace, still there today:

1938 was exceptional insofar as Aunt Natalie and Uncle Sergei invited me to come during the summer holidays to Switzerland. To travel abroad was not easy being the holder of a NANSSEN passport, issued to stateless persons . . . Senar was not a large building, but well constructed and comfortable.

Tatiana lived with her family in the small house at the entrance of the estate. Irina's daughter Sophinka was already staying there with her governess. She was a chubby teenager, twelve years old. Alexander Conus was four. Life in Senar was organised by Aunt Natalie according to a schedule around Uncle. Breakfast was served according to the convenience of those who came down to the glass verandah.

Uncle was ready fairly early and, after a walk around the garden, was ready to practise. The garden, or maybe it should be called a park, was Uncle's love, and he gave all orders what trees were planted and where. He himself did work occasionally there. His working schedule was set and hardly ever changed. After his walk he came to the music room and started practising, always beginning with scales. After that he played what he chose. The house had to be completely quiet but who would have had it otherwise? I often sat in a corner next to the music room and listened. This he did for a maximum of two hours. After his post lunch siesta everybody assembled in front of the house to have tea together.

With hindsight, Sophia Satin observed: 'I returned to Dresden with a strange feeling, that I would not see Uncle and Aunt for a long time.' A long time, in the event, was never. 'And so it happened, for they both died in America.'[44]

'The Man Will Perhaps Remain an Enigma'

Many of Rachmaninoff's friends, feeling the pressure and uncertainty of being stateless, had applied for American citizenship. As yet he resisted. Horizons were closing in. He had not played in Germany since Hitler came to power. Europe was, as he wrote anxiously to Somov, like a volcano. He felt trapped by indecision, knowing war was close, and that he and Natalia could find themselves stranded 'in a mousetrap'. At the same time, the sticking point: Tatiana was in Europe. His career in America was secure, but some were beginning to tire of the 'icicles personality', as the *Utah Evening Herald* expressed it (6 December 1938), when he played at the cavernous Provo Tabernacle:

Sergei Rachmaninoff has appeared – and gone . . .

To many his piano concert here will be the *ne plus ultra* of their musical lives for Rachmaninoff is Rachmaninoff and next to immortality.

Others, rebuffed by the icicles personality, vaguely tried to name within themselves what it was that disturbed: nor perhaps will ever know the answer [. . .]

Known, yet unknown; unbending yet not rude; taciturn, yet lighted by an inner flame, Rachmaninoff, the man, will perhaps remain an enigma.

Provo accorded him a mighty hand. As he rolled magnificently through the final brilliancies of Liszt's *Tarantella, Venezia e Napoli*, one could feel the ovation near. Then more than two-and-one-half minutes of clapping by 3,000 persons acclaimed [him]. Rachmaninoff (a symptom of a smile one fancied might appear) disappeared, acknowledged twice, and then, though perhaps it cost him effort, encored once with the multi-played 'Prelude in C sharp Minor', his own composition. He disappeared, was almost instantly out of the building and gone . . .

The *Salt Lake Tribune* (11 December 1938) was more encouraging: a 'wildly enthusiastic' crowd, queuing for hours in advance, appreciated the Russian's renowned artistry in Bach, Chopin and Liszt in this 'high water-mark' event. Nonetheless, the lead story that day was about an exhibition of original paintings from Walt Disney's recent 'masterpiece' *Snow White and the Seven Dwarfs* (1937).

Christmas 1938 was spent in New York. Sophie, now thirteen years old and musically talented, sang Gretel in a production of Humperdinck's *Hansel and Gretel*. In the spring of 1939, before going to Senar for the summer, Rachmaninoff was back on the

Queen Mary and made an extensive tour of Britain: it was the fortieth anniversary of his first London appearance, and would be his last.

Wirral-ites in Fur and Feathers

His programme for the season included Bach's Italian Concerto, Beethoven's Piano Sonata op. 111 and some transcriptions. Subjecting him to the inescapable press reception, the British newspapers said he looked exhausted but still grilled him on his opinion of the Soviet Union. The *Nottingham Journal* remarked on his 'tired face and curious hooded eyes'. Another Nottingham paper was more interested in his tobacco habit: 'He is an inveterate cigarette smoker, and a confirmed controversialist. He breaks his cigarettes into halves, and smokes them through a holder.' On a similar theme, on 21 February 1939, the *London Daily News* reported:

> Rachmaninoff, his face infinitely lined and creased, his English halting, is about to go on a tour of the English provincial cities. He talked about Russia. He is feeling more kindly towards the Soviet Union. 'They are not so cruel now.'

He gave, yet again, his reason for refusing to broadcast: how could he expect people to come to concerts if he was freely available on the wireless? The reporter noted in a sharp payoff that he was glad Toscanini did not hold the same view. The ubiquitousness of the C sharp minor Prelude attracted comment: it was to Rachmaninoff what 'Keep the Home Fires Burning' was to Ivor Novello.

In Liverpool the *Echo* praised his playing but regretted that the audience had provided a 'bronchial obbligato', which was 'simply terrible, this being Liverpool in February'. The city's rival paper, the

Evening Express (21 February 1939) had more important concerns:

> The audience was drawn from far and near. Miss Constance
> Cummings was in it, enjoying a 'night off' from the theatre.
> Mrs. Oscar Winterbottom had come over from Cheshire,
> in mink, and Wirral-ites included Mrs. John Dixon with her
> son. Miss Mary Corbett-Lowe, Miss Hazel Robins and Miss
> Gwenda Hodges. Miss June Napier caught the eye in the most
> alluring hat adorned with green feathers.

The Savage Club

In London Rachmaninoff had the comfort of being among friends.
One was the Russian-born pianist Benno Moiseiwitsch (1890–1963),
who had been in England since 1908. Another was Mark Hambourg
(1879–1960), also a Russian-born pianist, pupil of Anton Rubinstein
and frequent performer at the Proms. Both were members of the
Savage Club, and invited Rachmaninoff to join them as a guest. The
Evening News gossip columnist reported the event:

> After his concert at Queen's Hall on Saturday afternoon he
> was taken to the Savage Club, where, to his surprise, they made
> him an honorary member. A musician friend of mine who was a
> guest tells me it was amusing to see the great pianist's reaction
> to the carefree abandon of the gathering.

The current archivist of the Savage Club confirms that Rachmaninoff and Moiseiwitsch played duets in the club, but no further details
survive. Moiseiwitsch had a formidable reputation as a pianist but
took too much limelight without enough practice, according to some.
His errors were an irritant to the broadcaster John Amis, who

recalled on BBC Radio (in a programme repeated in 2015) that he once heard Moiseiwitsch three times in a week and each time he lost his place. Rachmaninoff was once tripped up – in one of his own compositions! – by Moiseiwitsch's lapses. The first time he heard 'Benno' play the *Rhapsody on a Theme of Paganini*, the pianist had a memory failure. After that, each time Rachmaninoff himself reached that particular point, he also experienced memory problems, once causing Ormandy to panic as his soloist-composer wandered into improvised territory. Amis also complained that Moiseiwitsch bored himself, as well as Amis, by playing nothing but Rachmaninoff's Piano Concerto no. 2 (the plain implication being that nothing could be more tedious), and that Benno would rather have been at his club – the Savage – playing bridge.

Rachmaninoff was delighted by his rendezvous there. The Savage at that time was based at 1 Carlton House Terrace. He was staying nearby in his usual luxury haunt, the Piccadilly Hotel, and wrote from there on 13 March 1939:

Gentlemen,

As I was driving to attend your dinner on the 11th March I kept on asking my friend, Mr Ibbs, who was accompanying me, for an explanation of the meaning of the word 'Savage' which I did not know. When my curiosity was satisfied I at once understood that the Savage Club is just the very place which I ought to have reached long ago, because from my childhood days this word has often been addressed in my direction. I suppose my pranks and my disregard of what is generally accepted as right and proper were the reason which called forth such an estimation. I must confess that even later when I had reached my years of discretion many of those who knew me bestowed on me the same nickname.

And now on the evening of the 11th March the members of the Savage Club elected me to be an Honorary Member! And what of it ! – This is the apotheosis, or shall we say, the last full stop in my life's career. For this honour, and for the place amongst you assigned to me I send my gratitude to all the savage people – the members of the Club of that name.

Signed Sergei Rachmaninoff.[45]

That last UK tour was mixed in all respects. After Sheffield he felt ill, and nearly cancelled Middlesborough. In Glasgow the local press called him a 'weary Titan', complained that his interpretation of Beethoven was pre-ordained ('he has made up his mind about it long ago'), and that he ought to be bringing new works. He had to cancel his Cardiff concert.[46] On 11 March he gave his last UK performance, one of his customary Saturday afternoon concerts, at Queen's Hall.

A young Robert Threlfall, later an authority on Rachmaninoff, was there. In 2015, by then in his nineties, Threlfall recalled the event for an interview on BBC Radio. As a teenager, he used to queue for the unreserved 'two bob' seats in the sunken arena of Queen's Hall.

The minute they opened the door, down you'd go. I got to go to [Rachmaninoff's] last recital he gave before the war. It was most extraordinary because he just walked up to the piano, sat down and played – incredibly difficult things. He just sat down, watching his fingers. Simple as that! Effortless. There was all the power that was needed, and yet his hands very rarely came up.[47]

'The Weather is Hitler-ian'

After the UK tour, as usual Rachmaninoff went to Paris, noting that his travel plans were uncertain: 'I'm not sure if Hitler will approve my plans.' He gave a concert in aid of L'Action Artistique but, judging from his correspondence, charitable intention aside, without enthusiasm. He and Tatiana had their own project; they drove through the suburbs of Paris looking for 'some villa or farm where she could live and shelter if Hitler flies here'. In May 1939, Rachmaninoff wrote to Somov about the growing tensions in Europe: 'I love my Senar very much. Whenever the sun peeps out, I walk in the garden and think, "God how good – if only war would not come." – But we have little sun now. Very little! The weather is Hitler-ian! . . .'[48] That month he fell heavily at Senar on the slippery parquet floor (still there, still slippery).

'The miracle is that I broke nothing. But the bruise was so bad that for three weeks I limp and walk with a cane.' Natalia described the accident to her sister; the lift came in useful: 'I was horrified: he was deathly pale. It was a miracle how we got him into the elevator and upstairs to his bed.'[49] This was the reason he was never able to witness Fokine's ballet version of the *Paganini Rhapsody* at Covent Garden in June 1939.

In August, Rachmaninoff appeared at the embryonic Lucerne festival, at this time called 'International Music Festival Weeks'. He had written to the Somovs on 5 July 1939, a sadness and inevitability hanging over his words:

We live as before – that is, not very calmly. Evidently calm has departed from those who live in Europe, even though war does not come. As you know, I've tied myself to a festival in Lucerne. My concert is on August 11. To be the first to run away seems improper in every way. But after the 11th I shall consider myself justified in displaying weakness. Perhaps we can then leave, or rather, take to our heels . . .

I just broke off this letter to glance at the local afternoon paper. News is again worse! So it goes from day to day. That there could be such possibilities in the world! Unthinkable![50]

Rachmaninoff performed Beethoven's Piano Concerto no. 1 in C major, and his own *Paganini Rhapsody*. The Swiss conductor (and professor of mathematics) Ernest Ansermet, a close associate of Diaghilev and Stravinsky and a founder of the festival, was on the podium. Richard Strauss, with the director Max Reinhardt and others, had considered Lucerne as a potential festival venue before settling, in 1920, on Salzburg. Lucerne had become a fulcrum for artistic freedom: Toscanini, Bruno Walter, Fritz Busch and other leading musicians of the time were unable or chose not to perform in Bayreuth or Salzburg because of Europe's darkening situation. The Sudetenland crisis, which would lead to the annexation of that region and the partition of Czechoslovakia, was unfolding. After the *Anschluss* of March 1938, many Austrian refugees fled to Switzerland.

Leaving Senar

As well as Rachmaninoff, star musicians such as Pablo Casals and Vladimir Horowitz performed at Lucerne, until war intervened and the concert hall was taken over by the military. Two days after his concert, his last in Europe, Rachmaninoff and Natalia left Senar, never to return, and went to Paris. In her memoir, their niece, Sophia Satin, captured the loss they faced:

207

It must have been a bitter feeling for Uncle when the family left Senar in 1939, as the war was imminent. The refuge in Switzerland was something which he had created and put his love and effort into building. And now again he had to leave something behind which was almost a replacement for Ivanovka.[51]

On 23 August 1939, the day the Hitler–Stalin non-aggression pact, also known as the Molotov–Ribbentrop pact, was signed, the Rachmaninoffs sailed from Cherbourg. This time their vessel was the Cunard liner RMS *Aquitania* (1914–50), called 'the ship beautiful' on account of its lavish interior, designed by the team responsible for the London Ritz. The portholes were already blacked out, an anti-submarine precaution. Tatiana, her husband Boris and their son, Alexander, remained in Paris. Within hours of the family's return to America, on 1 September 1939, Germany invaded Poland. A fortnight later RMS *Aquitania* was refitted as a war ship.

A sliver of joy for many, and a distraction from war, was the release by MGM, across the United States, of the Technicolor film *The Wizard of Oz*. Judy Garland shot to fame for her perform-ance of 'Over the Rainbow', which jostled with Glenn Miller's 'Moonlight Serenade' for top place on the Billboard charts. Art Tatum instantly recorded his own jazz piano version of 'Over the Rainbow'. As Horowitz used to say: 'If Art Tatum took up classi-cal music seriously, I'd quit my job the next day.' Toscanini once explained his late arrival for a Carnegie Hall concert by saying he had been in Harlem listening to Tatum play.

Rachmaninoff, too, is often credited (the original source lost in the sands of time) with calling Tatum the greatest pianist in any style. This almost-blind virtuoso pianist from Ohio, who had no proper training, may even have been an influence on the jazzier passages in Rachmaninoff's Piano Concerto no. 4. Can we detect a touch of left-hand stride in the last movement? And did Rachmaninoff ever join the other elite musicians who went to Harlem's Onyx Club to marvel at this dazzling improviser?

Swing with Russian Accents

Buried in the soundtrack of *The Wizard of Oz*, heard when Dorothy and friends try to escape from the Witch's castle, is Mussorgsky's *Night on Bald Mountain*. Rachmaninoff had conducted this work several times as a young man. It included a reference to the *Dies irae* which so preoccupied him (as well as, to a lesser degree, Mussorgsky). Likewise the distinctive Glenn Miller sound, which for millions epitomised the swing era and conjured the atmosphere of World War II, also had old Russia in its DNA. 'Moonlight Serenade' had started out as a composition exercise written by Miller under the guidance of his teacher, the Kharkiv-born Joseph Schillinger, popular music's 'unknown guru', also thought of by some as a crank.[52] Prokofiev, hearing a work of Schillinger's in Leningrad in 1927, disliked it so much he couldn't think what to say. Luckily, Schillinger explained it all in tedious analytical detail to Prokofiev, who was saved from having to say anything.[53]

Teaching was Schillinger's metier. A St Petersburg Conservatory student and friend of Shostakovich, he had been interrogated by the KGB for his interest in 'decadent' jazz, and left for New York in 1928. Soon his teaching sphere of influence extended to Benny Goodman, Tommy Dorsey, Paul Whiteman, John Cage and John Coltrane, and above all George Gershwin. Schillinger's association with Tin Pan Alley and Hollywood led to derision in musical circles, not that he needed to worry: he made huge sums of money, married a Ziegfeld girl-cum-nude model and owned a phenomenal number of shirts and pairs of socks. He was a friend of Horowitz and Nathan Milstein, both men at the heart of Rachmaninoff's circle. With the Russian physicist Léon Theremin (1896–1993), Schillinger invented the pioneering electronic instrument, the theremin.[54] (It was used in the soundtrack of Alfred Hitchcock's *Spellbound*, in which Michael Chekhov was nominated for an Oscar and Salvador Dalí created the dream sequence.) Theremin and Schillinger also collaborated with Rachmaninoff's pupil-friend, Henry Cowell, on the Rhythmicon, a form of early beat box, or drum machine.

This detail may seem to spin beyond Rachmaninoff's musical universe. That would be to overlook his innate curiosity. In January 1928 Rachmaninoff attended a concert given by the New York Philharmonic in which Theremin's spooky, whistling electronic instrument was demonstrated. Theremin had played it in 1922 to Lenin, who thought it would make a good burglar alarm. When the Russian-born Clara Rockmore, a pioneer theremin player, eventually made a solo recording on the instrument in 1977, the first track on her disc was Rachmaninoff's 'Vocalise'. It lends itself beautifully.

In this Russian dance to the music of time, Schillinger's many acknowledged disciples numbered two other familiar names: Vernon Duke, who as Vladimir Dukelsky made an arrangement of Rachmaninoff's 'Vocalise' in the 1920s, and that friend of all, Nina Koshetz, who sang it.

Webs and Connections

Rachmaninoff was in Europe from spring until late summer 1939, but a major enterprise in America, the New York World Fair, with music at its heart, might have been made for his interests. He was absent, but present via his many Russian musician friends who participated. For two seasons, 1939 and 1940, the World Fair was held in the shadow of war. The theme was 'world of tomorrow'. The site of this consumerist dream of chromium and glass, fluorescent light and sweeping curves and angular geometry, was New York's Flushing Meadows. Hitherto used for dumping rubbish and coal ashes, for F. Scott Fitzgerald in *The Great Gatsby* it was 'a valley of ashes – a fantastic farm where ashes grow like wheat into ridges and hills and grotesque gardens . . .'[55] The Fair's Perisphere globe and Trylon tower, known to every New Yorker, were visible from high buildings in Midtown Manhattan. President Roosevelt's opening speech was relayed on a new-fangled television. He hoped for peace among nations and said America had 'hitched her wagon to a star of goodwill'.[56]

Germany did not participate, supposedly on grounds of cost. The USSR, still trying to establish its identity as a country, declared it would take part as a gesture of friendship. Its contribution was grotesquely prominent, with three pavilions outstripping all other nations in size and footprint. The centre-piece was the Soviet Arctic Pavilion: hammer-and-sickle red flag fluttering above it. Conquering the Arctic was a priority rich with propaganda possibilities. 'Russia is distinguished by its vulgarity,' sniffed the *Russian Review*, not even dignifying the country with its new name.[57] At the same time, Russians in exile, including several musicians, were there representing not their old country but their new homeland.

Music of every kind featured, from the Dagenham Girl Pipers to a gamelan orchestra and a gypsy band. Finland's exhibit, in the Hall of Nations, described as a 'symphony of wood', was accompanied by the music of Sibelius (silent as a composer since his tone poem *Tapiola* more than a decade earlier).[58]

Despite racial controversy over the Fair's choice of an African American composer, William Grant Still, his piece, *Rising Tide*, was played on a loop at the Perisphere, conducted by André Kostelanetz. This Russian exile, born in St Petersburg, was described by the press as a 'middle-brow Toscanini', more crusader than conductor: 'He is to music what Billy Graham is to religion.'[59] Kostelanetz was a close associate of everyone from Stravinsky and Copland to Jerome Kern. His luscious string-rich arrangements and recordings of Rachmaninoff both spread the word and, for better or worse, helped condemn Rachmaninoff, for the next half-century, as an 'easy listening' composer of light classics.

A novelty electronic instrument, the Novachord made by Hammond Organs, was a major attraction. Ferde Grofé, so admired by Rachmaninoff as a writer of popular songs, led musicians playing the new-fangled keyboard outside the Garden Court of the Ford Motor Company's stunning white Art Deco building. That year, 1939, the young British singer Vera Lynn recorded a new song, written in anticipation of the coming war: 'We'll Meet Again'. It made pioneering use of the Novachord and was loosely based on Anton Rubinstein's popular Melody in F, op. 3 no. 1 (1852), a sweet piece with a somewhat repetitive tune. Now the pianist-composer whose influence had been so formative on Rachmaninoff's childhood – his playing 'gripped my whole imagination and had a marked influence on my ambition as a pianist',[60] he once said – haunted the world through the new mass media of gramophone and wireless.

The Fair's inaugural concert, on 30 April 1939, featured the New York Philharmonic-Symphony Orchestra under the baton of its British music director, John Barbirolli, with Josef Hofmann as soloist. Russians (that is, exiles) were embedded in the whole enterprise. The opening 'Star-Spangled Banner', now the official

US national anthem, was followed by a newly composed fanfare by Arcady Dubensky. This Kirov-born composer and one-time Moscow Conservatory student had made an orchestral arrangement of Rachmaninoff's 'Vocalise'. (By this time, the question might be: who hadn't?) As a young violinist, he played in the Moscow Imperial Opera orchestra when Chaliapin was making his name, and Rachmaninoff was a leading Russian conductor.

Steinway, struggling in the face of war and electronic invention, provided the Fair's official piano. Hofmann, his enthusiasm for gadgetry as bright as ever, had been working with the company's chief technicians on a new 'accelerated action', still the basis of American-made Steinway instruments today. Hofmann and Rachmaninoff, as well as the conductor, Damrosch, appeared in publicity material, providing glowing endorsements.[61]

JOSEF HOFMANN: The seemingly impossible has been achieved. The Steinway piano has been improved upon. The new Steinway accelerated action has done it. This invention not only facilitates and enhances tone production but also permits of greater precision and speed.

SERGEI RACHMANINOFF: This is to tell you that I consider the new Steinway accelerated action a great improvement, and that I have found your pianos more perfect during the past two seasons than ever before.

WALTER DAMROSCH: Your recent invention, the Steinway accelerated action, makes the manipulation of the keyboard still more sensitive to the most delicate emotional currents emanating from the fingers of the player.

In American music, this trio had close links. The German-born Damrosch was pivotal in the founding of Carnegie Hall, where Hofmann and Rachmaninoff had launched starry careers. Damrosch conducted Rachmaninoff on his first American tour in 1909, in the premiere of the Piano Concerto no. 3. He had also helped Rachmaninoff, in 1922, raise money for 'the relief of composers, artists and men of letters now destitute in the pianist's country'. By 1939 Damrosch, at seventy-seven, was a grand old man. A week after conducting Beethoven's Ninth at the Fair, he made news by beginning a new career in Hollywood. Playing himself, he conducted part of Beethoven's Fifth Symphony in a Bing Crosby picture, *The Star Maker*.

Part of the mythology and legend of those early Hollywood years, when any amateur could try to be a movie star, is that of exiles recreating themselves on the silver screen, especially the Russian aristocrat, or Tsarist military commander, but Germans and East Europeans too, playing themselves as lowly extras. In F. Scott Fitzgerald's unfinished novel, *The Last Tycoon* (1941), set in Hollywood, a White Russian prince is cast as a White Russian prince to ensure an 'authentic feel'. Vladimir Nabokov sums up the strange self-consciousness of Hollywood: 'The dovetailing of one phantasm into another produced upon a sensitive person the impression of living in a Hall of Mirrors, or rather a prison of mirrors, and not even knowing which was the glass and which was yourself.'[62]

Rachmaninoff would soon follow Damrosch and the rest to Hollywood, not to make a career in the movies but to find a new home. As always, he was playing himself.

English Soulmate

An important commission for the Fair was Vaughan Williams's *Five Variants of Dives and Lazarus*, as well as a piano concerto by Arthur Bliss (conducted by Adrian Boult) and Arnold Bax's Seventh Symphony. The previous year, in London, Rachmaninoff had been moved to tears by Vaughan Williams's *Serenade to Music* for sixteen solo singers. Rachmaninoff wrote to Henry Wood asking him to pass on his compliments, though the correspondence took a while to reach RVW, who wrote to Wood's wife, Jessie: 'I cannot remember ever having had a letter from Rachmaninoff – If I had I should certainly have treasured it.' And to Wood himself: 'Very many thanks for sending me Rachmaninoff's delightful letter. I am much gratified that he should have approved of my "Serenade".'[63]

The association between the two composers went back to 1910, when Rachmaninoff played his own Piano Concerto no. 2 at the Leeds Festival, with the premiere of Vaughan Williams's choral work *A Sea Symphony*, conducted by the composer, the other work on the programme. The two men, a year apart in age, had much in common, both regarded first as young radicals, then as outmoded romantics. Both believed in the infinite possibilities of the symphony. Rachmaninoff's own choral symphony, *The Bells* (1913) occupies a musical landscape Vaughan Williams would have recognised. The two each believed in the transcendent power of music, and carried their different religious traditions with them through life, as much a comfort and habit as a faith. RVW declared himself a youthful atheist, then an agnostic, yet gave heart and soul to his work on an *English Hymnal*. He liked to quote Virginia Woolf in *A Room of One's Own* (1929): 'Masterpieces are not single and solitary births; they are the outcome of many years of thinking in common, of thinking by the body of the people, so that the experience of the mass is behind the single voice.'[64]

Rachmaninoff was more circumspect, but his outlook has parallels. His *Liturgy of St John Chrysostom* (1910), for chorus and soloists, drew on Russian Orthodox music but using his own chants, rather than existing ones as he would in the *Vespers*. In this era of religious revivalism, the Orthodox Church wanted to excise any foreign influence in its music, especially German or Italian, or anything operatic, and return to old, pure styles. On hearing the *Liturgy*, the Russian church authorities condemned the work for its 'modernist' tendencies, unsuitable for use in a church. Ironically, to us it sounds thoroughly archaic.

Whatever his personal belief, a fool's game to speculate, the mythology, the ritual, the communal values of the Russian Orthodox Church were an indelible part of Rachmaninoff's being. In writing 'Thanks be to God' at the end of several of his manuscripts, he was only following an example set by Handel, Bach, Haydn and Mendelssohn. For him, as for them, faith was woven into the warp and weft of life, and served him to the end. (When Stravinsky wrote a choral symphony, the *Symphony of Psalms* [1930], he dedicated it, robustly, 'to God and the Boston Symphony Orchestra'.)

Stalin's Ginger Devil

Booked for the 1939 World Fair and arousing excited anticipation, Emil Gilels (1916–85) was due to be the first Soviet pianist to play in America. The new school of Russian, or Soviet, pianism, cut off from the international mainstream though in fact based on all the traditions with which Rachmaninoff and his peers had grown up, was keenly anticipated at Flushing Meadows. Back home Gilels was perceived as a pin-up boy of Soviet ideals, on a par with pilots and film-stars. As a teenager he had been spotted by Stalin (who called him 'the ginger devil' on account of his hair, and said, 'Hitler has his Goebbels.

I have my Gilels').[65] The plan was that the Odesa-born pianist would demonstrate the new nation's cultural supremacy, on a par with its technological prowess, through a show of virtuosic playing.

Gilels' name was known in the West already. That other Rubinstein, the pianist Arthur, had heard him in Russia and brought news of his brilliance. ('If that boy comes to the West, I might as well pack up my bags and go,' Rubinstein said, his remarks closely mirroring Horowitz's about Art Tatum.)[66] Rachmaninoff had heard of him through friends in Moscow after he won the all-Soviet prize. He had also managed to hear Gilels on radio broadcasts. The World Fair concert, with Rachmaninoff there or not, would be of enormous significance.

Instead, the event never happened. The outbreak of war meant Gilels' trip was cancelled. Following Germany's invasion of Poland in September 1939, the Soviet pavilion had to be protected by specially hired guards for fear of protests. After the Fair's first season closed, the USSR invaded Finland. Hostility between the Soviet Union and the West was open and raw. The majestic Soviet pavilions at the World Fair were razed and shipped back to Moscow, to be reconstructed in Stalin's new Gorky Park. For the 1940 season the fair's theme changed to 'Peace and Freedom'. The pavilions of war-torn Czechoslovakia and Poland remained closed. The expansive Soviet site was given over to 'the American commons', an area where people could meet freely and talk. Contributions from minority racial and ethnic groups were encouraged, via drama, dance, choral and symphony concerts, in 'Negro Week', 23 to 28 July 1940. Among those taking part was Marian Anderson, the singer, and a friend of Rachmaninoff's. A key speaker was the civil rights activist Mary McLeod Bethune. All this may have been an attempt to address the protests of the previous year, when five hundred African Americans picketed the gates because of the perceived racial imbalance in employment at the Fair. Music was one of the few areas where there was a (small) degree of African American representation.

Gilels did not make it to America until 1955, though he was still the first Soviet musician to perform there (he was aided in his attempts to get a visa by the violinist Yehudi Menuhin). Rachmaninoff had already made up his mind that Gilels was his pianistic successor. He sent Gilels his own medal and diploma, engraved with the profile of Anton Rubinstein, which the young Rachmaninoff had received, representing his own line in succession to the master.* In the words of the Emil Gilels Foundation website, the pianist 'treasured these relics all his life and through his incredible modesty kept the fact of these possessions shrouded in silence'.

The Soviet pianist remained devoted to Rachmaninoff's music, from a youthful recital in Leningrad's Great Philharmonic Hall in 1937, to his performances and recording of the Piano Concerto no. 3. During the war, now a member of the Communist Party, Gilels performed for Soviet soldiers on the front lines. A film from 1944 shows the handsome young pianist playing Rachmaninoff's G minor Prelude – sometimes nicknamed the 'Military Prelude' (marked *alla marcia* by the composer) – on a flatbed truck with planes flying overhead. The intention was to inspire Russian troops against the Nazi invasion. It was a decade since Rachmaninoff had been officially castigated, following the Tagore kerfuffle. His music was now played in the USSR, but he was categorically in exile. Who chose the Prelude? Was this a form of double propaganda on Gilels' part?

In *The Great Pianists*, published at the height of the Cold War in the early 1960s, the American critic Harold C. Schonberg noted

---

* According to the Emil Gilels Foundation website the medal was sent in 1955 by Sofia Satina.

that the Iron Curtain had made 'the Russian school' an enigma. When Gilels travelled to the West, together with his lustrous rival, the pianist Sviatoslav Richter, the violinist David Oistrakh and the cellist Mstislav Rostropovich, the rest of the world at last had a glimpse of Soviet performance. It began to be apparent 'that Russia was the last outpost of keyboard romanticism' in which, according to Schonberg, American pianists had no tradition and, when it came to playing Chopin, Liszt, Schumann – core Rachmaninoff repertoire – a degree of embarrassment.[67] They were better at Copland, Stravinsky, Bartók, Berg, Webern, composers Rachmaninoff studiously ignored.

The Long and the Short: Hands

Hofmann used to say that the hands of Anton Rubinstein were so big and meaty that his little finger must have been as thick as Hofmann's thumb. Gilels, in between the two in size, had small hands and short, muscular fingers. His *New York Times* obituarist described them as 'stubby'. None were like Rachmaninoff's. In his memoirs, Charles O'Connell, who in his recording career encountered many of the world's best, maintained that most pianists' hands were 'rather short, thick and somewhat ugly'. An exception were Rachmaninoff's: not only were they 'what romantic people' call artistic, with their long, slender, tapering fingers, but also powerful, cool and 'as smooth as a girl's'.[68]

In the *New Statesman* (25 February 1966), the American pianist Rosalyn Tureck vividly recalled her meeting with Rachmaninoff: 'His hands, which appeared bony and hard from a distance, were so large and soft that when I shook hands with him I lost mine in the cushions of his'. Similarly, the Cuban pianist Jorge Bolet, speaking in 1982, recalled shaking hands with Rachmaninoff as 'being enveloped in warm flesh – no bone, just meat'.[69] Neville Cardus, reserved about Rachmaninoff's cautious repertoire, as he saw it, could scarcely have been more enthusiastic about his hands:

> Rachmaninoff's hands are so expressive that a deaf man might well swear that he was hearing the music. The fingers curve and hover and sweep and dance; each supple finger is individual; every note in a harmony is alive and personal. He plays entirely with his finger and his feet; the rest of his body is amazingly still.[70]

To his Russian contemporaries the Pasternaks, whether father Leonid the painter, or son Boris the writer, neither great fans, Rachmaninoff's manner was dull. He may as well have been sitting in front of a bowl of soup, opined Leonid Pasternak, back at the turn of the century when the big-pawed pianist was still living in Russia.[71]

At the Villa Senar, a cast of Rachmaninoff's hands in plaster, resting on a sculpted keyboard in a glass case, holds eerie fascination. It was made in 1932 by Helen Liedloff. An article in the November 1935 issue of *Popular Science* describes how this New York artist sculpted hands as a study of personality. She worked on Einstein's, 'whose short and stubby hands are found resting on a globe' while Rachmaninoff's 'lean, agile fingers are depicted on a keyboard of a piano'.

When Rachmaninoff's cousin Siloti travelled to America, the *New York Herald* devoted an entire article to the musician visitor's hands. The catchline, which would not pass editorial muster today, read: 'Great Pianist's Hands: Siloti can strike an interval of eleven and a half notes'. Siloti, with hands larger, even, than Liszt's, acknowledged that though they were not necessarily beautiful, they were big. In size, at least, these hands ran in the family.

1939-1943

Gathering In

Music for Public Sorrow

On 3 September 1939, Neville Chamberlain announced that Britain and Germany were at war. Franklin D. Roosevelt gave his fireside chat, with a proclamation of American neutrality:

> It is easy for you and for me to shrug our shoulders and to say that conflicts taking place thousands of miles from the continental United States, and, indeed, thousands of miles from the whole American Hemisphere, do not seriously affect the Americas – and that all the United States has to do is to ignore them and go about its own business. Passionately though we may desire detachment, we are forced to realise that every word that comes through the air, every ship that sails the sea, every battle that is fought does affect the American future. Let no man or woman thoughtlessly or falsely talk of America sending its armies to European fields.[1]

In response to the situation abroad, on 10 September, New York City Mayor Fiorello La Guardia, speaking at the World Fair, announced a week of free music, designed to offset tension and 'allay the public sorrow and anxiety occasioned by the conflict in Europe'. The festival would be dedicated to art and to peace. It would also, fittingly, mark the twenty-fifth anniversary of the American Society of Composers, Authors and Publishers (ASCAP). Dr Serge Koussevitzky would conduct the Boston Symphony Orchestra in symphonic works. George Gershwin, Paul Whiteman, Benny Goodman and Cole Porter headed the line-up, alongside several

Russian-Americans: Irving Berlin, Leopold Godowsky, Vernon Duke and Sergei Rachmaninoff.

The festival programme promised 'a concert devoted to the works of Negro composers as played and sung by outstanding Negro singers, performers and organisations'. William Grant Still, the 'anonymous' choice at the World Fair, and Robert Nathaniel Dett (1882–1943) were among the names. Until the recent and vigorous renewal of interest, Grant Still and Nathaniel Dett, together with Florence Price and other Black American composers, were historically neglected. Dett was a pianist-composer like Rachmaninoff, inspired by Dvořák and Coleridge-Taylor in the use of spirituals, educated primarily in the German Romantic tradition together with a stint in Paris with Nadia Boulanger. He put himself in the crossfire of racial prejudice, negotiating with great dignity the obstacle course between different traditions of music in the search for an American style – another story, but of significance here for the way this music spills into the Russian tradition, even as far as Rachmaninoff.[2]

Ukrainians Come to Town

Dett's piano repertoire included studies by the near-inescapable Anton Rubinstein, as well as the English composers Henry Balfour Gardiner and Cyril Scott. He spoke of his kinship with Russian music, a sense of recognising the mood of oppression shared with 'Negro' music. There are parallels to be found between his melodic gift and pianistic style and those of Rachmaninoff and early Scriabin. As a busy choral conductor, presenting concerts at Carnegie Hall, Dett included Rachmaninoff's music in programmes, as well as Orthodox chant by the lesser-known Russian exile Konstantin Shwedoff.

The gesture was reciprocated. The visiting Ukrainian Chorus, singing *a cappella*, dressed up in 'Old World costume', also described in the press as 'gorgeous, native peasant costume', and performed folk and art songs, including music by Tchaikovsky, Scriabin and Rachmaninoff. They concluded their programme, as a courtesy to their host nation, with R. Nathaniel Dett's 'Listen to the Lambs'. The conductor was Alexander Koshetz, uncle of Nina Koshetz. His niece joined her uncle's choir, at Carnegie Hall and elsewhere, an august soloist in Rachmaninoff's *Vocalise* and other repertoire. Combining with Dett's Hampton Institute Chorus, 'composed of Negro voices', the Ukrainians and Americans sang folk music of East and West.[3] Afterwards, Alexander Koshetz said of Dett: 'This Negro composer's work is colossal in its significance of the cultural possibilities of Negroes. On my return to Ukrainia [*sic*] I shall put Professor Dett's compositions on my programme and have my students study and interpret Negro folk music.'[4]

Dett had enjoyed recent success with his epic Biblical choral work, *The Ordering of Moses* (1937), premiered in Cincinnati – it belatedly reached the UK in February 2022, with a performance at Symphony Hall, Birmingham. *Moses* had another performance, in 1938, at the five-day Seventy-Ninth Worcester Music Festival, Massachusetts, where Rachmaninoff's *The Bells* was also performed. This double thread of Black American and Russian music is a connection long overlooked. It sheds light on a remark Rachmaninoff made at the end of his life. Just before his final concert tour, he discussed American music with Victor Seroff. First, looking 'grave', he regretted the absence of good teachers, recalling what could be a description of his own encounter with the young Henry Cowell. 'I have had your men come to me with their compositions and when I point out to them what is obviously a wrong note, they tell me I do not understand, that this is a modern way of composing.' And then, after a long pause, he added: 'The seed of the future music of America lies in a true Negro music.'[5]

A reminder of some of the work from the period that might have informed Rachmaninoff's thinking: William Grant Still's *Afro-American Symphony*, performed by the Rochester Philharmonic in 1931; Florence Price's Symphony in E minor, performed by the Chicago Symphony in 1933; and William Levi Dawson's *Negro Folk Symphony*, premiered by Rachmaninoff's 'own' orchestra, the Philadelphia, conducted by Leopold Stokowski, in 1934, repeated in Carnegie Hall four days later, broadcast nationally and enthusiastically reviewed. Pitts Sanborn in the *New York Telegram* adored Dawson's symphony: 'One is eager to hear it again and again,' he wrote. This from the man who, despite being a radio commentator for the Philadelphia Orchestra, had been loudest and nastiest in his condemnation of Rachmaninoff's Fourth Concerto seven years earlier. When Rachmaninoff referred to 'Negro music' he was, as was his habit, being precise and particular.

Death Dance

Under the pall of Europe's crisis, Rachmaninoff carried on with concert work as usual. In November 1939 he performed with the Minneapolis Symphony Orchestra under its director, the Greek conductor Dimitri Mitropoulos: Beethoven's Piano Concerto no. 1 and Liszt's *Totentanz*. The choice of this apocalyptic 'Dance of Death' made sense. Rachmaninoff's daughter was stranded abroad. Europe was collapsing into war. Among Liszt's inspirations, as well as the *Dies irae*, were the macabre Renaissance woodcuts of Hans Holbein, on the theme of the *danse macabre*.

For the 1939–40 season, the Philadelphia Orchestra embarked on a 'Rachmaninoff Cycle': Eugene Ormandy now having succeeded the great showman, Stokowski, as its music director. The cycle consisted of three concerts at Carnegie Hall (26 November, 3 and 10 December), in one of which the composer-pianist was persuaded to conduct – taking up, once again, the baton he had laid down when he left Russia. The idea was to mark three decades since his American debut. All his major compositions, from different stages of his life, were performed, from the Piano Concerto no. 1 (in its revised form), to the Second Symphony and *The Bells*, to the *Paganini Rhapsody*, with Rachmaninoff an ecstatically cheered soloist. He recorded the Third Symphony with 'his' orchestra on 11 December 1939, the day after the festival ended.[6] This performance, taut, expressive, explosive, shows the dark-light contrasts in this work and remains as exciting as any since. The festival was a critical success, notably for the brilliance of his playing, to a lesser degree for his compositions. At least he escaped the worst kind of pasting he often received in his American years. The Fourth Concerto, so damned at its premiere – as having the 'richness of nougat' but 'neither futuristic music not music of the future' – was not included in the festival.[7]

At the end of 1939 Rachmaninoff described his circumstances to his musician friend Arthur Hirst, sharing his concerns about Tatiana. Touchingly he describes 'my wife and I' as having given concerts, reflecting his complete reliance on Natalia's presence and judgement.

Dear Mr. Hirst,

I received your letter of 4th December the day before yesterday. Thank you very much for it.

Since you ask, I can give you a brief summary of how we all are.

From the 20th October to the 10th December my wife and I gave twenty-three concerts. The last eight, in Philadelphia and New York, formed a cycle of my compositions. The final concerts I conducted myself. The cycle seems to have gone quite successfully. To conclude this discussion of my personal affairs, I can only add that we are all in good health, except that I feel very tired.

My elder daughter and my granddaughter had great difficulty in reaching New York. If it weren't for the efforts of Foley it is doubtful whether they would have succeeded at all. They came and brought four dogs with them, which is a little too much for wartime.

I am sad and worried about Tatiana. Before leaving Europe, I bought her a little estate within forty miles of Paris where she is living all alone, if you don't count her little boy. Her husband, happily, is not at the front but is serving, at present, as an instructor somewhere in France. It is only possible to bear up under such conditions with a character as strong as Tatiana's. In the past two months she managed to obtain a French passport and a driver's license. This last fact worries me no less than the war. I have never felt she had any talent for driving.

Well, I think that will be enough about my children.

In conclusion, may I send you my good wishes for next year which I trust will be a happier one for all of us.

With warmest greetings, S. Rachmaninoff[8]

On New Year's Eve 1939, four months into the war, a new musical tradition began in Vienna (it would soon switch to New Year's Day, where it has remained). A morale-lifting concert from the Golden Hall of the Musikverein, featuring music by the waltz-king Johann Strauss II, was broadcast to German-speaking countries. Proceeds would go to Hitler's war relief scheme. The orchestra was the

Vienna Philharmonic, some twenty per cent of whom were Nazi Party members. In 1938, several Jewish players had been forced into exile, in some cases murdered. The New Year concert became embroiled in the Nazi propaganda machine. The term 'degenerate music' was applied to music considered decadent. Wagner's music reigned supreme. The Jewish Mendelssohn was banned. Jazz and swing were the 'sin of Babylon'. Russian music, including Rachmaninoff's, was considered 'subhuman'.

A collection of records found in the Reich Chancellery, recovered by a Soviet intelligence officer at the fall of Berlin in 1945 then kept in a Moscow attic and not revealed until 2007, included Tchaikovsky's Violin Concerto played by the Polish Jewish violinist Bronisław Huberman, officially an enemy of the Third Reich. There is no evidence at all to prove it was 'Hitler's personal record collection' – an assertion that has been incorrectly made, and also roundly challenged. Here, however, with Führer HQ inventory number 'Führerhauptquartier 840', was a recording made in London in 1926, conducted by Eugene Goossens on the Electrola label: 'Russian Bass with Orchestra and Chorus: The Death of Boris Godunov', sung by Chaliapin. There was also a record of music by Rachmaninoff. This proves only, perhaps, the popularity at that time, in Nazi Germany and Soviet Moscow, of both these Russian musician-exiles, Chaliapin and Rachmaninoff.

Sitting by the Radio

In January 1940, Leningrad was in blackout. The Winter War between the Soviet Union and Finland was under way. Rachmaninoff found himself in the headlines when he joined nine exiled Russian writers in signing a protest against Soviet aggression in Finland. It was published in a Russian-French paper in Paris and stated that Russians, unlike Stalin's shameful government, could have no animosity towards the blameless Finnish people.

In this unstable climate, Prokofiev's ballet *Romeo and Juliet* was premiered at the Kirov Theatre – known now and in pre-Revolutionary times as the Mariinsky – the audience fumbling its way in darkness. Prokofiev had returned to live in the USSR four years earlier. Elsewhere war left its mark. The Nazi authorities established a Jewish ghetto in Łódź, Poland. The pianist Ignacy Paderewski became president of the Polish government in exile. In blackout England, foodstuffs were rationed and icy temperatures, enough to cause the Thames to freeze, sharpened the misery.

America had still not entered the war. To mark his birthday on 30 January, President Roosevelt took delivery of a Novachord electronic keyboard: his was labelled no. 1, though several had already been sold after the display at Flushing Meadows. War would soon make the instrument's components hard to access. By 1942, this huge, eerie-sounding instrument – the ghostly sound of Hollywood, in films such as *Gone with the Wind*, *Rebecca* and *The Maltese Falcon* – had ceased production. A slice of musical history, a prototype of the modern synthesiser, was a commercial flop.

In his own start to the year, Rachmaninoff had concerts planned in San Francisco and Los Angeles. He made his debut at the Pantages Theatre on Hollywood Boulevard, performing his Piano Concerto no. 2 under the baton of Stokowski. *The Firebird* was in the same programme. Stravinsky's ballet was not infrequently paired with music by Rachmaninoff, as in 1940 when it had been programmed in Ohio with the latter's Symphony no. 2. The 'modern Russian music' tag attached to the concert can scarcely have pleased either composer. Rachmaninoff was still trying, doggedly, to help Medtner come to America. He agreed with the Tolstoy Foundation that he would match any sums they raised up to $500, but Medtner was unable to leave England: they never met again.

As Rachmaninoff told the *Oakland Tribune*, he was still in a state of anxiety from having recently conducted again (in the Philadelphia Festival), for the first time for twenty years: 'Oh I have tireless piano-playing muscles, but conducting is something else. And perhaps I have forgotten some of the technic [*sic*] of conducting.' He went on to quote 'a friend, a very great pianist' who had warned him, on coming to America, not to say much about his compositions, 'because there, no one believes that a good composer can be a good pianist, or a good pianist a good composer.'

The reporter pressed on, asking whether Rachmaninoff had composed anything in Switzerland the previous summer:

[H]e bowed his head and raised it with tears in his eyes. 'No, he said, 'All last summer I sat by the radio, not by the piano. The things which were happening made me too sorrowful to create. Even here in America, it is hard to keep my courage. My children are in Europe. One of my daughters is married to a Frenchman already in the army. Each day I live in fear of a cablegram. Only when I am busy with music can I forget for a little while. It makes one's own grief and anxiety easier to bear if one can believe he is bringing the solace of music to others who are troubled.'[9]

After an unspecified 'minor operation' in May 1940, Rachmaninoff heard that Nabokov and his family had arrived in America, two years after the correspondence concerning possible publication of *The Gift*. Travel documentation, within Russian émigré circles, had been arranged by Koussevitzky. The Nabokovs sailed on the French liner SS *Champlain*, its last voyage to New York (on the return journey it was sunk by a German mine). Rachmaninoff and Nabokov established a working relationship: Rachmaninoff wanted help with a good English text of *The Bells*, in preparation for an American performance. Nabokov also reworked the monologue of Pushkin's *The Miserly Knight* for Rachmaninoff's opera. Was Nabokov serving his due and hoping that *The Gift* would be published with the composer's financial support? Despite good intentions, these plans came to nothing.

Long Island Sounds

That summer the Rachmaninoffs retreated to the Honeyman Estate at Orchard Point, on Little Neck Peninsula, Centerport, Huntington. The family had spent a short time there the previous year after hurrying from Europe, a continent now closed to them. Orchard Point was situated on the 'gold coast' northern shore of Long Island, with its early twentieth-century waterfront, affluent boating community and mansions of the kind immortalised in *The Great Gatsby* two decades earlier.

The estate belonged to the heiress Marian Stewart Honeyman, and her husband, Robert B. Honeyman Jr, a collector of books and rare manuscripts. William K. Vanderbilt II, part of the Vanderbilt dynasty, whose Spanish revival-style pile, the 'Eagle's Nest', is now a museum, was a near neighbour. Though not among the local party-givers, Vanderbilt was prominent locally: a keen sportsman and horse-racing enthusiast, a pilot and a yachtsman, president of the New York Central Railroad and, importantly in the history of motor racing, founder of the Vanderbilt Cup, held on the newly built Long Island Roosevelt Raceway – just Rachmaninoff's type.

There were aspects of the origins of the Honeymans' wealth that would surely have interested their guests in the summer of 1940. Mrs

Honeyman has a modest place in the early history of aviation, having flown as a child in 1914 on the biplane the *Benoist XIV*. This gave her the singular honour of being, as recorded in 1976, the oldest living female commercial flight passenger in the United States.

Her wealth came from her father, John K. Stewart, a Chicago entrepreneur whose patents included a mechanical pencil sharpener and the first domestic iron, the Sunbeam. His fame came, however, from the Stewart speedometers and car horns so vital for the early automobiles which Rachmaninoff himself took pleasure in owning and driving. Stewart's intention, at the time of his premature death, was to build a speedometer factory in Long Island City near the Ford factory. Stewart was also a music lover, and a pioneer in the early phonograph market. He and Rachmaninoff would have had much in common, though evidently the latter lacked Stewart's practical and boat-building skills. The *Syracuse Herald* (28 September 1941) reported that Rachmaninoff, for relaxation, 'passes part of each day during the summer' piloting his speedboat on Long Island Sound, but he is 'no good as a mechanic and can't make repairs if anything goes wrong'.

Sailing By

Today the land has been built on, but Sergei Bertensson described an idyllic setting: seventeen acres of seclusion, with groves, orchards, a mile-long beach, and pier for a new cabin cruiser, poignantly named *Senar*. The boat was equipped with kitchen and cabin. Rachmaninoff was usually at the wheel, with voyages made across the Sound to Connecticut, to visit Michael Chekhov, now living in America.[10]

Rachmaninoff's studio was isolated from all living quarters and swimming pool. He could practise and compose unembarrassed by the possibility of disturbing anyone. Bertensson wrote:

'Composition was possible only when he could feel that no one could hear or listen to him. On the other hand, he could not face being actually alone, especially in the evenings; he preferred to know that people were nearby, just out of ear range.'[11] He may have thought he was alone and not overheard, but tales were shared of Long Island locals tethering their boats in Northport harbour in order to listen to the celebrated visitor practising. He had programmes to prepare for his next concert season. A local piano teacher remembered that Rachmaninoff would 'sometimes drive his cabin cruiser to the home of the Northport harbour-master and play for small groups'.[12]

Many Russian friends spent the summer within close reach of his 'lair', as he called it. Horowitz visited several times to discuss changes to the Second Piano Sonata, whether in its original or its revised version. Horowitz eventually made his own edition, recording it in 1968.

Mikhail Fokine, the Somovs and the Greiners were there. Boris Chaliapin, the artist son of Fyodor, arrived from Hollywood: he was a cover artist for *Time* magazine, creating some four hundred portraits between 1942 and his death in 1979. This was the occasion he painted Rachmaninoff, with rare informality, in his shirtsleeves, practising: face in hangdog concentration, trousers crumpled, every vein of his large hands visible, gold wedding band on his right-hand ring finger in the Russian tradition. Seen in its entirety, this portrait gives a sense of the subject's height in relation to the keyboard, and conveys the self-possession of a musician at work, indifferent to the world.

Boris Chaliapin also painted Rachmaninoff's fifteen-year-old granddaughter, Sophie Volkonsky. She celebrated her sixteenth birthday with a party at Huntingdon, in which her grandfather was master of ceremonies, leading the family procession round the dining table and singing 'Happy Birthday', then making a speech in Russian. A talented musician, she had written a choral work during the summer, and was now busy orchestrating it. Her grandfather was preoccupied with revising his troublesome Fourth Piano Concerto.[13] Tatiana and her family were still in what was now 'Vichy France'. The country had fallen to Germany in June and was under the governance of Marshal Philippe Pétain: pro-Nazi, xenophobic, dictatorial. A postcard recently came to light in Senar, written by Natalia to her daughter on 28 September 1944, after Rachmaninoff's death:

> Dearest Tanya, This is the first postcard I'm officially allowed to send you by regular mail. I'm so happy I can do it now and hope you will answer me. I got your little note with the letter. I would like to know if you are still in the country and will stay there in the winter or if you will move to Paris. Please try to write to me. I'm anxious to know how you are and feel. Irina and my sister Sofia will also write to you. With many kisses and love, Natalia Rachmaninoff.[14]

I Thank Thee Lord

Before going to Orchard Point, Rachmaninoff had written to Yakov (Jacob) Weinberg (1879–1956), that he had been 'working a little' on composition. Like Rachmaninoff, the Odesa-born Jewish composer, yet another in the New York Russian circle, had studied in Moscow with Taneyev. Around 1914, Weinberg had made a two-piano tribute to Rachmaninoff, *Rachmaniana*. Eventually, in 1940, the pieces were published. He wrote to Rachmaninoff, asking him – rather belatedly – for his view on his arrangements. Abruptly, Rachmaninoff replied to the effect that since Weinberg's versions had now been published, any comments he had were not worth making. Here was a rare case of Rachmaninoff sounding tetchy.[15] He had reason. He also revealed to Weinberg that he was undergoing 'an unpleasant course of treatment', details unspecified, following his recent medical issues.

It did not prevent him, as recorded by Natalia, from observing a strict work regime. He was working on a substantial new composition, with the word 'Dances' in the title. He needed to exert discipline, not check over someone else's indifferent arrangement of his own music from long ago. Natalia set out the daily timetable as follows:

8.00 a.m.: Coffee
8.30 to 10 a.m.: composition
10 until noon: piano practice
Noon until 1 p.m.: composition
1 p.m. to 3 p.m.: lunch and rest
3 p.m. until 10 p.m. (with break for dinner): composition

Somewhere into all this – at weekends? – came the stream of friends, the boating, the motoring, the dining. According to his wife:

He wanted to finish the *Dances* for the beginning of the concert season, whatever the cost. Sergei Vasilievich achieved his goal, but the whole time I was worried looking after him. In the evening his eyes refused to focus because of the work of writing the score in his small hand. Afterwards too a lot of work was done when he was actually on his concert tour. At every large station at which we stopped, the proofs of the *Symphonic Dances* [as the work would become] awaited him, and Sergei Vasilievich quickly got down to the corrections of these green pages from the white sheets of music. How this tired his eyes! He carried on correcting both before and after the next concert.[16]

His usual preference was to keep composition and practice separate. Not on this occasion. *Symphonic Dances*, op. 45, for full orchestra, as noted in the published score, lasts thirty-seven minutes. It was his only large-scale composition written in the United States, and his last opus. He dedicated the new composition to Eugene Ormandy and the Philadelphia Orchestra. On 21 August 1930 he wrote to Ormandy.

My dear Mr Ormandy, Last week I finished a new symphonic piece, which I naturally want to give first to you and your orchestra. It is called *Fantastic Dances*. I am beginning the orchestration. Unfortunately my concert tour begins on 14th October and I must practise intensively, and so I do not know whether I shall be able to finish the orchestration until November.

He suggested that Ormandy visit. 'I should like to play the piece for you. We are staying at the Honeyman Estate, Huntingdon, Long Island, and only forty miles from New York, so that you can easily reach us.'[17] Ormandy responded enthusiastically. A week later, Rachmaninoff replied, now calling the piece by the title it would keep: *Symphonic Dances*. In late September, still at Orchard Point, composer and conductor went through the score together.

The change of name was prompted either by not wishing to duplicate Shostakovich's *Fantastic Dances* (1923), or simply because the new work was symphonic in scale. At the start of his concert tour he explained to the *New York World Telegram* (17

October 1940) that the work 'should have been called just *Dances*
but I was afraid people would think I had written dance music for
jazz orchestra'. Rachmaninoff had also made a two-piano version,
completing it on 10 August ahead of finishing the orchestral
version: he played it at home with Horowitz, a regular duo companion, in Senar and in California.

Tips on Playing the Sax

Another visitor to Orchard Point was a friend whose practical
help Rachmaninoff needed. Robert Russell Bennett (1894–1981),
a one-time student of Nadia Boulanger, was one of the all-time top
Broadway and Hollywood orchestrators. He had already worked
with Gershwin and Cole Porter; *Annie Get Your Gun*, *Oklahoma!*,
South Pacific, *Carmen Jones* and *My Fair Lady* were yet to come. Like
Rachmaninoff, he had a capacity for working intensive, long hours
when required. As Oscar Hammerstein said of him: 'Russell can
work twenty hours at a stretch, then have a shower and come out
looking as though he just had a vacation.'[18]

The previous summer Bennett had contributed six scores to the
World Fair, which were highly praised in the *New York Times* by
Olin Downes (who had pooh-poohed efforts by Arthur Honegger,
Florent Schmitt and Darius Milhaud at the Paris Fair two years
earlier). Bennett's music was written to accompany the spectacular
sound and light fountains display in the Lagoon of Nations, the
Fair's great tourist attraction. As coloured jets of water surged,
shooting from a thousand water nozzles, so Bennett's music likewise surged and the crowds gasped. (Disney cited the Fair as one
of his inspirations for Disneyland. It sounds irresistible.) Bennett
knew how and what every band and orchestral instrument could
do, and could himself play most of them.

Rachmaninoff needed guidance on the saxophone, never having used the instrument and having left it too late to get advice from Glazunov, who had already explored its charms. Bennett was his man. His witty recollection of their meeting, as told to Bertensson (29 October 1949), conjures both the single-mindedness and jubilation of the exchange:

Earlier in my life I had the great pleasure of making friends with [Rachmaninoff] and, like everyone who was exposed to his beautiful personality, I count the minutes spent with him as very precious. Our first meeting was at a time when Mr Fritz Kreisler and I were working something out together, and we happened by chance to meet in a studio . . . I was at that time working on the arrangements for *Of Thee I Sing* with music by George Gershwin. I had to excuse myself rather early during the afternoon because I had to begin work on the overture for the play.

Mr. Rachmaninoff asked me when I had to finish it, and I told him that the orchestra was rehearsing it the following afternoon at 4.00 p.m. [mid-December 1931]. He looked at me very gravely and said, —That is too little time, and he was perfectly right, but he understood already that that was show business in the USA. Later on, when he was doing his *Symphonic Dances*, he wanted to use a saxophone in the first movement and got in touch with me to advise him as to which of the saxophone family to use and just how to include it in his score – his experience with saxophones being extremely limited.

I therefore considered him as my pupil, or at least so I boast to my friends. At that time he played over his score for me on the piano and I was delighted to see his approach to the piano was quite the same as that of all of us when we try to imitate the sound of an orchestra at the keyboard. He sang, whistled, stomped, rolled his chords, and otherwise conducted himself not as one would expect of so great and impeccable a piano virtuoso. Some days later we had lunch together at his place in Huntington, Long Island. When he met my wife and me at the railroad station he was driving the car and after driving about one hundred yards, he stopped the car, turned to me, and said, —I start on A sharp? I said, —That's right, and he said, —Right! and drove on out to his place.[19]

Rachmaninoff did start the saxophone solo on A sharp: his question was not, as it sounds, about what note he, the composer, should start on, but whether the transposition was correct for an instrument pitched in E flat. He first planned to name the three movements Midday, Twilight and Midnight. He had a scheme that it might, with Fokine, become a ballet, an idea that took root but was thwarted by Fokine's death in 1942.

Before settling on the saxophone solo he had an idea that the African American contralto Marian Anderson should provide the first-movement solo melody.[20] A correspondence with Anderson, who filled huge venues with her classical recitals, continued until late in Rachmaninoff's life. A pioneer in the Civil Rights Movement, who had performed in the World Fair's 'Negro Week', Anderson won headlines for a major event in 1939. Helped by the intervention of Mrs Eleanor Roosevelt, she performed to a mixed-race crowd of seventy-five thousand at Washington's Lincoln Memorial. That year the Philadelphia-born singer had recorded Brahms songs with Eugene Ormandy and the Philadelphia Orchestra. She often performed Rachmaninoff's early song 'In the Silence of the Secret Night', op. 4 no. 3, in her recitals (in John McCormack's English translation). It is tantalising to imagine what Anderson might have brought to the first perform- ance, but Rachmaninoff was a practical musician: he would have seen the difficulty of hiring such a renowned singer for just a few bars of music.

By October 1940, the news was out: the American press announced the world premiere of Rachmaninoff's first orchestral work in four years. Entitled *Danses symphoniques*, it would be given by the Philadelphia Orchestra, conducted by Eugene Ormandy, the orchestra's fourth premiere of a work by this composer-pianist, following the Fourth Piano Concerto (1927), *Rhapsody on a Theme of Paganini* (1934) and the Third Symphony (1936). First Rachman- inoff had his own recital season to think about. He opened the new season (14 October) at a crammed Masonic Auditorium, Detroit, a 'long, lean and stooped figure' (*Detroit News*) but a 'marvel' given his nearly three-score-years and ten.

A correspondence in the gramophone section of the *New York Times*, alongside reviews of Bessie Smith and Louis Armstrong, wished that Rachmaninoff would record more major compositions, not just short works: 'It would seem that such recordings would be justified purely from a historical standpoint – a permanent preser- vation of some of the finest piano artistry the world has ever heard' (3 November 1940). A subsequent reply to the column noted that RCA Victor was 'filling these voids', following the Rachmaninoff festival the previous year, with the Piano Concerto no. 4. A greater regret, in retrospect, is that he did not record more of his songs too, so rich a part of his output in the fertile Russian years.

The Philadelphia Sound

In December he returned, after a long gap, to Havana, then allowed himself a short end-of-year break. Rehearsals were under way for *Symphonic Dances*. He wanted to be there. He addressed the men, as men they all were except the harpists, of the Philadelphia Orchestra at the final rehearsal: 'Years ago I composed for the great Chaliapin. Now he is dead and so I compose for a new kind of artist, the Philadelphia Orchestra.'[21] What was it about the orchestra Rachmaninoff so loved? Was it the now fabled 'Philadelphia sound', not in the jazz and soul sense of popular culture, but in the particular, orchestral manner Rachmaninoff would have understood? One answer is the rich, blended sound, without jagged edges, suited especially to Rachmaninoff's music, but (it might be argued) sounding too smooth and lush in some repertoire.

Stokowski, conducting without a baton, experimented with allowing the Philadelphia strings to bow freely, therefore creating an unbroken sound. Ormandy tried a different way of enriching and darkening the texture by having second violins double with violas. These are imprecise matters, since neither conductor followed these tendencies to the letter. It may, above all, be that after playing so frequently as a soloist with the orchestra, Rachmaninoff knew the musicians and felt them to be family. He was at home too, with its chief conductors, who knew what he wanted: that this was a two-way love affair, always an asset in achieving great performances, was without question.

In the last weeks of the year a cluster of other events made musical history. Walt Disney's third feature-length animated film, *Fantasia*, with music conducted by Stokowski, was released on 30 November. Old Russia was represented: Tchaikovsky's *Nutcracker* was in. Mussorgsky's *Night on Bald Mountain*, in the orchestration by Rimsky-Korsakov complete with *Dies irae* snatches and a ghoulish witches' sabbath, was in. So too was Stravinsky's *Rite of Spring*, with its monstrous animated battle between a Stegosaurus and a Tyrannosaurus rex. Rachmaninoff's *Troika* and G minor Prelude, however, ended up on the cutting-room floor, but he already had the distinction of having been honoured by Mickey Mouse. Prokofiev missed out too, but soon Disney would make an animated version of *Peter and the Wolf*.

On 6 December, the Violin Concerto by Arnold Schoenberg, living in Los Angeles, was premiered by the Philadelphia Orchestra (soloist Louis Krasner), conducted by Rachmaninoff's omnipresent ally, the ever-adaptable Stokowski. A day later, in the Café Rouge of Manhattan's Hotel Pennsylvania, Glenn Miller introduced a new number to the world. With a fleet of brass and saxophones blasting out a close harmony wah-wah chorus, the 'Song of the Volga Boatmen' now had a big-band Miller makeover: a total assimilation of the old Russian folk-song, Chaliapin's favourite, into the America Swing era.

Rachmaninoff had his own preoccupations, namely helping prepare Ormandy for the *Symphonic Dances*. The premiere was scheduled for 3 January 1941. A private recording, of historic importance, came to light in the Ormandy archive at the University of Pennsylvania (released commercially by Marston Records in 2018 as *Rachmaninoff Plays Symphonic Dances*, with notes by Richard Taruskin and Ira Levin). Rachmaninoff can be heard at the piano, working through the score with Ormandy, jumping from place to place, gravelly voice shouting comments in various languages. They, and others heard talking or laughing, are at Ormandy's house in Philadelphia. Rachmaninoff is off-microphone, not easy to decipher. Magnetic tape existed by the 1930s but the recording here was made on so-called 'acetate'. Disc machines for amateur use at home first appeared around 1940, still a luxury for the few but enabling instantaneous recording.

Given his profession, a musician of Ormandy's status would be an obvious client for this new gadget. We can imagine Rachmaninoff fascinated by the latest technology, never thinking that nearly eighty years later his own impromptu performance would reach the public. Ormandy kept it, faithfully, as a private document, though his own recording of *Symphonic Dances*, years later (1960), suggests he did not follow the composer's interpretation precisely. Rachmaninoff's performance at the start is brisk; the haunting second-movement waltz possesses an unsettling urgency, but at the same time is languid and moody. The last movement crackles and whirls between moods with rhapsodic freedom and fire. Ormandy's approach is more lush and, in speeds, lax. He never entirely took to the work that had his name as dedicatee on the title page. Nor, as it turned out, did Rachmaninoff much like Ormandy's performance.

Music for Weapons

By the end of the year the German bombing campaign had razed several British cities, among them those in which Rachmaninoff had performed the previous year: London, Birmingham, Liverpool, Sheffield, Glasgow. On 23 December, Manchester's Free Trade Hall, where he had given the UK premiere of the *Paganini Rhapsody*, was blitzed to an empty shell. The next year, hours after a performance of Elgar's *Dream of Gerontius* conducted by Malcolm Sargent in May 1941, the Queen's Hall, too, would be destroyed, not by explosives but by incendiaries, in the worst night of the London Blitz. The bust of Henry Wood, on display every year at the BBC Proms (adorned with a chaplet), was one of the few items left intact. Created by the sculptor Donald Gilbert, it had been made as part of the 1938 celebrations for Wood's fiftieth anniversary 'jubilee' as a conductor, during which Rachmaninoff had been star soloist.

On Christmas Eve, Mahatma Gandhi wrote to Hitler, calling him 'Dear friend', and begging him, 'in the name of humanity', to stop the war.[22] On Christmas Day, the Rodgers and Hart stage musical *Pal Joey*, starring Gene Kelly, premiered at the Ethel Barrymore Theatre on Broadway. Nearly forty blocks away off Broadway, at 505 West End Avenue on the Upper West Side, Rachmaninoff played Father Christmas to his granddaughter, who was quite old enough to know who might be beneath any Santa Claus disguise. The family still had no news from Tatiana in France.

In Britain, an armaments factory had found a new way of countering the exhaustion and repetitive tedium of making shells. By playing music, via gramophone and loudspeakers, to the workers, output increased by up to twelve per cent, according to the National Institute of Industrial Psychology. Artists came to give live 'factory concerts', in staff canteens at lunchtimes or sometimes at midnight. 'They're making shells to the tunes of Rachmaninoff,' reported the news wires, noting that his music, and that of Chopin, were particularly appreciated.

Alliluya

Rachmaninoff had a hunch the *Symphonic Dances*, written three years before his death, would be his last work, telling friends it was 'his last spark' or 'last flicker'. He was no great age but had physical ailments, some chronic. In many photographs he is seen with a cigarette, even when pictured informally at the piano, which may have contributed to failing health. His concert schedule suggested no yielding to age or infirmity, but his obsession with mortality was there from an early age. Did he consciously spin the strands of his entire life into this single work? A mood of longing for Russia, for the past, dominates this score.

Whether this sense of yearning is significantly different from the 'Russian melancholy' perceived in the works he wrote before 1917 – the grand sweep of the Piano Concerto no. 2, the poignant slow movement of the Second Symphony – is a matter for cautious debate. He was still in his homeland when he wrote those pieces, and therefore not missing it, so we should resist sentimental interpretation or meaning. His gift was lyricism and melody: this was Rachmaninoff's defining quality, his musical fingerprint.

The temptation to see the *Symphonic Dances* as a wrapping up of his creative output is nonetheless strong. The opening has an echo of Rimsky-Korsakov's *Le Coq d'or*, the one score by another composer that he carried with him in his case when he left Russia in 1917. The notion, suggested by some, that the solo saxophone, silent after that prominent, soulful solo, is Rachmaninoff's private farewell, is surely fanciful. It is curious and somewhat puzzling, all the same, at a live performance of the *Symphonic Dances*, to see the saxophone player sit on stage nursing his instrument for the work's remaining two and a half movements while the rest of the orchestra plays on. Rachmaninoff quotes several earlier works, often enigmatically, including *The Bells* and the *Études-Tableaux*. More pointedly, his Symphony no. 1, still unknown to his audiences after the crisis of its premiere and subsequent withdrawal, is given a brief, cascading star billing at the end of the first dance. Here, transformed, the main theme appears in a glistening shower of harp, piano and glockenspiel, now not in the minor but transformed to the redemptive major. Few if any would have spotted this self-quotation.

Whatever the musical impulse for using the plainsong chant *Dies irae*, audible in his music as early as the 1890s and occurring so many times since, its origin in the Requiem for the Dead is impossible to ignore. This faithful musical friend is present in the *Dances*, manically and hectoringly in the last movement, less blatantly elsewhere. In contrast he also includes the Resurrection doxology, 'Blessed art thou, Lord', the ninth movement of his *All-Night Vigil*, or *Vespers* (1915), writing the word 'Alliluya' in the score.

At the Philadelphia premiere on 3 January 1941, the composer received an ovation and was summoned from his circle box, reluctantly, to make an appearance on stage, shake Ormandy's hand, acknowledge his beloved orchestra, and the audience's applause. Four days later *Symphonic Dances* was performed at Carnegie Hall. Olin Downes reviewed the 'three pieces', as they were described, in the *New York Times*, damning them with faint praise as 'among the best works in the composer's later period'. He found no particular connection between each piece, regarding the first as pastoral, the second bitter-sweet with a Viennese lilt, the last fantastical and, like the composer himself, obsessed with the 'terrible old plainchant' of the *Dies irae*.[23]

Downes reflects that all music springs from a source which is 'deeper than any surgeon has yet probed', and which in Rachmaninoff's case was vested with a melancholy, 'a fatalism, not frantic or exhibitionist'. These dances, he wrote, formed a loose sequence of memories and reveries 'with some Dead Sea fruits in them – all unpretentious, melodic, sensuously coloured and admirably composed music'. Ormandy was not alone in his coolness towards the work. RCA Victor's music director, Charles O'Connell, felt it did not 'add lustre' to the composer's reputation, and was not much liked by the public either. O'Connell and Rachmaninoff disagreed over a proposed recording; Rachmaninoff wanted to conduct the Philadelphia Orchestra in the work himself; O'Connell preferred the Chicago Orchestra and Frederick Stock. Both lost out. The earliest surviving recording is by the New York Philharmonic-Symphony (as it was then called) and Dimitri Mitropoulos (released by Ward Marston on the set which includes Rachmaninoff playing through the work on the piano, for Ormandy's benefit). There is an early Soviet recording from the mid-1940s, of Nikolai Golovanov conducting the Moscow Radio Symphony Orchestra: hair-raising, expressive but never lush, edgy and dangerous – no Hollywood gloss here. The third dance is nothing short of savage.

Modernity Again: No Goooood

Mitropoulos, whom Rachmaninoff had come to like and admire, tried hard to interest him in music of his fellow composers. Most attempts were fruitless, as in the case of Paul Hindemith (1895–1963), a German in exile who, like Rachmaninoff, would eventually take American citizenship. The two composers were both in Minneapolis in 1941. Hindemith's symphony was being performed. Would Rachmaninoff come and listen? He could sit backstage where no audience would mob him. So Rachmaninoff went and sat behind the proscenium arch. The audience was enthusiastic, so too was the conductor, who demanded to know Rachmaninoff's view: 'Rachmaninoff looked up at him with a doleful expression and lugubriously intoned: "No goooood."'[24]

He was no more enthusiastic about the American composer David Diamond (1915–2005), a former student of Roger Sessions and Nadia Boulanger. Diamond's credentials would prove excellent, as mentor to the pianist Glenn Gould and, much later, as teacher of the choral composer Eric Whitacre. His First Symphony was being rehearsed in New York in 1942. Within moments of the music starting, the nervous young composer saw a tall figure leave the hall abruptly. Aghast, Diamond urged Mitropoulos to find out whether Rachmaninoff's exit was because he hated what he heard. Rachmaninoff, punctilious about time, and impatient to find rehearsal schedules had changed (other accounts tally with this), was expecting to hear his own Symphony no. 3 being played, not Diamond's Symphony no. 1. He said: 'Please tell Mr Diamond that it was nothing personal and no reflection on his symphony. I simply don't have time to spend listening to new music by American composers.'[25] One of that breed, Aaron Copland, made similar comments in reverse. Reportedly the prospect of having to sit through one of Rachmaninoff's protracted symphonies or piano concertos depressed him.

Rachmaninoff, throughout his life, articulated what many struggled to identify about 'modern' music: too much head and no heart, an excess of thought and analysis over feeling and exultation. As we retreat further from the period of these battles, 'modernity' becomes harder to define, or perhaps merely more meaningless. Everything grows old the minute it is born, 'for it comes into being contaminated with dry rot', as Rachmaninoff was not the first to observe. He said this, confidentially, to the editor of the *Musical Courier* in 1939 who, to his credit, waited until Rachmaninoff was dead to publish the entire exchange. This was the occasion on which, as well as describing himself as 'a ghost wandering in a world made alien', he said he could not acquire new methods of composition. 'Unlike Madame Butterfly, with her quick religious conversion, I cannot cast out my musical gods in a moment and bend the knee to new ones.'[26]

Even Schoenberg, who had posed the key question 'What is Modernism' in 1937, was now finding new answers, or old ones depending on your point of view. The 'bogey-man' of atonality had, to an extent, lost his way. In 1939, living in California, he finally completed the Chamber Symphony no. 2 which he had begun more than three decades earlier. In effect Schoenberg was revisiting a late Romantic style he had abandoned in his quest for experiment. In his essay '*On revient toujours*' (1948), Schoenberg said that he was not destined to continue in the lush, misty manner of his youth: 'The Supreme Commander had ordered me on a harder road. But a longing to return to the older style was always vigorous in me, and from time to time I had to yield to that urge.'[27]

Rachmaninoff never had that problem. His own personal 'Supreme Commander' had ordered him on a different hard road, which in his case meant pursuing a performing career and often writing nothing at all. It also entailed writing music in an essentially constant voice throughout his life, from his earliest Russian compositions to those late works of his American years. The net result is salutary. Schoenberg's *Verklärte Nacht* (1899) remains his most popular work. It inhabits a notably similar crepuscular sound world to Rachmaninoff's *Isle of the Dead* op. 29 (1908). However impassioned the advocacy of Schoenberg's devotees, his atonal music remains of specialist interest.

All but indifferent to fashion or experiment, Rachmaninoff's music outstrips, in terms of calculable success, that of nearly every other Western composer. A measure of this, if one is needed, is the top position of the Piano Concerto no. 2 in Classic FM's twenty-fifth anniversary 'Ultimate Hall of Fame' in 2021 – a chart of the charts – making it the most voted-for work in the past quarter of a century. Other Rachmaninoff works are in the list too. Finally the debate is sterile. Posterity is the only judge – as Van Gogh, who sold only one painting in his lifetime, would tell you were he here.

Sidestepping these arguments, Rachmaninoff might rather have styled himself as Sibelius did. The Finnish composer said, quite simply, that he was 'un-modern'.[28]

Leningrad, City of Dust

In June 1941, in Operation Barbarossa, Germany invaded the Soviet Union. The subsequent bombing of Leningrad led to millions dead, food shortages and a siege of more than two years. This was the city where Rachmaninoff's First Symphony had had its painful birth. As the last note had sounded the distraught composer ran to the Nevsky Prospect, 'boarded one of the trams, so familiar to me from my childhood, and drove incessantly up and down the endless street, through wind and mist, martyred by the thought of my failure'.[29]

That summer, Dmitry Shostakovich, working on his Seventh Symphony, had been on the rota to man the roof of the Conservatoire, the building where the young Rachmaninoff had made such unremarkable progress, preferring to spend his time ice-skating and skiing. The teenaged Shostakovich had fared better: crushed by Rachmaninoff's cousin Siloti's view that he would never make it as a pianist, he was saved by Glazunov, who recognised that the boy's genius was as a composer – a reminder, yet again, of Russia's close-knit musical community, across generations.

Reorganising his life in readiness to move to Los Angeles, Rachmaninoff followed events in the Soviet Union closely, with pain. Hearing broadcasts of Russian music, such as Rimsky-Korsakov's *Russian Easter Festival Overture* or Chaliapin singing Mussorgsky's *Boris Godunov*, provoked agitation. In the summer he went back to Orchard Point, set on reworking and tightening the Fourth Piano Concerto, op. 40, ready for performance and recording in the autumn. He also wanted to make a piano transcription of Tchaikovsky's 'Lullaby', which he completed on 12 August 1941, and premiered at Syracuse that October. Depressed by the situation at home, he gave the proceeds of his 1 November Carnegie Hall recital, $4,166, to those suffering from war in his homeland.

He sent complimentary tickets to Siloti and his wife who, hearing of the fundraising effort, insisted on paying for them. A few months later he received official thanks from the USSR consul in New York, and learnt that his donation had been used for X-ray equipment.

Many of his public statements from this period have a more than usually melancholy tone. In an interview with *Etude* magazine he said: 'I am a Russian composer, and the land of my birth has influenced my temperament and outlook. Music is the product of my temperament, and so it is Russian music.'[30] Both Seroff, and Bertensson and Leyda, use the word 'shudder' to describe his physical reaction to the darkening news, and his distress at the thought of the Russian cities of his youth being destroyed.

An urgent project was under way to address that issue. Four young mountaineers were ordered to camouflage the golden cupolas and spires of Leningrad. One was a champion skier, and the others were musicians, among them Olga Firsova, conductor of the children's choir at the Kirov Theatre. Risking their lives for the promise of food, under artillery fire, in freezing conditions, they concealed the city's gleaming landmarks. They painted them battleship grey, the colour of winter sky or water, or draped them in black sail-cloth. At night, they slept in the cathedral of St Peter and St Paul, among the tombs of the Romanovs, all that remained of Russia's last imperial dynasty. Ballerinas at the Kirov – where in 1912, at the Mariinsky, Rachmaninoff had conducted Tchaikovsky's *Queen of Spades* in his last opera engagement – tied bunches of scutched bast matting on to nets, to turn Leningrad's streets into ersatz 'fields'.

On 9 August 1942, the city still under siege, two of the climbers were in the audience to hear the Leningrad premiere of Shostakovich's Symphony no. 7, 'Leningrad'. Their two companions had died from starvation. One survivor was Firsova, whose husband, Misha, was playing violin in the shattered remnants of the

Leningrad Philharmonic Orchestra, assembled to perform the symphony, whose world premiere had taken place in Kuybyshev, in March 1942.

In 2018 Mikhail Bobrov, aged ninety-four, the other, and last, survivor of the quartet of climbers, recalled the concert for BBC Radio 4's *Witness* programme.

> I was sitting right up close to the musicians in the Philharmonic. It was close to the army hospital. Many wounded soldiers came to listen. It was summer, so they were just in their dressing gowns, some of them in white night shirts. There was a huge audience in the hall. People were sitting in the aisles, in the gallery. How could we have surrendered?[31]

Strange Meeting

Rachmaninoff knew all about the symphony by his younger colleague. The first performance outside the Soviet Union was given by his old friend Henry Wood in a broadcast from the Maida Vale Studios, an august event at which the Soviet Ambassador Ivan Maisky, and Sir Stafford Cripps, recently British ambassador in Moscow, were present. It was given again at that year's Proms, now taking place at the Royal Albert Hall. The 1942 season was launched in strong Russian-Soviet mood. Wood conducted Rachmaninoff's Piano Concerto no. 2 on the first night and the 'Leningrad' Symphony on the second. (More Rachmaninoff followed later: the *Rhapsody on a Theme of Paganini* and the Piano Concerto no. 1, with Benno Moiseiwitsch as soloist in both.) When Toscanini gave the American premiere of the 'Leningrad' Symphony with the NBC Symphony Orchestra, the first of sixty-two performances in the States that year, Rachmaninoff, at home in Hollywood, heard the broadcast. Reportedly his single response, according to Solomon Volkov in *Shostakovich and Stalin*, was 'Well, and now let's have some tea.'[32]

In an exchange with Victor Seroff, no doubt intended to be private, Rachmaninoff confessed his resistance to Shostakovich, as well as to his advocate, the ubiquitous Serge Koussevitzky. Inevitably Seroff put it straight into his biography. The episode is convoluted but revealing. Rachmaninoff was upset about a 'gala' performance of the 'Leningrad' Symphony at the Berkshire Festival, Tanglewood. In aid of Russian War Relief, it was organised and conducted by Koussevitzky. The sticking point was the presence of an invited guest, an old-time Bolshevik revolutionary, now Soviet ambassador to the US, Maxim Litvinov. It was he who had encouraged Roosevelt to recognise the USSR, helped by his English wife, Ivy. The pair were celebrity figures, with Mrs Litvinov the star of any Russian benefit event. In 1934, when the couple were still in Moscow, *Vanity Fair* celebrated her as the 'unofficial hostess of the Soviet Union, who 'befriended many Americans confused by a new regime'.[33]

Now they were part of American high society, must-have guests at any party. The press credited Ivy as oiling relations between Washington and Moscow, thanks to her Anglophone charm and linguistic abilities. She drank champagne in Hollywood with Harpo Marx and hung out around the film studios in the hope of getting her novel, *Moscow Mystery*, taken up by movie moguls. In every respect, these were people to irritate Rachmaninoff. Seroff writes:

> Rachmaninoff insisted on asking me for all the details. 'Where did Litvinov stay while in the Berkshires? Was it possible that he was Koussevitzky's guest? And was I sure that I saw Litvinov in a box at the concert, or perhaps I was mistaken?'

Finally, not able to control his emotions, he rose to his six feet and three inches and, throwing down on the desk a small silver paper-knife he had been gesticulating with, he walked out of the room. Later he returned, apologising and muttering something about how disgusted he was.[34]

Seroff's view is that Rachmaninoff had never forgiven Koussevitzky for differences in 'the Moscow days'. They performed only a handful of times together in America, Rachmaninoff aligning himself instead with Stokowski and Ormandy. Rachmaninoff paid close attention to new Soviet music as far as possible. When Koussevitzky claimed he had made a great musical discovery in the form of Shostakovich, however, Rachmaninoff lost patience, saying he had made a similar comment about Scriabin decades earlier, resulting in a terrible row over money which only ended at Scriabin's death.

Koussevitzky's taste was at odds with Rachmaninoff's. He gave first performances of all those American composers Rachmaninoff disdained: Aaron Copland, Roy Harris, Walter Piston. Founding the Koussevitzky Music Foundation in 1942 to commemorate the death of his Russian wife, Natalie, whose money had helped fund his activities, he commissioned Bartók's *Concerto for Orchestra* (1943), Britten's *Peter Grimes* (1945) and Messiaen's *Turangalîla-Symphonie* (1949). He was, above all, a great supporter of Stravinsky, and asked him to compose a work in his wife's memory. Stravinsky rejigged some music he had written, at Orson Welles's behest, for an abortive film version of *Jane Eyre*. In his haste, the orchestral parts had not been corrected. The trumpet was notated in the wrong key. The premiere was a fiasco. Stravinsky apologised profusely but it appears Koussevitzky, reputedly not the most fluent of score-readers, was not aware of any problem.

The Beverly Hills Set: Stravinsky

Facts are more important that speculation, but it would be inhuman not to wonder at the nature of the relationship between Rachmaninoff and Stravinsky, giants of the twentieth century and polar opposites. In Russia before the Revolution they had lived, for a time, within reach of each other in St Petersburg, but all their lives they inhabited different artistic planets and avoided each other by mutual, more or less respectful consent. By the 1920s, when both had left Russia (Stravinsky before the Revolution, Rachmaninoff after), their music continued to be programmed in the Soviet Union. Both were admired, though in terms of works performed, including *Aleko* and the *All-Night Vigil*, Rachmaninoff had the numerical advantage. By 1927, the Soviet-atheist tendency ruled and concert performances of sacred works, among them the *Vigil*, were shunned as relics of a derided past.[35] Both composers, for different reasons, fell from favour in the 1930s.

In the early 1940s the two ended up living three miles apart in California. From May 1942, the Rachmaninoffs rented 9941 Tower Lane, Beverly Hills, a large house, with views of the Pacific, a swimming pool, and a music room big enough for two grand pianos. They then bought their final home, 610 North Elm Drive. Rachmaninoff performed in California for the first time in 1923, and on many occasions subsequently, the popularity of his C sharp minor Prelude naturally having preceded him.

By the time Rachmaninoff became a Californian resident, he was held in esteem there, but referred to in sepia tones: 'One of the musical monarchs of an age almost past,' as the *Los Angeles Times* described him in 1941 (3 February). Confirming that impression, Rachmaninoff's debut at the Hollywood Bowl, on 17 and 18 July 1942, consisted of works by the Russian gods of his youth:

Rimsky-Korsakov, Tchaikovsky and Glazunov. In keeping with the unadulterated Russian spirit, the conductor was Vladimir Bakaleinikoff, Moscow-born and Moscow Conservatory-educated. This blanket of Russianness and familiarity, of language and background, was the kind of reassurance Rachmaninoff sought, or perhaps hid behind.

The Tower Lane house was near Horowitz and his wife and daughter. Rachmaninoff and his friend often played music together in private, with only family as audience – or, on occasion, Sergei Bertensson, who heard them play *Symphonic Dances*: 'The brilliance of this performance was such that for the first time I guessed what an experience it must have been to hear Liszt and Chopin playing together, or Anton and Nikolai Rubinstein.'[36] Together Horowitz and Rachmaninoff visited Disney's studios, where they were photographed together with the American animator.

'It's true, I've bought a house,' Rachmaninoff wrote to his new secretary: another Russian, Nikolai Mandrovsky, who served him from 1939 until 1943. Calling it small, neat and in a good residential street, he praised its 'tiny' garden with lots of flowers and several trees: an orange tree, a lemon and a nectarine. He lamented, however, his lack of nous with property. 'In my lifetime I've bought six houses. Of these only the one in New York was a success, and I sold it satisfactorily. The others I've either lost, as in Russia, or practically lost, as in Germany and Switzerland. The last one here will probably be taken from me by the Japanese' – Japan having attacked Pearl Harbour six months earlier, triggering America's entry into World War II. 'Though, frankly, I scarcely believe they will get here. If they do come, it will only be for the sake of my house. Such is fortune!'[37] He joked to the Somovs – or perhaps it was not a joke – that fifty glass cigarette-holders would make a good housewarming present.

Goat's Milk

Stravinsky, like many other émigré Russians, had been drawn at first to Paris. After a long period in France, he left Europe on 30 September 1939 to conduct concerts on the West Coast of America. Stravinsky was in his late fifties, and needed a change. A combination of circumstance and desire marked the start, for him, of a new phase in life. In the past year, first his twenty-nine-year-old daughter, then his wife of thirty-three years (Catherine), and his mother had died. (Catherine had once complained, in March 1935, that Rachmaninoff was in Paris at the same time as their son, who was trying to make a career as a pianist: 'Rachmaninoff will have a recital [the following week at the Salle Gaveau], and many people, especially Russians, will spend their money to hear him rather than Svetik.'[38])

Stravinsky himself had been ill. Finances were a challenge, his income depleted by the onset of war and the cancellation of concerts. He liked money. He needed it, too, to support not only his family but also his long-term mistress, the Russian-born dancer and painter Vera de Bosset. Occupied France was no longer an option. Vera joined him in America in January 1940. They soon married, one year after Catherine's death, the small wedding breakfast held at Serge Koussevitzky's home. The newlyweds then settled at 1260 North Wetherly Drive, just above Sunset Strip at the foot of the Hollywood Hills: a comfortable but not extravagant one-storey house.

They would stay there more than two decades, taking American citizenship in 1945, keeping a tethered goat for its milk and receiving, among other visitors, W. H. Auden, Christopher Isherwood, Aldous Huxley and Dylan Thomas. Stravinsky was less interested than Rachmaninoff in securing himself within Russian circles. Like

Rachmaninoff, he chose a warm climate for his health, also confessing to a taste for the 'neon glitter' and mechanised speed and glamour of LA. On Stravinsky's first trip in 1935, to conduct his early ballets, a local critic noted that only a visit by Einstein would prompt such public fascination. A second visit in 1937 was a *succès d'estime*: the West Coast revered Stravinsky as a fashionable figure of modernism while not wholly embracing his music.

Rachmaninoff had once been a 'modern' composer, too. Now even his recitals were thought dated by some, and 'could have been performed before gas lamps, with horses hitched to carriages outside' as one critic, in St Louis, put it.[39] Stravinsky was the voice of the new, the fashionable and radical torch-bearer. And now he and Rachmaninoff were near-neighbours. It was only a matter of time before one or the other of them would break the ice.

Stravinsky's coolness towards Rachmaninoff started almost as early as their first encounters in pre-Revolutionary Russia. Their names appeared on the same concert lists. The Stravinsky 'family', together with Chaliapin and others, was present at Rimsky-Korsakov's house in St Petersburg early in 1906 for a run-through of Rachmaninoff's *The Miserly Knight*. Stravinsky was closely associated with Rachmaninoff's cousin, Siloti. At one of his concerts, we should remember, Siloti introduced the young Stravinsky to Sergei Diaghilev. Stravinsky said that encounter was vital to the whole future of his musical career. 'It was at this point that I began the close relationship with Diaghilev, which lasted for twenty years.'[40]

While Rachmaninoff often remarked on his enthusiasm for *Firebird*, he was resistant to the musical advances he perceived in *Petrushka* (1911). As a board member of Koussevitzky's publishing firm, Éditions Russes de Musique, Rachmaninoff had been known, no surprise, to be sceptical of overtly modernist works. In this he was able to rely on the support of his friend, the ultra-conservative

Medtner. Scriabin and Prokofiev – all these composers were published by Koussevitzky at that time in pre-Revolutionary Russia – provided hotly opposing views. Board meetings must have been animated, to say the least. *Petrushka* was premiered in Paris by the Ballets Russes. Nijinsky danced the title role, with choreography by Fokine, who would, twenty-eight years later, choreograph Rachmaninoff's *Rhapsody on a Theme of Paganini*. In this tight artistic web of Russians abroad, everyone knew each other even if they pretended not to.

Six-and-a-Half-Foot Scowl

In lists of catty remarks made by composers about their colleagues, Stravinsky's always comes near the top: 'Rachmaninoff's immortalizing totality was his scowl. He was a six-and-a-half-foot-tall scowl.'[41] According to his application form for American citizenship, Rachmaninoff was six feet three inches. Other descriptions say six feet two inches but never six and a half feet (except perhaps when 'heightened' by wearing the Homburg hat which appears in several photos of him). He was considered good-looking, his appearance admired. He was a virtuoso pianist without equal, and he was exceedingly rich.

At five feet three inches Stravinsky was a foot shorter and not handsome, though he presented himself with immense care. Romain Rolland, with no mercy, noted: 'He is small, sickly looking, ugly, yellow-faced, thin and tired, with a narrow brow, thin, receding hair, his eyes screwed up behind a pince-nez, a fleshy nose, big lips, a disproportionately long face in relation to his forehead.'[42] Today such remarks would have the lawyers in. Cocteau, in 1924, made a different observation: 'Rings, gaiters, scarves, half-belts, ties, tiepins, wristwatches, mufflers, fetishes, pinces-nez [*sic*], monocles, glasses, chain bracelets, describe him badly. Put simply, they prove on the surface that Stravinsky goes out of his way for no one. He composes, dresses himself, and speaks as he wishes.'[43] He also possessed some sort of animal magnetism that captivated women, famously among them Gabrielle 'Coco' Chanel (his biographer, Robert Craft, refers to their 'deep affair' in 1920, which was only interrupted by a 'steamy affair' with a dancer, Zhenya Nikita, which ended when he met Vera).[44] Rachmaninoff had no problem attracting female fans. The difference was that he appears, in those long celebrity years, to have sheltered in the safe carapace of his steady and happy marriage and family, with Natalia as a loyal protector. Beyond any usual habits or irritations of a long marriage, and the occasional flirtatious glance from the corner of his eye, there is no evidence to suggest otherwise.

In America, the composers lived separate lives, but occasionally found themselves in the same room. A gilded Steinway reception, in the peak golden era of gilded receptions, was given, on 11 January 1925, for Josef Hofmann. A famous photograph shows the cream of New York musical life (all men, mostly exiles) staring out with various degrees of attitude: at the edge, a debonair Albert Coates just makes it into the picture; Medtner looks somewhat askance; Wilhelm Furtwängler exudes sombre authority; George Engles, the New York-born cabaret pianist, a regular at the Rainbow Room, allows himself a smile; behind him Alexander Siloti wears the benign expression that characterised so much of his being; Fritz Kreisler looks handsome and distracted; Hofmann, it being his event, is at the front, but overshadowed by 'mein host' Frederick Steinway; on the other edge is Pierre Monteux, looking distinctly like Albert Einstein. This leaves two others: Stravinsky, arms folded, detached, looking cross and bored; and Rachmaninoff, a safe distance away, protected by his friends Kreisler and Hofmann.

GOODBYE RUSSIA

In 1942, Rachmaninoff made the first move. He took Bertensson, a well-connected Russian-about-Hollywood and not yet Rachman-inoff's co-biographer, into his trust:

I'm eager to meet someone whose family, like mine, is over there, and with whom I could discuss ways of sending money and other things. As I know how much Igor Fyodorovich has always disliked my compositions, even though he respects me as a pianist, and he must know my attitude to modern music, I'm not sure whether I could invite him and his wife to my house – which I'd love to do – because I don't know how he would receive my invitation. Would you be so kind as to send out a feeler to gauge his reaction to such an idea?[45]

The dinner was a modest success. The two couples dined again that year, the invitation returned by the Stravinskys. The occasion sounds uneasy. Stravinsky found Rachmaninoff's company a challenge: 'To sustain social relations with [Rachmaninoff] required perseverance. In fact my meetings with him during our mutual California period were rather with his wife, for he remained silent.'[46] Learning that Stravinsky liked honey, Rachmaninoff delivered a pot, leaving it on his doorstep, a gesture of sweet amity. The story has often been told, with ever greater gloss depending which of Craft's versions you read. One has the tall composer creeping up to the shorter composer's front door in the middle of the night, with an oversized honeypot, trying not to make a noise. Who needs cartoons?

Hollywood Bowl

On 4 August 1942 Rachmaninoff had written to his sister-in-law Sofia Satina in carping mood:

Tomorrow, Thursday, we're dining at Stravinsky's. The day
after tomorrow everyone except me is going to the concert
at the Hollywood Bowl in which Horowitz is playing my
Third Concerto. On Monday, dinner with [Olga] Samarova-
Stokowski in Pasadena, after which I have to listen to Horowitz
and the Third Concerto, etc. Don't imagine that is all: there's
another dinner the same week. Nor must you think that
because of this lifestyle I am not practising. No, actually I'm
practising very diligently. True, what I'm not doing is any
composing, that is completely impossible. And even if it were
possible, what would come out is probably something like
Shostakovich's latest symphony [the 'Leningrad']. No! Any free
time I have I'm reading novels of doubtful value but absorbing
interest. I'm also gulping down [the Russian historical novelist]
Vsevolod Soloviov. And, by the way, quantities of iodine as well.
On the whole I'm not feeling too bad.[47]

At the end of the month, he wrote to his secretary Mandrovsky,
expressing his devotion to Russia and his desire to help his country
in a time of war. He said he could not accept Nathan Milstein's
invitation to play in an American fundraising concert when funds
should instead be raised for Russia. He also discussed playing the
Symphonic Dances in Minneapolis and playing his own concertos
in New York and elsewhere. Other letters to Mandrovsky show
human concerns: he complains of lumbago, saying he looks 'like a
comma', wants money sent to needy Bulgarian children in Russia,
orders plentiful supplies of cigarettes while expressing concern
for Mandrovsky's health and telling him not to smoke too much
himself, adding that he will cover any of his secretary's medical
fees. When Mandrovsky's papers were sold at Sotheby's in 2011,
including handwritten and typed concert schedules, photographs,

financial accounts, press cuttings and draft programmes, there was also a 'Route Book' plotting Rachmaninoff's travels for the 1941–2 season, and a sugar ration book.

By now the Rachmaninoffs had established a tentative foothold in Hollywood circles. Charlie Chaplin's studios, resembling a group of English country cottages, were on Sunset Boulevard, with Chaplin a focus of Los Angeles society, dining with Schoenberg, Eisler, Stravinsky and (at Horowitz's house, as his memoirs recall) Rachmaninoff:

> Rachmaninoff was a strange-looking man, with something aesthetic and cloistral about him . . . Someone brought the topic round to religion and I confessed I was not a believer. Rachmaninoff quickly interposed: 'But how can you have art without religion?' I was stumped for a moment. 'I don't think we are talking about the same thing,' I said. 'My concept of religion is a belief in a dogma – and art is a feeling more than a belief.' 'So is religion,' he answered. After that I shut up.[48]

'What a Neighbourhood'

Stravinsky and Rachmaninoff met once more in the presence of the pianist Arthur Rubinstein, who noted that most of their conversation was about money and royalties, and that they sat in a corner comparing sums. The composers would not have found common interest in cars. Craft notes that Vera, who had recently passed her driving test, 'purchased a "goose-turd green" jalopy in Aldous Huxley's words'. The same car was still in use in 1948, 'followed by other vehicles of which I only remember a maroon Buick and a black Jaguar'. Had they been important to Stravinsky, Craft might have been obliged to remember them better.[49]

Rubinstein added that Rachmaninoff ate scarcely a morsel of pressed caviar, owing to a stomach-ache, perhaps a sign of his advancing illness.[50] Usually his appetite was robust, as his wife recalled in her short memoir:

> As far as food was concerned Sergei Vasilievich was not particularly demanding. He liked Russian cuisine, *pelmeni* [meat dumplings], *bliny*, cabbage pies, dumplings with sour cream, and especially bream with buckwheat *kasha* [grains], and crabmeat. But most of all: coffee. He would drink coffee with cream round the clock. How I tormented the poor man after the doctor recommended substituting *sanka*, decaffeinated coffee, for the real thing. He categorically refused to drink it and got angry if we tried to fool him into accepting it.[51]

In 1948, when Gary Graffman, then a twenty-year-old pianist, opened a recital with Stravinsky's *Serenade* and two Rachmaninoff preludes, Stravinsky added some crisp marginalia to a letter from Graffman: 'What a neighbourhood.' (Recalling that exchange in 2022 – seventy-four years after the event – the nonagenarian Graffman, speaking to the author on a telephone call from New York, was instantly reduced to gales of laughter.) Some time earlier, Prokofiev had been dining and gossiping with Vernon Duke. They agreed that Stravinsky's *Serenade*, 'which has just come out in print, contains melodic turns of phrase derived from Rachmaninoff and sonorities that sound like Medtner. Ha ha!'[52] What a neighbourhood indeed. Stravinsky would not have been amused.

In *Memories and Commentaries* Stravinsky makes a perceptive remark, showing admiration, if not warmth, for Rachmaninoff. Having referred to Rachmaninoff's early pieces as 'water colours', he complains that too soon he turned to oils and became, though merely in his twenties, old. Then Stravinsky pulls back:

> But do not expect me to denigrate him for that. In fact he was an awesome man, and there are too many others to be denigrated long before him. As I think about him, his silence looms as a noble contrast to the self-approbations that are the only conversation of most musicians. Besides, he was the only pianist I have ever seen who did not grimace when he played. That says a great deal.

In 1951, when asked to take part in an article about his fellow Russian Stravinský declined, saying, 'I knew Rachmaninoff very little.'[53]

Amnesty: the USSR Responds

In those war years, when Rachmaninoff and Stravinsky, in Beverly Hills, were cautiously sniffing at each other like well-bred hounds, a shift had begun to take place in the Soviet Union towards Rachmaninoff's music. The supposedly retrograde musical style that so vexed his American critics was now winning him favour in the USSR. A report in the *Aberdeen Press & Journal* of 20 June 1942, from the Moscow correspondent, sums it up:

> Rachmaninoff, the Russian composer, whose fame is known the world over, is in the Soviet news. 'Blood is thicker than water,' and Rachmaninoff, now aged sixty-nine, who left Russia after the Revolution and dissociated himself from the Soviet Union, has been greatly stirred by his people's struggle against the invader. Prominence is today given in the Soviet

Press to numerous concerts Rachmaninoff has been giving in America in aid of the Soviet Red Cross. His wife and daughters have been knitting socks for the Red Army. At the composer's request the Soviet Committee for Cultural Relations Abroad have sent him a set of the Soviet edition of his works and particulars of their performance in Russia in recent years. Rachmaninoff has been requested to send scores of his latest compositions – notably the Third Symphony and Fourth Piano Concerto for performance in the Soviet Union.

This report observes the changing mood in the Soviet Union towards Rachmaninoff's music. While some, including Stravinsky, thought the composer had sold out to the sound of Hollywood, especially in his recent, unloved Third Symphony (the musicologist Peter Franklin notes an upward-sweeping 'American' quality and a possible allusion to 'Shenandoah' and the big-band style of Paul Whiteman[54]), in the USSR the view was quite the opposite. His sister-in-law, Sofia Satina, also commented on the work's Russian character. When some American critics made the same observation, after its muted premieres by Stokowski and the Philadelphia Orchestra in 1936, it was only to emphasise Rachmaninoff's retrograde, sentimental style.

The step-like opening, reminiscent of moments in Rimsky-Korsakov, Borodin, Mussorgsky, has echoes of old Orthodox chant. The mournful oboe melody, yearning string theme and melancholy second subject all, to Soviet ears, confirmed the view that Rachmaninoff was conjuring his homeland in music (not, it might be said, for the first time). Given his vigorous fundraising efforts, Rachmaninoff was now effectively exonerated. The symphony was premiered, to acclaim, in the Soviet Union on 11 July 1943, four months after the composer's death. *Pravda* praised it as a lyrical hymn to Russia, imbued with love for the homeland.

Decades later, in advance of a Rachmaninoff festival in London in 1991, Vladimir Ashkenazy – who himself left Russia at the age of twenty-six – gave an interview in which he spoke of the essential qualities of Rachmaninoff's 'Russianness': a combination of generosity and fatalism, present both in his character and his music. 'The *Dies irae* theme, which he frequently uses, represents fatalism; and the generosity is there all the time, such as in the way the harmonies rise up from the bass and help the music to glow and expand.' A recent newspaper article, however, had made Ashkenazy angry. The object of his vitriol was a review in a Berlin newspaper following a performance of Rachmaninoff's Third Symphony. The headline was: Dr Zhivago's Music. 'Just like that, dismissing it like film music. I thought, "You miserable idiots! There is so much in this symphony. Can you not hear it?" I think it's unbelievably arrogant, so small-minded.'[55]

Rachmaninoff did not live long enough to appreciate, or not, the moment in David Lean's 1965 film *Dr Zhivago*, based on Boris Pasternak's novel, in which his G minor Prelude is played at a concert. A woman remarks to her neighbour: 'But Boris, this is genius.' The bored medical professor responds: 'Really? I thought it was Rachmaninoff. I'm going for a smoke.' Pasternak, a musician himself, was more of a Scriabin man.

And Again: Koshetz

In all this period, at a safe distance, Nina Koshetz continued her career, with distinction but not with the adulation she might have had in Russia. With her second husband, Gabriel Leonoff, a one-time tenor, she moved to Laguna Beach, California. A review of 1934 (in the *San Bernardino Daily Sun*) complimented her dramatic fervour and sense of humour, and her ability to sing well in eight languages, as well as praising the size of her voice, 'adequate for an auditorium five times the size' of the town's Women's Clubhouse. She gave many recitals and in 1939–40 made her last disc with Schirmer.

That recording included songs by Rachmaninoff and that favourite folk-song of his, 'Dark Eyes'. As a fabled Russian in California, she began taking bit parts in Hollywood movies and teaching voice to young actresses, among them Claudette Colbert and Marlene Dietrich. Koshetz and her husband opened a Russian restaurant in Los Angeles, but the enterprise failed, rendering them bankrupt. Her daughter Marina (1912–2000), the child who had sailed into New York with her as witnessed by Prokofiev, became an opera singer and actor. At her death, it was reported in the *LA Times* that she had donated the op. 38 songs manuscript belonging to her mother to the Library of Congress in 1970. She was also working on a screenplay 'about the long-secret love story of Rachmaninoff and her mother, called *The Last Love Song*'.[56] Given Nina Koshetz's propensity for talking about her affairs, real or imagined, helped by the likes of Prokofiev, it might more accurately have been called 'the not-secret' love affair. Nothing came of the screenplay.

At some stage in California, when relations were friendly, any rift healed, Rachmaninoff allegedly gave Koshetz the two-piano score of the *Symphonic Dances*. When it came up for auction at Sotheby's some years ago, the catalogue note stated, without qualm or qualification, that Rachmaninoff had had an affair with Koshetz. The manuscript was removed from the sale. Controversy continues. At the time of writing, the US branch of the family (the Wanamakers, descendants of Sophie Volkonsky, Rachmaninoff's granddaughter) had hired a lawyer to clarify ownership. In affairs of the heart, some controversies radiate heat long beyond the grave.

After further enquiry, one more piece of information arrived, via the Rachmaninoff authority Francis Crociata, as this book was being completed in summer 2022.

> The manuscript was purchased by the Library of Congress. I [Francis] attended the celebratory concert and reception to recognise the acquisition that was hosted by Natalie and Jeff Javier [descendants]. The manuscript was never possessed nor owned by Nina Koshetz. That story was provably false. There are legal restrictions on saying anything more, but that's all that is really significant.[57]

Last Tour

Christmas 1942 and New Year 1943 were bleak, for the family, for the world. America had joined the war, following the attack on Pearl Harbour. In his Christmas Eve message, President Roosevelt offered solace to those millions with families scattered far from home: 'Christmas prayers follow you wherever you may be.' Nothing had been heard from Tatiana, in Vichy France, a silence which tormented her father. 'There is no way of hearing from them. I don't know if they are hungry or not,' Rachmaninoff confessed to an interviewer, referring to his daughter and grandson. 'There's such anguish in my soul it could be measured in yards,' he wrote, in sorrow, to Somov.[58]

In addition, Rachmaninoff's health was bad, the symptoms not yet identified: fatigue, weight loss, pallor, pains on his left side. He was worried about his capacity to perform, and urged the loyal Somovs not to travel to his concert in Ohio, near their home in Yellow Springs. 'I shall play badly and I shall be ashamed that you should have taken such a trip for the sake of such playing.'[59] The compassion that so shaped his character, the great constant in his life, was never more evident than in letters to intimate friends such as the Somovs, the Swans, Vilshau, Medtner.

Shortly before Christmas he enjoyed a musical boost. Mitropoulos had conducted the New York Philharmonic-Symphony Orchestra in the *Symphonic Dances*, recorded live. Having consulted Rachmaninoff in microscopic detail about the score, the Greek conductor became the composer's preferred interpreter of the work. Rachmaninoff and 'the monk of Minneapolis', as Mitropoulos was now nicknamed in the press, had programmes scheduled in New York in early 1943. 'They make an odd pair,' as one newspaper remarked: Rachmaninoff the 'height of chill' on the stage; tiny Mitropoulos, who dressed entirely in black and conducted with 'religious frenzy', looking as if he were about to leap off it altogether.[60]

The New Year was taken up with thinking about the forthcoming tour, physically arduous but providing the mental distraction Rachmaninoff always needed. The car, and the need to secure fuel, were as usual at the top of his worry list. He wrote to Paul Schmidt (perhaps a Steinway rep) from New York on 31 January 1943:

Many thanks for your letter of the 26th, which arrived today. Your letter was so delightful that I would certainly appeal to you for any help that I might need. But for the present everything at home is in the charge of the woman who lives-in with us.

All my car's tyres have been checked and both licences are in my name. At present, the car is in a rented garage in Beverly Hills. The only thing I need is a new number plate for the car. I have an 'A' card to buy fuel. If your friend were able to get me some additional gasoline, I would be very glad.

271

The woman who works for us in the house is leaving as soon as we arrive, and it will not be easy to find a replacement. We therefore will have to do our own shopping for supplies, and with my Packard I'm not going to get very far on three gallons of gasoline in a week.[61]

In February 1943, after a quarter of a century in America and having delayed so long, the Rachmaninoffs took a brave step. With 218 other people, they went to New York to obtain their naturalisation papers in the Federal Court at 641 Washington Street. They were now United States citizens, their new status reported on news wires across the land, from Oregon to West Virginia, Wyoming to Louisiana. Rachmaninoff told the *New York Times* that he was 'very happy to become a United States citizen in this land of opportunity and equality'. He and his wife would be leaving next day for a concert tour 'that will take them across the continent'. In conclusion it was noted that the couple had 'bought a house at Beverly Hills'.

Jitterbug Talk

A few days later Rachmaninoff played at Pennsylvania State College. His dreadful appearance was hard to ignore. On the front page, alongside a headline about Penn State college men being called up for war service, *The Daily Collegian* reported: 'A tired old man walked on the Schwab auditorium stage last night and enthralled a capacity audience with a brilliant performance. Although Sergei Rachmaninoff will be seventy years old in April, his playing was that of an ageless master of the keys.'[62] He surprised his audience by making the C sharp minor Prelude his first encore. 'After playing this number over 1,400 times, he is becoming tired of it, according to Mr Howard Heck, his personal secretary.' He performed on one of his four pianos which are sent on ahead of concerts. Mrs Rachmaninoff 'who has never missed a concert' (true in spirit, but not to the letter) explained that though this was an expensive habit, 'my husband prefers it'.

Most of Rachmaninoff's compositions, the newspaper added, were written before the copyright law was passed. 'He has received royalties only on his later pieces – last of which is *Symphonic Dances* for orchestration.' The reporter disclosed, randomly, that one of the maestro's favourite pastimes 'is playing with children'; he lives simply in Beverly Hills; he still practises two hours a day and one of his closest friends is Fritz Kreisler.

The same journal reports how Rachmaninoff stopped to chat to three Penn students on the pavement after the concert, signing their programmes. The conversation, mundane as conversations go, shows Rachmaninoff's interest in others. 'He asked about the fraternity houses on the campus, how many men could live in one, and how large they were inside . . . After five minutes of conversation [surely enough given the subjects discussed], Rachmaninoff declared he and his companions must return to Nittany Lion Inn, where they were to have lunch before leaving State College at 1 p.m.'

This generosity in speaking to the young fostered many posthumous stories of kindness. A music student, Pasquale 'Joe' Verdure, was working in his vacation as a doorman at Orchestra Hall, Chicago. Speaking in 1943, he recalled being asked by Mrs Rachmaninoff to help her assist her husband, weakened by illness, from the hall. By chance they met again during his final tour, weeks before his death. The couple remembered the young man. Natalia asked him to assist her in calling a taxi. In the forty-five-minute wait for it to arrive, the 'elderly musician' sat in the empty hall and chatted to the young bass-baritone, telling him that alas no one understood his songs, and he, Joe, should understand them before trying to sing them. They discussed the current 'jitterbug' craze. Rachmaninoff regretted that modern music lacked what was most important: heart.[63]

'I Am Too Tired'

Ignoring Rachmaninoff's entreaties, Somov and his wife, Yelena, travelled to the concert at Columbus on 5 February. Mme Somov recorded their meeting:

> I remember how angry he once became when a doctor prescribed total rest and a halt to all musical activity. 'Does he really think that I could sit in the sun and feed pigeons! No, such a life is not for me – better, death . . .'
> I recalled these words when we saw him in the Columbus dressing room. My heart contracted when I saw his thin and suffering face.

At her suggestion that he stop giving concerts and spend his time, instead, on composition, he had a plain response:

> 'I am too tired for that, too. Where should I find the strength and the fire?' I reminded him of the fire and inspiration in his *Symphonic Dances*. 'Yes,' he replied. 'I don't know how that happened. That was my last flicker.'[64]

Rachmaninoff and the Somovs never met again. Years later, in 1950, Yevgeny Somov would escort Sophie Volkonsky, without father or grandfather still living, to her short-lived first marriage.

Fyodor Chaliapin (junior) was an usher. It took place at the Russian Orthodox Church of Christ the Saviour, Madison Avenue and 121st Street, to which her grandfather, in 1925, with his four hundred dollars, had been one of the earliest donors.

Despite fatigue, his concerts in Chicago (playing the same programme he had played when he left Switzerland: Beethoven's Piano Concerto no. 1 and the *Paganini Rhapsody*) were a success. An unnamed Russian doctor attended him the next day when he complained of pains in his side. Pleurisy and neuralgia were diagnosed, sunshine prescribed.

Not Yet a Ghost

Perusing the press from this period, near the end of his life, numerous concert reports confirm that other musicians gave regular performances of his music. He may have been scorned in some quarters, but he was a favourite with audiences. A sample of reviews gives the flavour: on 7 February 1943, his *Italian Polka*, the piece he had playfully persuaded Natalia to perform with him in France so many summers earlier, was included in a concert in Nebraska City alongside works by Florence Price (*Three Negro Dances*) and Sousa (including *Stars and Stripes*). A week later a young Viennese pianist (Hilde Somer) performed a selection of Rachmaninoff's music in Maryland, the review showing pointed interest in her black-taffeta and pink net gown. Someone sang 'Lilacs' in a song recital. At a school founder's day in Montana, a parent opened proceedings with a performance of the C sharp minor Prelude.

The British conductor John Barbirolli conducted a broadcast of the Piano Concerto no. 2 with Eugene List, a young US Army sergeant, as soloist. Of Russian heritage, List had signed up for the military immediately after the attack on Pearl Harbour. Nevertheless he kept his high-profile musical career going, becoming known as the 'Potsdam Pianist' after playing for Winston Churchill, Joseph Stalin and Harry S. Truman at the 'Big Three' conference of June 1945. Rachmaninoff was central to his repertoire.

Amid the turbulence of war, Rachmaninoff himself was still a revered star performer. His US tour was anticipated in every regional newspaper. As usual he gave interviews. *The Long Beach Independent* (28 February 1943), intending to be reverential, sounded elegiac. The overwhelmed reporter wrote that speaking to the star pianist 'would seem at first to be like interviewing some legendary and awe-inspiring figure out of the past. The great Russian pianist and composer has been an acknowledged virtuoso for so long now, that he scarcely seems like a contemporary.'

Instead, when he opens his mouth, he turns out to be not a ghost from the past but a vital, living creature: 'no legend but an extremely charming, quiet gentleman. He is reserved and serious but his sombre Slavic countenance becomes considerably lightened in more intimate conversation. Occasional flashes of dry humor [sic] belie his sombreness and, when he talks of his grandchildren, his face lights up with pleasure.' The short column ends poignantly: 'I am myself only in music,' he says. 'Music is enough for a whole lifetime – but a lifetime is not enough for music.'

Then to widespread consternation, Rachmaninoff was taken ill, forced to pull out of concerts. 'Chief topic for grumbling this week,' as one newspaper ungenerously put it. In Denton his replacement was Claudio Arrau, the 'brilliant South American pianist' unknown to American audiences until World War II. In Pasadena, Vladimir Horowitz would step in for the indisposed Rachmaninoff.

Last Concert

He did, however, manage to play at Knoxville, Tennessee, arriving by train from Louisville, Kentucky. Having had to cancel there in a previous season, he was determined to honour his promise to come back. The date was 17 February 1943.[65] The venue was the University of Tennessee's Alumni Memorial Gymnasium/Auditorium, an imposing 1930s building of red brick and stone, with gothic flourishes, gargoyles, leaded windows and wrought-iron sconces, built to honour alumni who had died in World War I.

The interior resembled a basketball arena, the floor in the middle, surrounded on four sides by seating and balconies. This building was no mere student sports hall. It had civic importance. 'Townies' came to the new campus auditorium and heard Glenn Miller, Paul Whiteman, Jascha Heifetz, Benny Goodman and, in this area of the segregated south, leading black musicians who wanted to play there, too: Noble Sissie and Chick Webb among them.

It was in this unlikely venue that the ailing and exhausted Rachmaninoff gave his last ever concert. It was sold out. The programme opened with Bach's English Suite no. 2 in B flat minor. As well as Schumann's *Les Papillons*, some Wagner transcriptions and some of his own works – the *Études-Tableaux* op. 39, nos 4 and 6 – he played Chopin's Piano Sonata no. 2 in B flat minor. Rachmaninoff was one of the first pianists, in 1931, to record the work – that recording still prized. The sonata's taut perfection had made him rethink his own sprawling Piano Sonata no. 2, in the same key. 'Chopin's Sonata lasts nineteen minutes, and all has been said,' he once protested to the Swans. The third movement is the *Marche funèbre*, though Chopin preferred the simple title 'March'. It was played at Chopin's graveside in Père Lachaise cemetery, Paris. It was played by Rachmaninoff at Knoxville, in his final concert.

No one had realised the sombre truth. Sergei Vasilievich Rachmaninoff had made his last public appearance. He was mortally ill. In a matter of weeks he would be dead. He had made 1,457 appearances as a pianist by the end of his career, 1,189 of them during the period of his new life in exile.[66]

Leaving Tennessee, on the way to Florida, Rachmaninoff felt so unwell that he and Natalia left the train at Atlanta. Florida was cancelled. They decided instead to spend two days in New Orleans, so that he could recuperate in the warmth. According to their usual habit, they chose a luxury hotel, the Roosevelt, a favourite of band leaders Glenn Miller and Tommy Dorsey, but offering no panacea to Rachmaninoff. He wrote from there, on 22 February 1943, to Nikolai Rashevsky. This fellow Russian was from a rich sugar-factory owning family in Ukraine. He was now a pioneer in mathematical biophysics and early ideas of quantum theory, working as a professor at the University of Chicago.

Dear Nikolai Petrovich
   Yesterday I cancelled a concert, and I am cancelling three concerts this week, for tomorrow I leave for 'summer quarters' in California. There's little I can brag about – for my health is definitely run down: the pains in my side seem stronger and I feel terrific weakness. It's hard for me to play. I should see a doctor, but on this question I am a narrow-minded nationalist: I recognise only Russian doctors, and there's one I can see in California but not before. He's from Moscow University. I'll talk with him about my side, and we can recall old times. It will be good for body and soul.

The letter to Professor Rashevsky ends with an urgent request. 'Please send me as quickly as possible what we have asked. Otherwise we shall starve. My wife is already saying, when she looks at me, that I look like Gandhi. This is unfortunate because an uglier face than his would be hard to find.'[67] Let us assume that Natalia was referring to her husband's wasted appearance, and that Rachmaninoff's comment in turn refers to Gandhi's emaciated state (given his habit, since 1932, of intermittent fasting as a means of political resistance). The exact request to Rashevsky is not stated, but the Russian word indicates supplements or vitamins which presumably could be found by an able-bodied professor in Chicago but not by a sick pianist in New Orleans.

The sign-off to Rachmaninoff's letter, sending warm greetings to Rashevsky's family in Chicago, was extended to another friend and resident of the city, Vladimir Nikolayevich Ipatieff, a father of petroleum chemistry in the US, and holder of more than two hundred patents. (At times it seems that Rachmaninoff had few friends who were not holders of several patents.) Ipatieff, stripped of his Russian citizenship and living in a hotel in Chicago, had defected to America via an international energy conference in Berlin (having instructed his wife, accompanying him, to bring her jewels 'in the event that we go dancing'). He had close links with the Romanovs: the Tsar and his household had been murdered in the basement of the family's summer residence, Ipatieff House, in Yekaterinburg. No wonder he was a figure of suspicion in Soviet eyes. Once again, we see the tight-knit intellectual circle in which Rachmaninoff moved and who supported him, emotionally, even in his by-now extreme state of frailty.

Unwell though he was, Rachmaninoff also wrote on the same day as his letter to Rashevsky, 22 February, to his future biographer, Victor Seroff: 'I am ailing all the time. And I play fewer concerts than the number I cancel.'

Hospital, Home

Priority for the use of trains, in wartime, was given to the movement of troops. Rachmaninoff and Natalia had to wait three days to secure a reservation, and then spent three days on a slow train to Los Angeles. There, with Fyodor Chaliapin (junior), an ambulance met him, and took him to the Hospital of the Good Samaritan. Rachmaninoff's account in a letter to Somov, dated 27 February, makes painful reading. Typically, he had been seen by a Russian doctor in Chicago, and was under a Muscovite doctor at the hospital. Somov must have read this letter with alarm:

After sitting with me all day, Natasha has just left; so here I lie in hospital . . . I'll try to tell you briefly how it happened. Leaving you, I went to Chicago. There a Russian doctor was summoned. He discovered a slight pleurisy, but the severe pain in the side can't be pleurisy – it is a nervous symptom. Some knot in the nerves aches and it would be useless to expect it to pass soon. Only with heat and lots of sun! After three days the doctor found nothing in the lungs, but the side began to ache with more severe pain. We went on and gave two more concerts. It was so hard for me to play! Oh, how hard! We decided to cancel the next concert and go to New Orleans, from where I was to go for three concerts in Texas. In New Orleans I noticed that the cough had definitely increased, as well as the pain in the side, and that soon I shouldn't be able to stand, or to sit, or to lie down.

We took desperate measures, cancelled three concerts, took a terrible train from Texas (sixty hours), and moved straight on to Los Angeles . . . Irinochka left for here last night. Dr Russell arranged for a doctor friend of his, who wired us on the train, to meet us at the station with an ambulance. So last night, then, we landed here. Two fellows grabbed me under the arms and brought me here. That was nine in the evening. A specialist was waiting and at once they began to sound me and listen. And early this morning an X-ray. Now all grows clear. Here's a report for you. There are only two small spots on the lungs, with a not very large inflammation . . . As you see, much ado about nothing. I scared Irina almost to death, and Sonichka nearly quit her job, and so forth. So now I feel embarrassed and guilty . . .[68]

He stayed in hospital for three days, undergoing tests, but eventually, depressed and longing for home, on 2 March 1943, he was allowed back to Elm Drive. The choice of a Russian doctor demonstrated, once more, Rachmaninoff's unwillingness, even in this circumstance, to venture beyond the world he knew, in which he felt safe and protected. Dr Alexander Golitzin was no mere Los Angeles doctor, but a scion of one the richest noble families in the Russian Empire, associated with the Romanovs, born a prince. Escaping the Red Army, Golitzin settled in Los Angeles in 1927, running a successful medical practice, his family variously embedded in the nascent movie industry. His daughter appeared in cameo roles in silent movies starring the likes of Rudolph Valentino and Charlie Chaplin. One son worked as a producer at Universal and Walt Disney Studios; the other son, also Alexander, was an art director for Fritz Lang, Alfred Hitchcock and later Clint Eastwood.

As Rachmaninoff lay dying, the local LA papers were reporting on the nominations for the 15th Academy Awards: *Mrs Miniver* swept the board in several categories. Best song was Irving Berlin's 'White Christmas' from *Holiday Inn*. Alexander Golitzin would miss out on an award as art director on *Arabian Nights*, but he would win an Oscar the next year for *Phantom of the Opera*. Walt Disney won best cartoon for the Donald Duck animation, *Der Fuehrer's Face*.

A Russian nurse, Olga Mordovskaya, was there to care for Rachmaninoff when he arrived home by ambulance at lunchtime. He was tired, and went straight to bed, but expressed relief at being home. Given his wife's recent remark, he might have been glad to know that Gandhi, in prison, had given up his latest fast.

Face to Face with The Creator

News from Russia was getting worse. Stalin promoted himself to 'Marshal' of the Soviet Union. Word was spreading, for the first time, via the Polish government in exile, about a Nazi German 'murder camp' at the Polish town of Oświęcim, or in German, Auschwitz. The Soviet Union had suffered heavy losses in the Battle of Stalingrad – taking place in and around that industrial city, named after the Soviet leader, on the banks of the Volga. Eventually Soviet troops regained control of Stalingrad, the defeat a blow to Hitler. 'Praise the Lord. God grant them strength,' Rachmaninoff exclaimed, his voice weak.

Rachmaninoff kept up his other interests. What was happening in the garden, he asked daily. What about the furniture overdue from New York? His sister-in-law, Sofia Satina, now a research botanist at the Genetics Experimental Station at Smith College, Massachusetts, was there. A few very close friends were allowed to visit. Drowsy from sleep, Rachmaninoff asked who it was who kept playing the piano, his fingers moving on the sheets. Natalia said that no one was playing. It dawned on him that the playing must be in his head. At times Natalia read Pushkin to him. Perhaps his friends the Swans were thinking of those final days when they wrote in their 1944 recollections that, in spite of success, money and a loving family, 'Rachmaninoff lived shut up within himself, alone in spirit, and everlastingly homesick for Russia.'[69]

He could no longer eat. To provide pain relief, Dr Golitzin upped the level of morphine. On 26 March 1943, Rachmaninoff went into a coma. A telegram from Moscow dated 22 March, from eleven Soviet composers wishing him a happy seventieth birthday, arrived too late.

> Dear Sergei Vasilievich!
>
> On the day of your seventieth anniversary the Union of Soviet Composers sends you warm congratulations and hearty wishes for good spirits, strength and health for many years to come. We greet you as a composer of whom Russian musical culture is proud, the greatest pianist of our time, a brilliant conductor and public man who in these times has shown patriotic feelings that have found a response in the heart of every Russian. We greet you as a creator of musical works penetrating in their depth and expressiveness. Your piano concertos and symphonies, your chamber works, songs and other compositions are often played in the Soviet Union, and the public here watches with close attention your creative activity and is proud of your triumphs.

The signatories were Reinhold Glière (1875–1956), Nikolai Myaskovsky (1881–1950), Sergei Prokofiev (1891–1953), Dmitry Shostakovich (1906–75), Aram Khachaturian (1903–78), Dmitry Kabalevsky (1904–87), Vano Muradeli (1908–70), Vissarion Shebalin (1902–63), Tikhon Khrennikov (1913–2007), Yuri Shaporin

(1887–1966), Nikolai Chemberdzhi (1903–48), Viktor Bely (1904–83) and Ivan Dzerzhinsky (1909–78).[70]

Rachmaninoff never regained consciousness. On 28 March 1943, aged sixty-nine, he died.

LAST RITES

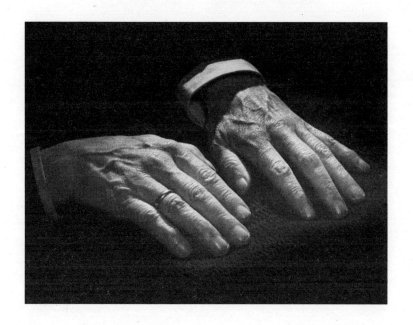

Two Medical Reports

The medical reports, of his doctor and nurse, have been widely quoted but not given, as here, in full.* Each rewards close reading, providing insight into Rachmaninoff's fortitude in his final days.

Illness and death of S. V. Rachmaninoff
By Dr Alexander Vladimirovich Golitzin
The whole of S. V. Rachmaninoff's life was unusual, and his last illness was no exception: he died of cancer (but a particular, and rare, form) which in the space of two months brought him to the grave.

Notions of cancer are usually associated with long-drawn-out suffering lasting for months or even years, lesions that refuse to heal, painful operations, and so on. It is hard to understand how a person suffering from cancer of almost all his organs could get about, work and pursue his creative activities right up to six weeks before dying from it, but Sergei Vasilievich played his last concert in Knoxville on the 17th February. Anyone who ever attended his concerts will know what level of emotional and physical power he invested in his performance.

Only in the middle of January did Sergei Vasilievich begin to experience feelings of failing health, while those close to him noticed that he was losing weight. A troubling cough manifested itself, also mysterious pains in the side of his body, and a general feeling of weakness. Initially none of these symptoms were severe enough to prevent him from continuing with his concert schedule. They were

* In new translations by Anthony Phillips

ascribed to a cold, to the general state of his wellbeing, in part to getting old; in mid-January Sergei Vasilievich himself said to me, half-jokingly but the same time half-seriously, that he had been eating *bliny* and since then had not been feeling quite up to the mark.

As long ago as the previous summer, when he and his family were living here* he was indicating to me that this would probably be his last concert tour; in the spring of 1943 he would be playing at venues on the Pacific Coast, after which he would withdraw from public appearances and rest. As his doctor I regarded this decision as entirely sensible: some sclerosis of the heart and raised blood pressure mandated an end to the nervous tension necessarily endured by a working pianist, to be replaced by the more restful activity of composition. But the dream was not destined to become reality.

In the last ten days of February, when Sergei Vasilievich arrived at New Orleans, he began coughing up blood and the pain in his side increased. The local doctors had him admitted to hospital, but neither he nor his wife Natalia Alexandrovna wished to stay there and as soon as the blood flow from the coughing ceased they set off for Los Angeles, where they arrived on 26 February.

On arrival at the train station he was met by ambulance and taken to one of the hospitals where he spent a few days undergoing necessary clinical investigations and consultations.

Sergei Vasilievich, finding the atmosphere of a hospital, particularly an American one, extremely oppressive, longed to be home in a Russian environment with his family; there he believed he would immediately start to recover and benefit from the sunny climate. Indeed once home, over the first few days he did feel better; the pain was susceptible to relief from tablets and occasional injections of codeine.

* Still in the Tower Road Boardman House, not yet Elm Drive.

Following a small operation performed by Dr Moore, the diagnosis of his illness was confirmed and the family was informed as to the conclusion of the analysis. The patient himself was, however, not told. It was not that Sergei Vasilievich feared death, or at least not more so than any person in a terminal condition, but his was a life so exceptionally rich in content, he so loved life, the light, his family, that the very thought of death would have been insupportable to him. It fell to Natalia Alexandrovna, and to us who were with him, to shoulder the difficult task of concealing so far as possible the truth and keeping his spirits up. For a time this was quite successful, the more so as Sergei Vasilievich, in common with most artists, had no idea of medicine or of the structure and functions of the body. For him they held no interest at all, therefore he readily accepted the vague and inaccurate explanations we were obliged to offer him for the various distressing manifestations his illness was now inflicting on him.

Despite suffering such a painful illness, Sergei Vasilievich was invariably cordial and affectionate, often joked and welcomed visits from those few close friends who were allowed in to see him when the painful episodes were sufficiently in abeyance. But soon these brighter intervals became shorter and more infrequent, and the doses of narcotics, small as they were, had to be increased. For a man who had always lived a normal life never resorting to drugs or alcohol, even minimal doses of morphine, twice a day, were enough to maintain him in a comparatively equable state. His weakness, however, increased daily and in consequence his morale declined; when he gave voice to his complaints one could hear a note of hopelessness; it is possible that he sensed the approach of death, and in those moments when the pain was resurfacing but before the injections had taken effect, he may even have wished it. This phase was not of long duration; the disease was advancing not by the day but by the hour, an arrested pneumonia developed, the pulse weakened, and three days before he died the patient began to have periods of unconsciousness and at other times was delirious. Natalia Alexandrovna, who never left his side even for a minute, said that in his delirium he would move his hands as if conducting the orchestra or playing the piano. I can never forget the feeling I experienced when taking his hand to feel for the pulse, the sadness that overcame me when thinking that these beautiful, slender hands would never again touch a keyboard nor give the pleasure, the joy, that for fifty years they had been giving to people.

On the morning of Saturday 27 March he received Communion and early on Sunday morning, without regaining consciousness, he died quietly, surrounded by his family.

The report by Rachmaninoff's nurse, modest and heartfelt, gives a tender impression of her patient's longing for the embrace of Russia in those final days:

By Olga Georgievna Mordovskaya [Nurse]
At the end of February 1943 Dr Alexander Golitzin telephoned me to inform me that Sergei Vasilievich Rachmaninoff was in hospital but would soon be taken back to his home. He wanted to be cared for there by a Russian nurse, and thus it happened that I had the great honour of being the person to take care of his needs.

Despite my many years of experience I was a prey to great anxiety, believing myself neither worthy nor knowledgeable enough to look after such a person as Rachmaninoff. At the same time my desire was to do everything humanly possible to help him. On the 1st of March the doctor asked me to go to Sergei Vasilievich's apartment and make everything ready for the sick man. Naturally I was nervous, as I had been since the first moment I was approached for the task, and so doubtful was I of my ability to be of real service to him that I hardly slept that night.

On the 2nd March at ten o'clock in the morning I found myself in the Rachmaninoff house at No. 10, Elm Drive, Beverly Hills. The generous and cordial welcome I received from the family greatly eased my feelings, since I felt immediately that I had come to a true Russian home. At one o'clock Sergei Vasilievich was brought home in an ambulance. His face lit up with joy that he was at last home, but also bore traces of the fatigue and anxiety he had suffered from the journey. Lying in bed he looked attentively round the room, his glance resting on the old family icon of Saint Panteleimon, and said:

'How good it is to be home.'

Dr Golitzin arrived at four o'clock and issued a series of instructions and dietary requirements. In the first week of his indisposition, Sergei Vasilievich showed a lively interest in everything, and spent a great deal of his time reading American newspapers. He was concerned about his garden, asking each day which flowers were coming into bloom and where they were. He inquired about newly planted trees, asked for seed catalogues, and spoke of getting back to work in his beloved garden as soon as he was well again.

He was worried about the furnishings for the new home that were being sent over from New York. As soon as a new radio set was installed he asked for it to be tuned to Moscow, as he wanted to listen to music from there. He continually worried that Natalia Alexandrovna was spending so much of her time with him and not getting out enough into the fresh air. He would say:

'Natasha, you must go into the garden. Olga Georgievna will stay with me.'

He said the same thing to Irina Sergeyevna, wanting her to go out to be with friends or go to the cinema, but they both seemed to think that he would not be much longer with them, and tried not to leave him.

Sergei Vasilievich did have some visitors, with whom he would talk and joke, so it was hard to imagine that such a serious condition was progressing at a rapid tempo.

He was also concerned about me, insisting that I go out at least for a while each evening, or sit in the garden even for an hour, and repeatedly asked me if I was not getting too tired.

Even though he continually complained of pain in his arm, he kept up his wrist and finger exercises. I was all the time in awe of the exceptional beauty of his hands. It was as though they had been sculpted by a master.

Sergei Vasilievich, by nature an extremely active person, found it hard to lie all the time in bed, and with the doctor's permission would sometimes get up to sit in a chair, a feat he always attempted to manage unaided. He would sometimes have his meal sitting in the chair, and even stayed there when friends visited, although this would soon tire him.

Some time around the 10th to 13th March the pains in his forearm increased, and spread to the right side of his body. At the same time small swellings began to appear on his body, and he began to lose his appetite. He asked me:

'Why does the doctor concentrate on these little lumps, but doesn't seem to think my loss of appetite matters?'

The doctor was trying various remedies to relieve the pain. His patient stoically waited for improvements, and suffered in silence.

We tried everything to get him to eat, and Irina Sergeyevna took charge of her father's diet, preparing all his favourite dishes. But he asked all of us not to force him to eat, saying that he would much prefer to do so only when he felt like it. Alas! what little appetite he still had steadily diminished, so that any desire for food was replaced by revulsion. The illness was now progressing at pace, and Sergei Vasilievich was increasingly anxious that the pain allowed him no respite from being conscious of it so that he could rest.

The arrival of Natalia Alexandrovna's sister, Sofia Alexandrovna, whom Sergei Vasilievich had known and dearly loved since child-hood, brought him a measure of relief. His appetite showed signs of returning. But the improvement was short-lived and he started to doubt that his treatment was proceeding in the right direction.

It was decided that a well-known American surgeon should be asked to attend for a joint consultation. The conclusion of the consultation was that Sergei Vasilievich was suffering from cancer.* I should mention that Dr Golitzin had already for some time been sharing with me his suspicion that the cause of the illness was cancer. I cannot find the words to describe how crushed the family was by this news. But at the same time every member of the family heroic-ally concealed their feelings, going to great lengths not to reveal to Sergei Vasilievich the slightest hint that he was terminally ill and was gradually approaching the end of his life.

Sergei Vasilievich continued to battle against the inroads of his illness, but whenever he got out of bed could not but be aware that he was becoming weaker. He often said:

'My powers are slipping from me and I'm losing strength. Surely the doctors can see that?'

We all did our best to encourage him and assured him that it was a passing phase, and that the medicines he was being given would gradually restore his strength. We did everything we could to relieve his anxieties.

---

* The doctors present at the consultation decided to remove one of the swell-ings in order to determine the form of the cancer.

I must say that we were largely successful in concealing from him the seriousness of his condition, while he, who had always shown such vital interest in every aspect of life, showed almost no interest in his medication, and for that reason did not suspect how ill he actually was.

Only once while he was being examined did Sergei Vasilievich draw the doctor's attention to his increasing weakness, and complain of his loss of appetite. The doctor replied that the most important remedy was sound sleep: sleep would restore the appetite and with it his general health. At that, directing his gaze fixedly on the doctor, Sergei Vasilievich asked:

'Are you quite sure of that? Could it not be that it is already too late? And why are you so concerned about that little lump you took out?'

Before long he became weaker still, and he was no longer strong enough to read.

I was always deeply impressed by Sergei Vasilievich's strength of will and his refusal to submit to the pain he was subjected to, no matter how grievous. He could never get out of his mind the sufferings of the fighting forces of his motherland, sharing and enduring them alongside his compatriots.

Every day he would ask Sofia Alexandrovna for the latest news from the front, what successes the Russian forces were having, and where their present position was. At this time the Russian forces had already begun their counter-attack, and on hearing that the Russians had retaken several cities, Sergei Vasilievich sighed with relief and said:

'Well, thanks be to God. May He give them all strength!'

Whenever he asked her to, which was often, Sofia Alexandrovna would read to him Pushkin, his favourite poet.

Despite his increasing feebleness and generally deplorable

condition, Sergei Vasilievich went on trying to do everything for himself, refusing all offers of help often when he obviously needed them. It was how he had always lived, and it was difficult for him to abandon his ingrained habits. He maintained to the last his interest in his garden, in the furnishings of the house and generally all his surroundings.

When the furniture arrived from New York he insisted that it be unpacked immediately. Wanting to do as he requested and yet not overly disturb his rest, the family had all the boxes first hidden away in the garage, and their contents subsequently brought gradually into the house as quietly as possible and without involving the workmen. This was done by Fyodor Fyodorovich Chaliapin and Sofia Alexandrovna.

The family, sensing the imminence of his demise, scarcely left his presence. Natalia Alexandrovna was by his side day and night, leaving him only for the briefest time possible to have something to eat or to greet visitors wanting to know how Sergei Vasilievich was. Himself he could no longer see his friends, because their presence tired him too extremely. The only exception to this among the closest friends was the daily visit of Fyodor Chaliapin. As well as him, if S. V. was feeling a little more up to it, he could manage a few minutes with Vladimir Horowitz and his wife, née Toscanini. The moment Charles Foley learned of his serious condition, about two weeks before Sergei Vasilievich died, he flew from New York, upon which he stayed throughout in the house, striving to do whatever he could to support both his friend and the members of the family. It was clear how much Foley loved Sergei Vasilievich and shared his distress.

From the 20th March Sergei Vasilievich's health took a sharp turn for the worse. He developed an acute aversion to food, responding to all appeals to eat something by saying that he found the very sight of food, not to mention the smell of it, revolting, and begged for it to be taken away. It was a red-letter day for all of us if in the morning he could be persuaded to drink half a cup of coffee and eat half a rusk. But our delight was, of course, no more than clutching at straws, because the disease was already advancing at full speed. Sometimes in his agony he would say:

'How dreadful I feel . . . everything in my body hurts, my hands, my side . . . it is hard to breathe; I can't even decide which side is less painful to lie on. The doctors can do nothing to help me. Perhaps they don't even know what is wrong with me? I can't take any food at all, and am simply losing all my strength.' Once Natasha Alexandrovna asked him if he would like her to help him turn so that he could lie on the other side, and he replied:

'I can't answer you because I am in such terrible pain. You must decide what is best.'

This was the first time, and it was very noticeable, that he started to lose all interest in himself. He even ceased to ask any of us to read to him as we had been doing, spoke more rarely and often groaned from pain. It was at this stage of his illness that news came of the Germans having destroyed the Tchaikovsky Museum at Klin. Needless to say we could not think of telling him about such a tragedy.

Two days before the end, Sergei Vasilievich lapsed into uncon-sciousness. His temperature rose sharply and his pulse accelerated, his cheeks burned and he groaned only rarely.

On one of these days a telegram was received from Moscow, signed by a cohort of Russian composers. It was a telegram of congratulations to Sergei Vasilievich on his birthday with many expressions of warm wishes, but sadly by the time it arrived it was too late for the recipient to read it.

The following morning we succeeded in administering to Sergei

Vasilievich a few teaspoons of coffee. Towards midday, the pulse perceptibly weakened, and Sergei Vasilievich lay motionless, his eyes closed. Naturally, we tried to make his position as comfortable as possible. We raised him up a little and smoothed out the sheets, but he made no reaction.

Between one and two o'clock in the afternoon Dr Golitzin came, and gave as his opinion that the end was very near. The family decided to call a priest, who came between three and four o'clock and administered Silent Confession* and Holy Communion to the dying man. With that Sergei Vasilievich visibly began to depart from life: his breathing became even and peaceful, but the pulse grew weaker and weaker. By eleven o'clock it was difficult to discern any pulse; the hands and the soles of the feet became cold to the touch. It was suggested to me that I should go and rest so that I could relieve others if needed later in the night. When I reached my room I was in a state of great nervous tension, I could not sleep and kept on thinking how it could possibly be that such a great man as Sergei Vasilievich should no longer live when he had so much still to give to the world, such great service to offer to mankind. How can such things come to pass? I even began to lose faith in medicine and in my profession.

At half past one, Sofia Alexandrovna came to me with the terrible but long-awaited news:

'Sergei Vasilievich has passed away. Please come and help us.'

I ran upstairs, where Natalia Alexandrovna and Irina Sergeyevna were waiting. Sergei Vasilievich lay perfectly still and quiet, as if sleeping, while all the lines of suffering seemed to have vanished

---

* A rite of the Russian Orthodox Church administered to those too near death to be able to communicate. It includes a form of extreme unction and is part of the Last Rites.

from his face. Once we had performed all our final obligations and said our farewells, we went our separate ways, but of course nobody could sleep. It was hard to reconcile oneself to the thought that our dear Sergei Vasilievich was no longer among us. All the time he was lying there, unconscious but breathing, it was easier for us because we were aware he was still with us. Yes, it was a terrible thing to accept that death had conquered and the unforgettable Sergei Vasilievich had left us for ever.

According to the wishes of the deceased and of his family, the funeral arrangements were modest, since he had no love for graveside perorations and generally all the portentous trappings of funerals.

I wish to record how simple, kind and considerate Sergei Vasilievich invariably was to me. He would often say: 'Don't be offended, Olga Georgievna, when I tell you that nothing is of any help to me. It's just that I have grown very irritable, but you mustn't think that I am dissatisfied with anything you do.'

He often asked me to give him his injection before the prescribed time so that I would be able to leave him and go to rest myself. And he was always very appreciative of even the most trivial thing I might do for him.

Remembering Rachmaninoff, I cannot forebear to mention his family. As I wrote at the beginning of this note it was a truly Russian household and I quickly became accustomed to it. I so much wanted to help in every way I could, and their sorrow was my sorrow too. I understood them without the need for words. Natalia Alexandrovna, Irina Sergeyevna and Sofia Alexandrovna were like family to me, and in spite of the distressing condition of their loved one not a day passed without their showing me every conceivable care and consideration. After he died they expressed most touchingly their gratitude for the help I had given them and that I, as a member of their family, had shared their grief. But sadly I was still left with a strange feeling of dissatisfaction with myself, that I had not done more for this great man.

Funeral, Burial

Rachmaninoff's funeral was held at Holy Virgin Mary Russian Orthodox Cathedral in the Silver Lake district of Los Angeles. Founded by Tsarist exiles and opened in 1928, the church was immersed in the Hollywood film industry in more ways than one. For decades a rumour circulated that it had been built as a set for *The Cossacks* (1928) – a high-budget silent film based on Tolstoy which hired sixty local Russians and two dozen Cossacks as extras – then given to the Russian community. The architect was Alexander Toluboff, who was also art director of *The Cossacks*. Dr Golitzin and his family were parishioners. A Golitzin family icon was given to the church. The church in the film, in actuality, was a temporary set erected on land owned by MGM, but the edifice proper was built and flourished thanks to financial support from all the Russians working in the Hollywood studios. Among those named as donors, one name catches the eye: Nina Koshetz.

Rachmaninoff, too, was listed as a member of the parish. An account of the funeral appeared in *New Dawn* (San Francisco) on 2 April 1943. After his death in the early hours of Sunday, a family mass was held at home. At 7 p.m. the body was carried in a coffin to the church, for another mass, with singing, at 8 p.m. The place was packed with mourners, and filled with flowers. A cross of white gardenias stood in front of the coffin, with azalea bushes either side. The Vice-Consul of the USSR was present, and laid a wreath. On Monday at 8 p.m. and on Tuesday at 11 a.m., two further services were held. At the request of the family, there were

no speeches. After a final rite led by Archpriest Grigory Prozorov
(1894–1946), with much singing, the ceremonies were over. The
family gave the cathedral their old icon of St Nicholas, which had
hung in Rachmaninoff's bedroom. It had once belonged to his late
son-in-law, Prince Volkonsky, given to him by his grandmother,
Countess Maria Alexandrovna Shuvalova, on the christening of her
first grandson.

Rachmaninoff had expressed a wish to be buried in Russia in
the cemetery of Novodevichy Monastery, Moscow. Here, Rimsky-
Korsakov, Scriabin and Chekhov had been laid to rest. When he built
Senar, he imagined this lakeside paradise being his final resting place.
Instead, his mortal journey would end on the East Coast of America
where he had been welcomed, amid the joyful celebrations of Armistice and the tribulations of a flu epidemic, a quarter of a century
earlier. After temporary safeguard in a vault in Los Angeles, on 2
June 1943 his body was interred in the hillside cemetery of Kensico
at Valhalla, Westchester County, New York. Later his wife Natalia
(in 1951) and his daughter Irina, Princess Volkonsky (in 1969),
were buried alongside him. Tatiana, the daughter whose absence he
so mourned, died in 1961 and was buried in France. The grave at
Kensico, now walled on three sides by tall hedges, is marked by a
simple engraved panel and a Russian Orthodox Cross, that is, with
three horizontal cross beams, the lowest of which slants downward.

In 2015 Russia's culture minister, Vladimir Medinsky, called
on the United States to repatriate the composer's remains, for
burial in a 'lavish mausoleum' in Ivanovka. The minister, claiming
Rachmaninoff as one of their own and 'of Russian origin', accused
the USA of neglecting the grave. Speaking for the family, his
great-great-granddaughter, Susan Sophia Rachmaninoff Volkonskaya Wanamaker, said no: 'To dig up and move his body would be
an immense violation of the privacy he so prized,' Ms Wanamaker

said. 'After fleeing from one country to the next in life, as he did, is it too much to ask that he be allowed to rest in peace with his family? I don't think so.'[1] His mortal remains rest in the country which gave him refuge.

On 2 April 1943, Eugene Ormandy conducted the Philadelphia Orchestra in a performance of *The Isle of the Dead*, a memorial to the composer, played by the musicians he loved. In New York, Josef Hofmann, career now teetering but still, as Rachmaninoff had described him, a 'sky high' genius when on form, performed Chopin's funeral march. In London Benno Moiseiwitsch, referred to by Rachmaninoff as his 'spiritual heir', did likewise. Audiences rose to their feet in homage.

Addressing his telegram simply to 'Madame Sergei Rachmaninoff, Beverly Hills, California', Henry Wood wrote:

Our deepest sympathy goes out to you in your sorrow STOP
I mourn your dear husband not only as a friend but as an
irreplaceable figure in the world of music STOP We shall miss
him but his name will live for all time[2]

WILD STRAWBERRIES

Remembering Ivanovka

Vera Skalon's Diary

We now leave that burial site in Westchester County and return one final time to Ivanovka, in that happy summer of 1890. Rachmaninoff was there with the Silotis and the Satins, including his future wife, Natalia and her sister Sofia, and the three Skalon sisters. For once he experienced the warmth of family life, extended through these cousins and friends. The long, hot summer days were spent picnicking, boating, walking, eating wild strawberries, but working too. Ivanovka was the place that remained in his heart to the end.

Below is a short, edited extract from the vivacious diary of fifteen-year-old Vera Dmitrievna Skalon, Rachmaninoff's teenage sweetheart, which captures that idyllic summer in the country.* Names are explained in brackets, but as in a Russian novel, can be mastered or skipped depending on the reader's inclinations.

14 June 1890

Today Alexander Ilyich [Siloti] was firmly convinced he was dying. During the night he had an attack of our famous colic, which led him to imagine that he was suffering from cholera or even cancer. He is the hypochondria champion of the world. At lunch as we contemplated the mournful expression on his face, we couldn't stop laughing. Afterwards we all set out to pick the season's first wild strawberries from the beds in the garden. No one who doesn't live in the country can know the ecstasy of eating berries straight from the bush.

* New translation by Anthony Phillips

[. . .] Sergei Vasilievich sat down beside me, his long legs stretching out so that they reached right down to the bottom step. 'What a bean-pole,' I thought, smiling at the idea. 'That's better,' he said, observing my smile. 'Do I have your permission to tease you a little?' Naturally, permission was granted, and we started talking. But only about rather serious matters. He told me about his childhood and living with Zverev; poor man, how much he had to endure! It's no wonder his character has become so unpredictable. I now understand what a mistake it is to judge anyone on first impressions, because when we first met in Moscow none of us could stand him! But now, I don't know, but my sisters and I find him a really dear person. [. . .]

Today I want to describe exactly how we spend our days at Ivanovka. Everyone is ready by eight o'clock in the morning, except the Siloti parents. Uncle often gets up at five a.m. in order to get into the fields before it gets too hot. At half past eight begins a general stampede around the garden, mostly along Red Alley: some of us drink kumiss,* some water, some nibble herbs. Meanwhile Mlle. Jeanne is preparing coffee . . .

It's always good fun at coffee-time, everyone chatters and laughs, at the same time devouring incredible quantities of wonderful pretzels and doughnuts. From up above come the plaintive sounds of the piano: this is Sonya [Sofia Satina, Natalia's sister] practising her detested 'music'. From eight in the morning until five in the evening a continuous stream of musicians takes it in turn to play the poor old piano, which never gets a moment's peace.

After coffee we all go outside to continue talking for a few minutes on the long bench in front of the house, until we are dragged off by main force to our various tasks from nine o'clock until eleven o'clock. During these two hours I often have to run over to the

* Fermented mare's milk.

house to get an exercise book or a pencil, and I grab a caramel or a chocolate. Sergei Vasilievich doesn't sit still for long either, he's always dashing over to get paper, or some score or other, or to ask advice from Alexander Ilyich.

Twice a week at half past ten Natasha goes to Sergei Vasilievich in the billiard room so that he can work with her on assignments from Zverev, and every time without fail they quarrel: he insists that the appointed hour has only just struck and Natasha deliberately came early. Natasha loses her temper and her voice goes right up to the top as she screeches: 'You simply don't want to work with me, that's all it is.'

Promptly at eleven o'clock we run out of the balcony, and Natasha the billiard room, it's then Sergei Vasilievich's time at the piano and for two hours he practises the same study by Schlözer. Alexander Ilyich also continues practising in his study, so there is no corner of Ivanovka free from the thunder of music. My sisters and I often visit Sergei Vasilievich to distract him with our chatter, for which he is always very grateful; I bring him some berries and every time he says: 'Well, thank you, Psychopatushka. What a kind, good person you are!'

Between eleven and twelve, my sisters and I, Natasha, Sonechka, Mlle. Jeanne, and along with them Sonya and Marina [daughter of the cook], all like to go swimming even though it always takes at least a quarter of an hour to find the key to the bathing-shed. I am terribly envious of them so usually don't go to watch, but when I do I sit in a boat, rocking with the waves and seeing them swimming and getting up to all sorts of tricks on a big flat board. In a few days' time they are going to bring a big bath from Tambov in which I can bathe. Of course, it's not so enjoyable, but at least it will refresh me. Over the last days the heat has become unbearable, and there is no prospect of much change in the weather.

At half past twelve there starts up a frenzied racket from the bell in the courtyard. Everyone makes a dash for lunch because we are all so hungry. But the music doesn't stop during lunch: poor Sergei Vasilievich carries on working at his eternal étude until precisely one o'clock and so has to have lunch on his own.

Being at Ivanovka always puts everybody in the best of spirits, therefore the laughter and jokes never let up at meal times.

At one o'clock Natasha goes back to her room to study, Lyolya goes to write her composition, Tatusha does some sewing or reads, and Missochka drags me upstairs for piano practice. The billiard room is always very warm, and my playing is extremely lethargic anyhow, but when it comes to us playing duets, poor Missochka completely loses patience. Sometimes it can happen towards the end of the lesson that Alexander Ilyich and Sergei Vasilievich will come upstairs for a game of billiards, which makes both our hearts sink to our boots, our eyes glaze over, our fingers stumble and we aren't together for a single bar. Alexander Ilyich merely shakes his head and says with the utmost seriousness: 'Seryozha, these young ladies play really well, don't you think?' He obviously can't under-stand why such talentless girls should be forced to learn music.

This is the time when Sergei Vasilievich comes to our wing to work on his four-hand transcription [he is making of Tchaikovsky's *Sleeping Beauty*] and Alexander Ilyich goes back to the piano in his study and does not emerge until five o'clock.

At five o'clock Lyolya, I and the cousins are free: I always run to find Auntie and drink water with syrup or eat sweets and jam. Then I go for a natter with Sergei Vasilievich who has yet again been rattling through his étude from three until five. I cannot conceive how he has the patience and strength to do it, although he does admit that he finds it hard and his spine gets tired. Lyolya often sits there too, on the sofa in the corner, reading *War and Peace* in spite of her elder sister complaining she is too young to be reading anything like that.

On the way back from the lake we stop to drink a glass of hot milk. At nine there is more frenzied bellringing which means we go in for tea and laughter, because laughter is an absolute necessity at night-time. Everyone fights to get to the table as we all have our assigned chairs.

Everyone else, as soon as tea is finished, heads outside. The older generation sits on the long bench; we young ones make great strides to the summerhouse, or maybe to the park. We all adore this moment of the day; a special kind of stillness and contentment descends on the whole of Ivanovka, one's soul feels light and consoled. The gaiety of our mood is transformed into seriousness, and our conversations become loving and intimate. We go out on to the balcony and gaze our fill at the sky and the stars, carry on talking and laughing, until at long last tiredness takes over and forces us to sleep.

EPILOGUE

Today the Villa Senar, on the shores of Lake Lucerne, still closely resembles the place Rachmaninoff knew. The original open-work Art Deco iron gate has been replaced by a long wooden fence and shuttered gate which hides all sight of the property. The grounds are minimally maintained, but without the horticulturalist's eye of the original creator, back in the 1930s, to add colour and contrast. The gardens have identifiable areas: border plantings, fruit grove, park, driveway with lawn, shoreside area. A wooded path, now carpeted in moss, sweeps down to the boathouse. Trees Rachmaninoff planted as saplings, now mature, mostly shade the house from public view. Some, nearing the end of their lifespan, must soon be felled before their roots erode the rocky cliff behind. The farmhouse next door, which once provided the Rachmaninoffs with fruit and vegetables and other produce, is still there. The gardener's house stands in angular, visual echo of the large house ahead. Both buildings are white, where once they were ochre. The main dwelling has a presence which is austere but not overbearing. The stepped roof line, made up of three interlocking cubes, gives a sense of the house crouching, a ship afloat in the landscape.

The bars of the iron and mirrored glass front door have the initials S. R. worked in beautiful, elongated Art Deco font. Inside, according to modernist aesthetics, rooms flow into one another: salon to dining room to terrace. The south-west orientation of the house gives an airy, light feel. Much of the furniture has survived. Rachmaninoff's Steinway piano, his sixtieth-birthday gift from the company, is in the studio. The distinctive Art Deco clock, seen in photographs, stands on the walnut veneer desk. On a cabinet at the far end, scores and books are stored. Photos of friends (now copies) line the top: Rimsky-Korsakov (1844–1908), Tchaikovsky (1840–1893), Chaliapin, Frederick Steinway, Josef Hofmann, the Russian writer Ivan Bunin, the English writer Noël Coward, Thomas Edison and Vladimir Horowitz. This little gallery may have been amended over the years, by his daughter Tatiana, or grandson Alexander, who lived there after Natalia's death in 1951. There is no obvious explanation for the presence of Coward: he wrote the screenplay for *Brief Encounter* – which, through its soundtrack, immortalised the Second Piano Concerto for new audiences – but not until 1945. They could have met in New York in the early 1920s.

The house is free from ornament but luxurious: the Bauhaus banister, the bespoke Schindler lift made of wood, steel and glass; large rooms, long dining table for populous family gatherings, cabinet full of classic German porcelain, Russian cutlery in the Baroque style, tableware bearing the S. N. R. monogram. Upstairs, a built-in linen cupboard, discreetly hidden on the broad first-floor landing, is stocked with monogrammed sheets and pillowcases.

The tweed suit with plus-four trousers, which Rachmaninoff can be seen wearing in so many photographs from Senar, hangs in a bedroom. He had commissioned it in Jermyn Street, London, in the 1930s, as casual attire for his Swiss summers. This style of trousers, traditionally cut to end, fastened, four inches below the knee, allowed the wearer freedom of movement: for hunting and shooting, or in Rachmaninoff's case for boating and gardening. The length of the pair at Senar gives an indication of the wearer's height.

The 'master' bedroom, with a view of Pilatus, is in some disarray, awaiting decoration after a leak. The bathrooms retain their original fittings. In the 'master bathroom', the bath has elegant, rounded corners, Art Deco fluting, and a mechanism familiar from Russia: a means of piping hot water into the cavity between the interior and exterior wall of the bath, keeping the bather heated as if in their own samovar.

The property passed to Natalia after Rachmaninoff's death, and after her death in 1951, to Tatiana [Conus], then to her son Alexander Conus (1933–2012), who added Rachmaninoff to his name and founded the Sergei Rachmaninoff Foundation in 2000. After his death, Senar passed to a 'community of heirs' consisting of Alexander's four children and the Foundation. Vladimir Putin instructed his government to prepare a formal report on the possible repatriation of Rachmaninoff's property, part of a new desire to reclaim Russia's cultural legacy. Putin proposed that Russia purchase the estate and archive. The sale came to nothing, allegedly blocked by the canton of Lucerne.

In November 2021, the canton of Lucerne put in a bid of CHF 15.45 million (approximately £13.2 million) to purchase Senar, with plans to renovate it and turn it into a cultural centre. According to the Rachmaninoff Foundation website: 'Of the 15.45 million francs, 8 million are earmarked for the purchase of Villa Senar, including furniture and inventory.' On 6 December 2021, the parliament of the canton of Lucerne voted in favour of purchasing Senar. A nine-year deadlock, concerning the settlement of the inheritance of Rachmaninoff's grandson, has at last been broken. On 1 July 2022 the Swiss musician, Andrea Loetscher, became managing director of the Sergei Rachmaninoff Foundation, incorporating the new role of Director of Cultural and Educational Centre 'Villa Senar'. Its future looks secure, and full of promise.

I saw the house just in time, its privacy and spirit intact. The atmosphere Sergei and Natalia Rachmaninoff created, for that short, fragile time of happiness in the 1930s, was precious and alive. Mount Pilatus, sometimes called the mountain of dragons, often cloud-topped, retains its weighty presence. The lake shimmers. The boathouse stands ready. Water laps against the steps, clear and inviting.

The 'Exile' Works
compositions written after 1917

Piano Concerto no. 4 in G minor, op. 40
(1926, revised 1941)

The seeds of this work were planted as early as 1913–14, but Rachmaninoff composed most of it in his sabbatical year, 1926, in New York and Dresden, and dedicated it to Medtner. The premiere took place on 18 March 1927 in Philadelphia, conducted by Stokowski with the composer as soloist. Reviews were negative. Rachmaninoff, worried by its length and, especially, aspects of the third movement, cut it by 114 bars, in 1927, then put it aside, returning to it to make further cuts and revisions in 1941. He recorded it in December of that year.

Trois Chansons Russes for chorus and orchestra,
op. 41 (1926)

Composed in 1926, this was Rachmaninoff's last work for chorus and orchestra (following *Spring* and *The Bells*). The first song, for altos and basses in unison, is about a drake and his loss of the grey duck he loves. The second is for women's voices. The third is a version of the song Rachmaninoff recorded in 1926 with the 'gypsy' singer Nadezhda Plevitskaya. The songs are dedicated to Stokowski, who conducted the premiere on 18 March 1927 in Philadelphia in the same concert as the premiere of the Fourth Piano Concerto.

Variations on a Theme of Corelli for piano, op. 42 (1931)

Twenty variations, all but two in the key of D minor, on the theme *La Folia* – not by Corelli but used in his Violin Sonata no. 12. Rachmaninoff dedicated his op. 42 to the violinist Fritz Kreisler. An intermezzo separates Variations 13 and 14. The piece ends with a coda. Rachmaninoff maintained that he sometimes omitted variations, according to the concentration levels of his audience. When once there was too much coughing – 'I don't remember where. Some small town' – he played only ten variations. He did not record the work.

Rhapsody on a Theme of Paganini for piano and orchestra, op. 43 (1934)

Most of this single-movement work for piano and orchestra was written in the summer of 1934, in Villa Senar, Lucerne. The twenty-four variations, based on Paganini's Caprice no. 24 in A minor, for solo violin, fall loosely into three groups, mirroring a concerto with a central slow movement. Variation 18 in D flat major, the work's most popular (Rachmaninoff allegedly joked 'This one is for my agent'), is an inversion of the main theme, which is, in effect, played 'upside down'. Variation 24, which like Variation 6 quotes the *Dies irae*, presents particular pianistic challenges. Fokine's ballet version was premiered in 1939 at the Royal Opera House, Covent Garden, under the title *Paganini*.

Symphony no. 3 in A minor, op. 44 (1936)

Rachmaninoff completed the symphony at Senar in June 1936, revising it in 1939, his last summer in Europe. Unlike his first two symphonies, it is in three movements, with the central one acting both as slow movement and scherzo (also the case in Piano Concertos nos 2 and 3). Especially in the step-like motif of the opening movement, and in its lyricism, the symphony has been characterised as Russian in mood, a positive in the Soviet Union at the time, but less of an asset to American critics. Lean in texture compared to earlier works, it is scored for full orchestra including xylophone, two harps and celesta. The *Dies irae* makes a notable appearance in the work's coda. The last movement nods back at themes in the first movement. Rachmaninoff considered the symphony a strong work, despite the negative reaction. The Philadelphia Orchestra gave the premiere, conducted by Leopold Stokowski, on 6 November 1936. Rachmaninoff made adjustments to the score, leading to a revised edition in 1939.

Symphonic Dances, op. 45, and version for two pianos, op. 45a (1940)

Most of this three-movement work was written on Long Island in the summer of 1940. Rachmaninoff worked on the two-piano version at the same time. Originally intending to call it *Fantastic Dances*, with movement titles of 'Midday', 'Twilight' and 'Midnight', he settled on *Symphonic Dances*. The first dance is marked *non allegro*, which some interpreters have taken to mean 'at a moderate speed', whereas Rachmaninoff's own evidence (in the Marston recording: *Rachmaninoff Plays Symphonic Dances: Newly Discovered 1940 Recording*) suggest he wanted a brisker pace. The first movement's distinctive saxophone theme, a unique use of the instrument in his output, emerges from a chatter of woodwind then falls silent. The second movement, rich in mystery, is a waltz which finally collapses. While the *Dies irae* appears earlier, its most conspicuous statement is in the final movement. The work ends with a feature still debated, and played different ways, by conductors: did Rachmaninoff want the tam-tam's sound to be stopped, or to continue resonating after the orchestra's final fortissimo chord? His last work ends with an enigma. *Symphonic Dances* was premiered by Eugene Ormandy and the Philadelphia Orchestra on 3 January 1941.

Select Bibliography

Apetian, Z. A. (ed.), *S. Rakhmaninov, Literaturnoe nasledie*, 3 vols (Moscow: Sovetskii kompozitor, 1978–80)

—— *Vospominaniia o Rakhmaninove*, 2 vols, 5th edition (Moscow: Muzyka, 1988)

Barber, Charles, *Lost in the Stars: The Forgotten Musical Life of Alexander Siloti* (Lanham, MD: Scarecrow Press, 2002)

Bertensson, Sergei and Jay Leyda, *Sergei Rachmaninoff: A Lifetime in Music* (New York: New York University Press, 1956; revised edition, Bloomington and Indianapolis, IN: Indiana University Press, 2001)

Bullock, Philip Ross (ed.), *Rachmaninoff and His World* (Chicago, IL: University of Chicago Press, 2022)

Bullock, Philip Ross and Pauline Fairclough (eds), *1917 and Beyond: Continuity, Rupture and Memory in Russian Music* (Cambridge: Modern Humanities Research Association, 2019)

Cannata, David Butler, *Rachmaninoff and the Symphony* (Innsbruck and Vienna: Studien Verlag/Lucca: Libreria Musica 1999)

Frolova-Walker, Marina, and Jonathan Walker, *Music and Soviet Power 1917–1932* (Woodbridge: The Boydell Press, 2012)

Gelernter, David, *1939: The Lost World of the Fair* (New York: Avon Books, 1995)

Harrison, Max, *Rachmaninoff: Life, Works, Recordings* (London: Continuum, 2005)

Lieberman, Richard K., *Steinway & Sons* (New Haven and London: Yale University Press, 1995)

Martyn, Barrie, *Nicolas Medtner: His Life and Music* (London: Scolar Press, 1995)

—— *Rachmaninoff: Composer, Pianist, Conductor* (London: Routledge, 1990)

Mitchell, Rebecca, *Sergei Rachmaninoff* (London: Reaktion Books, 2022)

Norris, Geoffrey, *Rachmaninoff: Master Musicians* (London: Dent, 1975; second edition, Oxford: Oxford University Press, 1996)

—— *Sergei Rachmaninoff: The Collected Interviews* [forthcoming 2023]

Prokofiev, Sergei, translated and annotated by Anthony Phillips, *Diaries 1915–1923: Behind the Mask* (London: Faber, 2008); *Diaries 1924–1933: Prodigal Son* (London: Faber, 2012)

Riesemann, Oskar von, *Rachmaninoff's Recollections, told to Oskar von Riesemann* (New York: Macmillan, 1934)

Swan, A. J. [Alfred] and Katherine Swan, 'Rachmaninoff: Personal Reminiscences', *Musical Quarterly* Vol. 30 nos 1 and 2 (1944), pp. 1–19; pp. 174–91

Sylvester, Richard D., *Rachmaninoff's Complete Songs: A Companion with Texts and Translations* (Bloomington and Indianapolis, IN: Indiana University Press, 2002)

Taruskin, Richard, *Defining Russia Musically* (Princeton, NJ: Princeton University Press, 1997)

—— *Russian Music at Home and Abroad, New Essays* (Berkeley: University of California Press, 2016)

Threlfall, Robert and Geoffrey Norris, *A Catalogue of the Compositions of S. Rachmaninoff* (London: Scolar Press, 1982)

Zelensky, Natalie K., *Performing Tsarist Russia in New York: Music, Émigrés and the American Imagination* (Bloomington and Indianapolis, IN: Indiana University Press, 2019)

Short note on recordings

Rachmaninoff's own recordings, including those with the Philadelphia Orchestra, are an inspiring starting point, but not the final word. Most have been repackaged and remastered, and made available commercially. Others are easy to locate online, as are the home movies, touching evidence of Rachmaninoff the family man. Of the countless pianists who have specialised in his music over the decades, the following are worth investigation (in chronological order): Vladimir Horowitz, Sviatoslav Richter, Van Cliburn, Vladimir Ashkenazy, Martha Argerich, Stephen Hough, Leif Ove Andsnes, Nikolai Lugansky, Kirill Gerstein, Yuja Wang, Anna Fedorova, Daniil Trifonov. On YouTube, watch the remarkable South Korean newcomer Yuncham Lim who, aged eighteen, won the Van Cliburn Competition 2022, with the Piano Concerto no. 3, conducted by Marin Alsop. In orchestral music, the conductors of Rachmaninoff's own era – Stokowski, Ormandy, Mitropoulos among them – can be sampled online. Recordings of the Soviet era give a sharp and fascinating sense of contrasting performance styles. Of the many conductors who respond to Rachmaninoff's music, these are current or recent ones that stand out: Vladimir Ashkenazy, Semyon Bychkov, Mariss Jansons, Paavo Järvi, Vladimir Jurowski, Yannick Nézet-Séguin, Antonio Pappano, Simon Rattle.

For a complete recording of the songs, sung by native Russian speakers, Delphian's box set, with Evelina Dobračeva, Ekaterina Siurina (sopranos), Justina Gringyetė (mezzo-soprano), Daniil Shtoda (tenor), Andrei Bondarenko, Rodion Pogossov (baritones), Alexander Vinogradov (bass) and Iain Burnside (piano), is recommended. For a selection, try the album *Dissonance*, by Asmik Grigorian (soprano) and Lukas Geniušas (piano).

Many fine musicians, including those listed above, have joined forces to perform the chamber music, and most top cellists have recorded the Sonata for Cello and Piano, from Mstislav Rostropovich with Alexander Dedyuhkin, to Alisa Weilerstein with Inon

Barnatan, to Sheku Kanneh-Mason with Isata Kanneh-Mason.

These suggestions are offered as a guide, open-ended and in no sense dogmatic, to a well-populated world of recordings.

Acknowledgements

Julia Boyd's early enthusiasm acted as a set of jump-leads, jolting me out of lockdown inertia by trawling through newspaper archives when she had a book of her own to write. Gerard McBurney steered me towards Anthony Phillips who put his warm heart, sharp brain and exemplary translations at my disposal freely; I cannot thank him enough. Laura Tunbridge, at a key moment, connected me with Philip Ross Bullock, who was kindness itself. Sunita Sharma Gibson was, as ever, the best possible picture researcher: unflustered, quick, patient.

My *Observer* colleagues, Sarah Donaldson, Jane Ferguson and Carol McDaid, models of constancy and non-interference, deserve their own paragraph of thanks.

So too do Lucy Shortis and Alice Wood, unfazed, rock-like, in a year of alarums.

Thank you to my agent, Carrie Plitt, at Felicity Bryan Associates. At Faber Belinda Matthews and her excellent team were always there and veiled their panics in soothing words as deadlines came and went. Joanna Harwood and Kate Hopkins have been meticulous and inexhaustible. Michael Downes took in my endless changes with a charming nonchalance as if this were a highlight of the editing process, when we all know it is every editor's worst headache.

Friends and family – the list is long, and headed by my loyal daughters – gave endless support, the walks or cups of coffee every bit as vital as the leads on Nabokov or Mitropoulos or Gary Graffman. The gates close early on a book. I know from experience there will be others who join late and make critical, perhaps face-saving, contributions. So rather than risk a catalogue of omissions, I will thank each of you in my own way.

My husband Tom Phillips, dealing with dispiriting ill health throughout the period I was writing this, still found the willpower and devotion to read, read and read again. The accounts of Rachmaninoff's final illness caused both of us anguish. I am sad Tom did not live to see the finished book but, in its own way, his fingerprint is on every page.

I thank everyone and take responsibility for anything that isn't as it should be.

Notes

All quoted matter without sources listed is from the five volumes of letters and documentary accounts edited by Z. A. Apetian: *Literaturnoe nasledie (Literary Legacy)*, 3 vols, and *Vospominaniia o Rakhmaninove* (*Reminiscences about Rachmaninoff*), 2 vols, 5th edition (see Bibliography), only available in Russian, or from the Rachmaninoff Archive, Library of Congress, Washington DC. Translations are by Anthony Phillips, or drawn from the exhaustive work of Sergei Bertensson and Jay Leyda in *Sergei Rachmaninoff: A Lifetime in Music* (New York: New York University Press, 1956; revised edition, Bloomington and Indianapolis, IN: Indiana University Press, 2001, with a new introduction by David Butler Cannata). If I have inadvertently quoted, without credit, anyone else's translation, I hope in the spirit of Rachmaninoff understanding I can be forgiven. Newspaper articles have been located, mainly, through online subscription archives including the *New York Times*, Newspaper Archives Online and British Newspaper Archive.

Every effort has been made to contact copyright holders. The publisher and author will be pleased to hear from any whom they have not been able to locate, so that acknowledgement can be made in any digital or future editions.

Preface

1 *New York Times*, 14 April 1968.
2 Both Malcolm quotations from *Guardian*, 1 July 2021, obituary by Ian Jack.
3 Nathan Milstein and Solomon Volkov, *From Russia to the West: The Musical Memoirs and Reminiscences of Nathan Milstein*, trans. Antonina W. Bouis (London: Barrie & Jenkins, 1990), p. 108.

1915–1918: Revolution, Departure, Arrival

1 N. K. Krupskaya, *Reminiscences of Lenin* (1933), Part II: 'The Years of the War: Last Months of Emigration', sourced from the Marxist Internet Archive: https://www.marxists.org/archive/krupskaya/works/rol/index.htm

2 See Catherine Merridale, *Lenin on the Train* (London: Penguin, 2016).

3 Review of *The Diaries of Marius Petipa*, trans. and ed. by Lynn Garafola, *Studies in Dance History* Vol. 3 no. 1 (Spring 1992), published in *Dance Research: The Journal of the Society for Dance Research* (Edinburgh: Edinburgh University Press, 1992), p. 80.

4 See Douglas Smith, *Former People: The Last Days of the Russian Aristocracy* (London: Macmillan, 2012).

5 Oskar von Riesemann, *Rachmaninoff's Recollections, told to Oskar von Riesemann* (New York: Macmillan, 1934), p. 186.

6 Lyudmila Skalon, under her married name Rostovtsova, wrote a memoir of Rachmaninoff. See Z. A. Apetian (ed.), *Vospominaniia o Rakhmaninove*, 2 vols, 5th edition (Moscow: Muzyka, 1988), Vol. 1, pp. 232–50.

7 Sergei Bertensson and Jay Leyda, *Sergei Rachmaninoff: A Lifetime in Music* (New York: New York University Press, 1956; revised edition, Bloomington and Indianapolis, IN: Indiana University Press, 2001), p. 287.

8 Michael Kennedy, *Portrait of Elgar* (third ed., Oxford: Clarendon Press, 1987), p. 115.

9 Barrie Martyn, *Rachmaninoff: Composer, Pianist, Conductor* (London: Routledge, 1990), p. 235.

10 Bertensson and Leyda, *Sergei Rachmaninoff: A Lifetime in Music*, p. 197.

11 Vladimir Bezobrazov, *Diary of the Commander of the Russian Imperial Guard 1914–1917*, ed. Marvin Lyons (Boynton Beach, FL: Dramco, 1994), p. 116.

12 Marietta Shaginian, 'Rachmaninoff, Pisma k Re', *Novyi Mir* (Moscow), 1943, No. 4.

13 Michael Scott, *Rachmaninoff* (Stroud: The History Press, 2008), p. 95.

14 Letter from Rachmaninoff to Shaginian, 14 February 1912. See Z. A. Apetian (ed.) *S. Rakhmaninov, Literaturnoe nasledie*, 3 vols (Moscow: Sovetskii kompozitor, 1978–80), Vol. 2, p. 43.

15 Martyn, *Rachmaninoff: Composer, Pianist, Conductor*, p. 262.

16 Bertensson and Leyda, *Rachmaninoff: A Lifetime in Music*, p. 199.

17 Bertensson and Leyda, *Rachmaninoff: A Lifetime in Music*, p. 199.

18 From Rachmaninoff's dictated *Reminiscences*, quoted in Bertensson and Leyda, *Sergei Rachmaninoff: A Lifetime in Music*, p. 184.

19 Sergei Prokofiev, translated and annotated by Anthony Phillips, *Diaries 1915–1923: Behind the Mask* (London: Faber, 2008), p. 171.

20 Vladimir Nabokov, *Collected Stories* (London: Penguin Modern Classics, Kindle edition), p. 853.

21 Charles O'Connell, *The Other Side of the Record* (New York: Alfred A. Knopf, 1947), p. 160.

22 Apetian (ed.), *Vospominaniia o Rakhmaninove*, Vol. 2, p. 320 (from the chapter entitled 'Sergei Vasilievich's Character').

23 Riesemann, *Rachmaninoff's Recollections*, pp. 184–5.

24 Riesemann, *Rachmaninoff's Recollections*, p. 185.

25 Natalia Rachmaninoff's memoir in Apetian (ed.), *Vospominaniia o Rakhmaninove*, Vol. 2, p. 299.

26 Letter from Rachmaninoff to Mikhail Tereshchenko, 1 June 1917, quoted in Bertensson and Leyda, *Sergei Rachmaninoff: A Lifetime in Music*, p. 205.

27 Prokofiev, *Diaries 1915–1923: Behind the Mask*, p. 216.

28 Prokofiev, *Diaries 1915–1923: Behind the Mask*, p. 217.

29 Prokofiev, *Diaries 1915–1923: Behind the Mask*, p. 218.

30 Prokofiev, *Diaries 1915–1923: Behind the Mask*, p. 217.

31 Marietta Shaginian, 'Rachmaninoff, Pisma k Re', *Novyi Mir* (Moscow), 1943, No. 4.

32 In *Rachmaninoff: A Biography* (London: Cassell, 1951), Victor I. Seroff quotes extensively from Rachmaninoff's letters to Shaginian, which were published in *Novy Mir*, Moscow, 1943, No. 4, by which time Shaginian was an honoured Soviet figure. This extract, however, is from an article she wrote after his death. Seroff states that it was written for publication in 1946. Seroff, *Rachmaninoff: A Biography*, p. 119.

33 Taken from Zoya Arkadievna Pribytkova's memoir of Rachmaninoff, written in Tashkent (1952) and reproduced in Apetian (ed.), *Vospominaniia o Rakhmaninove*, Vol. 2, pp. 52–89 (new translation by Anthony Phillips). In this memoir Zoya states that

she accompanied the Rachmaninoffs to the Finland station as they departed their homeland in December 1917 and that 'I was the only person who saw him off as he left Russia for ever.' This contradicts the generally reported view that the Rachmaninoffs were accompanied by Nikolai Struve and no one else saw them go. We can never know the truth.

34 Sophia Satin, *A 20th Century Life: The Memoirs of Sophia Satin* (London: The Rachmaninoff Society, 1997), p. 5.

35 Riesemann, *Rachmaninoff's Recollections*, p. 185.

36 Riesemann, *Rachmaninoff's Recollections*, pp. 185–6

37 Watson Lyle, *Rachmaninoff: A Biography* (London: William Reeves, 1938), p. 167.

38 Quoted in Rebecca Mitchell, *Sergei Rachmaninoff* (London: Reaktion Books, 2022), p. 154.

39 Lyle, *Rachmaninoff: A Biography*, p. 173.

Rewind: Life before Exile

1 *Rachmaninoff* (Boxed 140th Anniversary Album of Ivanovka and surroundings), p. 19. The notes for this book (which is mostly in Russian) credit the Glinka Museum of Musical Culture, the Library of Congress, the Russian State Library and the Russian State University for the Humanities as sources for texts.

2 *The Times*, 27 May 1928.

3 Oskar von Riesemann, *Rachmaninoff's Recollections, told to Oskar von Riesemann* (New York: Macmillan, 1934), p. 25.

4 Z. A. Apetian (ed.), *Vospominaniia o Rakhmaninove*, 2 vols, 5th edition (Moscow: Muzyka, 1988), Vol. 1, pp. 17–18.

5 Dictated memoirs from 1931, quoted in Sergei Bertensson and Jay Leyda, *Sergei Rachmaninoff: A Lifetime in Music* (New York: New York University Press, 1956; revised edition, Bloomington and Indianapolis, IN: Indiana University Press, 2001), p. 25.

6 *Rachmaninoff: A Biography*, Victor I. Seroff (London: Cassell, 1951) pp. 57–66.

1918–1930: America, the Glory Years

1 https://www.loc.gov/item/today-in-history/november-11/

2 *New York Times*, Wednesday 13 November 1918.

3 Sergei Prokofiev, translated and annotated by Anthony Phillips, *Diaries 1915–1923: Behind the Mask* (London: Faber, 2008), p. 341 (entry for 20 September 1918).

4 *The Delineator* 75 (1910), p. 127. See Philip Ross Bullock in Philip Ross Bullock (ed.), *Rachmaninoff and His World* (Chicago, IL: University of Chicago Press, 2022), pp. 187–90, for full article.

5 *Philadelphia Inquirer*, 22 December 1918.

6 *Boston Herald*, 16 December 1918.

7 *Boston Evening Transcript*, 16 December 1918.

8 Abram Chasins, *Speaking of Pianists* (New York: Alfred A. Knopf, 1957), p. 25.

9 Barrie Martyn, *Rachmaninoff: Composer, Pianist, Conductor* (London: Routledge, 1990), p. 379. Martyn cites it as an obituary written by Josef Hofmann and signed Los Angeles, 16 May 1945.

10 *New York Times*, 22 December 1918.

11 Sergei Prokofiev, translated and annotated by Anthony Phillips, *Diaries 1924–1933: Prodigal Son* (London: Faber, 2012), p. 366.

12 Prokofiev, *Diaries 1915–1923: Behind the Mask*, p. 384.

13 Paul Rosenfeld, *Musical Portraits: Interpretations of Twenty Modern Composers* (1920), available online via: https://www.gutenberg.org/ebooks/19557

14 Virgil Thomson, *Music Chronicles 1950–54* (New York: Library of America, 2014), p. 477. The entry, from 31 January 1945, reads: 'Even through the mud and sugar of Rachmaninoff's Second Symphony, it was clear in Carnegie Hall last night that Karl Krueger is a virtuoso conductor and the Detroit Symphony Orchestra is one of our top professional outfits.'

15 Jerome Davis, *The Russian Immigrant* (New York: The Macmillan Company, 1922), p. 178.

16 Brian Holder, 'The Bolshevik Revolution and Tin Pan Alley', PhD thesis, University of Florida.

17 *Kharkiv News*, 1931, quoted in Holder, 'The Bolshevik Revolution and Tin Pan Alley', p. 96. See also Oskar von Riesemann,

Rachmaninoff's Recollections, told to Oskar von Riesemann (New York: Macmillan, 1934), p. 204.

18 Rachmaninoff to Dagmar Rybner, letter, 15 June 1919, the Rachmaninoff Archive, Library of Congress, Washington.

19 All quoted without reference in *Rachmaninoff* (Boxed 140th Anniversary Album of Ivanovka and surroundings), p. 100.

20 Riesemann, *Rachmaninoff's Recollections*, p. 155.

21 All letters and telegrams to Ibbs and Tillett (written in English) are from Christopher Fifield, *Ibbs and Tillett: The Rise and Fall of A Musical Empire* (Farnham: Ashgate, 2005) Appendix 14, pp. 539–40.

22 Theodore Dreiser, *A Traveler at Forty* (1913), Chapter II: Miss X, Project Gutenberg e-book: https://www.gutenberg.org/ebooks/65765

23 11 February 1937. New translation by Anthony Phillips.

24 Virginia Woolf, *Orlando* (first published 1928, this edition London: Vintage, 2016), p. 35.

25 Somerset Maugham, *Ashenden: or The British Agent* (first published 1928), Preface (both quotes). See Project Gutenberg: https://gutenberg.ca/ebooks/maughamws-ashenden/maughamws-ashenden-00-h.html

26 All information about the film comes from the AFI Catalog: https://catalog.afi.com/Catalog/MovieDetails/13047.

27 *New York Times*, 10 June 1923.

28 This and the previous quotation: *New York Times*, 10 June 1923.

29 *New York Times*, 10 June 1923.

30 Marina Raku, '"The Case of Rachmaninoff": The Music of a White Emigré in the USSR', translated by Jonathan Walker, in Bullock (ed.), *Rachmaninoff and His World*, p. 274.

31 Max Harrison, *Rachmaninoff: Life, Work, Recordings* (London and New York: Continuum, 2005).

32 Harrison, *Rachmaninoff: Life, Work, Recordings*, p. 227.

33 Quoted in the article 'A century ago America saved millions of Russians from starvation'. *The Economist*, 11 November 2019.

34 *New York Times*, 3 April 1922.

35 *New York Times*, 4 January 1922.

36 Rachmaninoff, letter to Nikolai Avierino, 1 November 1920, quoted in Sergei Bertensson and Jay Leyda, *Sergei Rachmaninoff:*

A Lifetime in Music (New York: New York University Press, 1956; revised edition, Bloomington and Indianapolis, IN: Indiana University Press, 2001), p. 222.

37 Marietta Shaginian, 'Rachmaninoff, Pisma k Re', *Novyi Mir* (Moscow), 1943, No. 4.

38 Sophia Satin, *A 20th Century Life: The Memoirs of Sophia Satin* (London: The Rachmaninoff Society, 1997), p. 12.

39 See Harrison, *Rachmaninoff: Life, Work, Recordings*, pp. 221–3 for full discussion of recordings.

40 Interview, *Etude* Magazine, October 1919.

41 Prokofiev, *Diaries 1915–1923: Behind the Mask*, p. 519.

42 'Siloti, pupil of Liszt', *New York Tribune*, 16 October 1921.

43 From an interview with Kyriena Siloti by Charles Barber, quoted in Charles Barber, *Lost in the Stars: The Forgotten Musical Life of Alexander Siloti* (Lanham, MD: Scarecrow Press, 2002), p. 111.

44 Igor Stravinsky and Robert Craft, *Expositions and Developments* (Berkeley and Los Angeles: University of California Press, 1962), pp. 94–5.

45 Prokofiev, *Diaries 1915–1923: Behind the Mask*, pp. 542–3.

46 Simon Morrison, *The Love & Wars of Lina Prokofiev* (New York: Vintage, 2014), p. 57. Koshetz is mentioned in Chapters 3, 5, 6 and 7 of this book.

47 Prokofiev, *Diaries 1915–1923: Behind the Mask*, pp. 543–4.

48 New translation by Anthony Phillips who notes: 'Apetian, in what appears to be a rare error, gives the year as 1921 and most unusually has no comments about this letter, except to state its whereabouts (Library of Congress, marked ML, 30, 55)'.

49 *New York Times*, 28 March 1921.

50 See Morrison, *The Love & Wars of Lina Prokofiev*, pp. 56–7.

51 *New York Times*, 15 February 1922.

52 Leonid Sabaneyev, *Modern Russian Composers* (London: Martin Lawrence, 1927), pp. 104–7.

53 From Sofia Satina's Reminiscences in Z. A. Apetian (ed.), *Vospominaniia o Rakhmaninove*, 2 vols, 5th edition (Moscow: Muzyka, 1988), Vol. 1, pp. 62–3.

54 Letter from Konstantin Balmont to Sergei Rachmaninoff, translation by Anthony Phillips.

55 Bertensson and Leyda, *Sergei Rachmaninoff: A Lifetime in Music*, p. 227.

56 Watson Lyle, *Rachmaninoff: A Biography* (London: William Reeves, 1938), p. 182.

57 Quoted on Struve Family website: https://www.struvefamily. org/?page_id=264

58 Bertensson and Leyda, *Sergei Rachmaninoff: A Lifetime in Music*, p. 233.

59 *New York Times*, 18 January 1969.

60 *Buffalo Times*, 26 April 1923.

61 *Musical Observer*, May 1927.

62 All Sikorsky quotes from: https://sikorskyarchives.com/ igor-sikorsky-sergei-rachmaninoff/

63 Olin Downes, the *New York Times*, 13 February 1924, quoted by Allan Kozinn in the *New York Times*, 17 January 2014.

64 John Culshaw, *Sergei Rachmaninov* (London: Dennis Dobson Ltd, 1949), p. 161.

65 Rachmaninoff letter to the Somovs, 12 May 1924; Medtner letter to Rachmaninoff, 28 May 1924.

66 Bertensson and Leyda, *Sergei Rachmaninoff: A Lifetime in Music*, p. 236.

67 *New Orleans Item*, 21 January 1925.

68 *New Orleans Item*, 21 January 1925.

69 Quoted in Barrie Martyn, *Rachmaninoff: Composer, Pianist, Conductor* (London: Routledge, 1990), p. 148.

70 Z. A. Apetian (ed.), *S. Rakhmaninov, Literaturnoe nasledie*, 3 vols (Moscow: Sovetskii kompozitor, 1978–80), Vol. 2, pp. 178–80 and 458–9.

71 Apetian (ed.), *S. Rakhmaninov, Literaturnoe nasledie*, Vol. 2, p. 180.

72 From Sofia Satina's Reminiscences in Apetian (ed.), *Vospominaniia o Rakhmaninove*, Vol. 1, p. 25.

73 David Butler Cannata, *Rachmaninoff and the Symphony* (Innsbruck and Vienna: Studien Verlag/Lucca: Libreria Musica, 1999), p. 22 note 20.

74 Letter to Dagmar Rybner (later Rybner-Barclay), The Rachmaninoff Archive, Library of Congress.

75 See Richard K. Lieberman, *Steinway & Sons* (New Haven and London: Yale University Press, 1995).

76   David Dubal, *The World of the Concert Pianist* (London: Victor Gollancz, 1985), p. 198 (from interview with Vladimir Horowitz).

77   https://www.openculture.com/2012/11/sergei_rachmaninoff_home_movies_.html

78   Translation by Anthony Phillips.

79   *Coronado Eagle and Journal*, 18 January 1940.

80   Bertensson and Leyda, *Sergei Rachmaninoff: A Lifetime in Music*, p. 253.

81   *The Madisonian*, 31 October 1941.

82   https://youtu.be/99HNCfVx4xA

83   Described as 'The Russian "Mata Hari" presents a rare signed portrait to Rachmaninoff', this photo came up for sale with RR Auction, Boston, Mass., Lot #170, in January 2022, and sold for $4,886.

84   Vladimir Nabokov, *Collected Stories* (Penguin Modern Classics, Kindle Edition), p. 846.

85   *The Evening World*, Philadelphia, 23 March 1927.

86   Pitts Sanborn in the *New York Evening Telegram*, 23 March 1927.

87   Stephen Hough, *Rough Ideas* (London: Faber, 2019), p. 193.

88   Rachmaninoff, in a letter to Somov, 29 September 1929.

89   'Beyond my expectations, this barn's acoustics turned out to be very good': Rachmaninoff in a letter to the Somovs, November 1929.

90   Le Corbusier, translated by John Goodman, *Towards an Architecture* (Los Angeles, CA: Getty Research Institute, 2007), p. 158.

91   Bertensson and Leyda, *Sergei Rachmaninoff: A Lifetime in Music*, p. 261.

92   All quotes from Prokofiev on pp. 134–5 from Prokofiev, *Diaries 1924–1933: Prodigal Son*, pp. 893–4 (entries for 24–31 December 1929).

93   Nicolas Nabokov, *Old Friends and New Music* (Boston, MA: Little, Brown and Company, 1951), pp. 146–7.

94   *La Nation Belge*, 6 May 1933.

95   For full discussion see Susan Jeanne Woodward, 'The Dies Irae as used by Sergei Rachmaninoff', DMA thesis, Ohio State University, 1984.

96 *Etude* (Vol. 28 no. 3), pp. 153–4.

97 René Leibowitz, from his pamphlet *Sibelius, le plus mauvais compositeur du monde* (Liège: Éditions Dynamo, 1955). Leibowitz's students included Pierre Boulez.

98 Quoted in 'Jean Sibelius' by James Hepokoski in Stanley Sadie (ed.), *The New Grove Dictionary of Music and Musicians*, second edition, 29 vols (London: Macmillan, 2001), Vol. 23, p. 339.

99 Foreword to Victor I. Seroff, *Rachmaninoff: A Biography* (New York: Simon & Schuster, 1950), pp. xi–xiv.

100 John Cage, 'History of Experimental Music in the United States' (1959), reprinted in *Silence: Lectures and Writings* (Middletown, CT: Wesleyan University Press, 1961), pp. 65–7.

101 Joel Sachs, *Henry Cowell: A Man Made of Music* (New York: Oxford University Press, 2015), p. 87.

102 Henry Cowell interviewed by Beate Gordon in 1962 for the Columbia Oral History Project, quoted by Sachs, *Henry Cowell: A Man Made of Music*, p. 87.

103 Sachs, *Henry Cowell: A Man Made of Music*, p. 87.

104 Sachs, *Henry Cowell: A Man Made of Music*, p. 329.

105 Harpo Marx with Rowland Barber, *Harpo Speaks!* (London: Victor Gollancz, 1961), pp. 284–5.

106 Herman Finck, *My Melodious Memoirs* (first published 1937; facsimile edition Binsted: Noverre Press, 2012), p. 182.

107 Abram Chasins, sleeve notes to *The Four Rachmaninoff Concertos and Rhapsody on a Theme of Paganini*, RCA Victor LM–6123.

1930–1939: France, Switzerland, Second Exile

1 Oskar von Riesemann, *Rachmaninoff's Recollections, told to Oskar von Riesemann* (New York: Macmillan, 1934), Preface.

2 Sergei Bertensson and Jay Leyda, *Sergei Rachmaninoff: A Lifetime in Music* (New York: New York University Press, 1956; revised edition, Bloomington and Indianapolis, IN: Indiana University Press, 2001), p. 267.

3 A. J. [Alfred] and Katherine Swan, 'Rachmaninoff: Personal Reminiscences – Part II', *Musical Quarterly*, Vol. 30 no. 2 (April 1944), pp. 174–91.

4 Nathan Milstein and Solomon Volkov, *From Russia to the West: The Musical Memoirs and Reminiscences of Nathan Milstein*, trans. Antonina W. Bouis (London: Barrie & Jenkins, 1990), pp. 110–11.

5 Milstein and Volkov, *From Russia to the West*, pp. 110–11.

6 Sergei Prokofiev, translated and annotated by Anthony Phillips, *Diaries 1924–1933: Prodigal Son* (London: Faber, 2012), p. 650.

7 Heinz Horat, 'The Story of the Construction of Villa Senar', in *Villa Senar, Sergei Rachmaninoff's Dream of a House* (Weggis: Sergei Rachmaninoff Foundation, Villa Senar, 2016), p. 9. Heinz Horat kindly showed me round Senar in August 2021.

8 Heinz Horat, 'The Story of the Construction of Villa Senar', in *Villa Senar, Sergei Rachmaninoff's Dream of a House*, p. 9.

9 Nikolai Vygodsky, 'Heavenly "Idyll" or Fascism in Priestly Garb', in Marina Frolova-Walker and Jonathan Walker, *Music and Soviet Power, 1917–1932* (Woodbridge: The Boydell Press, 2017), pp. 298–301.

10 *Syracuse Herald*, 24 October 1931.

11 *Villa Senar, Sergei Rachmaninoff's Dream of a House*, p. 2.

12 Bertensson and Leyda, *Sergei Rachmaninoff: A Lifetime in Music*, p. 275.

13 Joseph Vissarionovich Stalin, *Problems of Leninism* (Moscow: Foreign Languages Publishing House, 1945), pp. 454–8.

14 Marilyn Monroe forged her own association with Rachmaninoff's music via Billy Wilder's film *The Seven Year Itch* (1955), which features Piano Concerto No 2. 'It makes me feel goose-pimply all over' her character gasps. The appropriation of Rachmaninoff's music in popular culture after his lifetime, outside the scope of this book, is a subject worthy of exploration.

15 Charles O'Connell, *The Other Side of the Record* (New York: Alfred A. Knopf, 1947), pp. 159–71.

16 Bertensson and Leyda, *Sergei Rachmaninoff: A Lifetime in Music*, p. 275.

17 A. J. and Katherine Swan, 'Rachmaninoff: Personal Reminiscences – Part I', *Musical Quarterly*, Vol. 30 no. 1 (January 1944), pp. 8–9.

18 *Tempo*, Vol. 58 no. 231 (Jan 2005), pp. 14–16.

19 Related to the author by the American cellist Fred Sherry.

20 Letter written to Cyril Bourne-Newton, musical director of the Brighton and Hove Musical Society, from unpublished

correspondence of thirty-seven autograph letters (1945–51) sold at Sotheby's, London, Musical Manuscripts Lot 12, 2006.

21 Sophia Satin, *A 20th Century Life: The Memoirs of Sophia Satin* (London: The Rachmaninoff Society, 1996), p. 34.

22 Robert Roper, *Nabokov in America: On the Road to Lolita* (New York: Bloomsbury, 2015), p. 25.

23 All Prokofiev quotes from Prokofiev, *Diaries 1924–1933: Prodigal Son*, pp. 745–6, 838, 890.

24 Victor I. Seroff, *Rachmaninoff: A Biography* (New York: Simon & Schuster, 1950), p. 57.

25 All translations by Anthony Phillips.

26 *Spokane Chronicle*, 17 November 1958.

27 Translation by Anthony Phillips.

28 Translation by Anthony Phillips.

29 Translation by Anthony Phillips.

30 Milstein and Volkov, *From Russia to the West*, p. 172.

31 O'Connell, *The Other Side of the Record*, p. 165.

32 *Brooklyn Times Union*, 28 December 1934.

33 Translation by Anthony Phillips.

34 Victor I. Seroff, *Rachmaninoff: A Biography* (London: Cassell, 1951), pp. 194–5.

35 Translation by Anthony Phillips.

36 *Morning Oregonian*, 23 January 1937.

37 Henry Wood, *About Conducting* (London: Sylvan Press, 1945), p. 75.

38 Translation by Anthony Phillips.

39 *Posledniye Novosti* (Paris), 17 April 1938, quoted in Bertensson and Leyda, *Sergei Rachmaninoff: A Lifetime in Music*, p. 341.

40 All letters and reminiscences pp. 193–7 in new translations by Anthony Phillips.

41 A. J. and Katherine Swan, 'Rachmaninoff: Personal Reminiscences – Part II', *Musical Quarterly*, Vol. 30 no. 2 (April 1944), pp. 189–90.

42 Satin, *A 20th Century Life: The Memoirs of Sophia Satin*, p. 38.

43 *New York Times*, 2 October 1938.

44 Satin, *A 20th Century Life: The Memoirs of Sophia Satin*, p. 37.

45 I am grateful to Michael Gray, Honorary Archivist of the Savage Club, who gave me access to this letter, which is still held by the Club.

NOTES

46 *Glasgow Herald*, 20 February 1939.

47 This radio interview pre-dates the existence of BBC Sounds with its powerful search engine. I found it by chance and transcribed the relevant passage. When I later tried to locate it again, it proved impossible to find. If anyone can supply details of its whereabouts I would be grateful.

48 Letter to Somov from Paris, 2 April 1949.

49 Bertensson and Leyda, *Sergei Rachmaninoff: A Lifetime in Music*, p. 349.

50 Bertensson and Leyda, *Sergei Rachmaninoff: A Lifetime in Music*, p. 351.

51 Satin, *A 20th Century Life: The Memoirs of Sophia Satin*, p. 39.

52 See Warren Brodsky: 'Joseph Schillinger (1895–1943): Music Science Promethean', *American Music*, Vol. 21 no. 1 (2003), pp. 45–73. https://www.jstor.org/stable/3250556

53 Prokofiev, *Diaries 1924–1933: Prodigal Son*, p. 517.

54 See Albert Glinsky, *Theremin: Ether Music and Espionage* (Champaign, IL: University of Illinois Press, 2000).

55 F. Scott Fitzgerald, *The Great Gatsby*, edited with notes by Philip McGowan (first published 1925; this edition published London: Penguin Books, 2021), p. 27.

56 From President Franklin D. Roosevelt's opening day speech at the Court of Peace in New York City's Flushing Meadows on 30 April 1939. See David Gelernter, *1939: The Lost World of the Fair* (New York: Avon Books, 1995), p. 348.

57 Anthony Swift, 'The Soviet World of Tomorrow at the New York World's Fair, 1939', *The Russian Review*, Vol. 57 no. 3 (1998), pp. 364–79. https://www.jstor.org/stable/131952

58 Finland's exhibit, in the Hall of Nations, was designed by celebrated architects Alvar Aalto and Aino Maria Marsio-Aalto as a 'Symphony of Wood', accompanied by Sibelius's music. See Stanley Appelbaum (ed.), *The New York World's Fair 1939/1940 in 155 Photographs by Richard Wurts and Others* (New York: Dover Publications, 2013), p. 117.

59 From an interview late in Kostelanetz's life, *New York Times*, 6 May 1973.

60 Riesemann, *Rachmaninoff's Recollections*, p. 49.

61 Richard K. Lieberman, *Steinway & Sons* (New Haven and London: Yale University Press, 1995), p. 202.

62 Vladimir Nabokov, *Collected Stories* (Penguin Modern Classics, Kindle Edition), pp. 854–5.

63 Arthur Jacobs, *Henry J. Wood, Maker of the Proms* (London: Methuen, 1994), pp. 314–15.

64 Virginia Woolf, *A Room of One's Own* (first published by the Hogarth Press in 1929; ebook edition published by Global Grey, 2021), p. 32.

65 Quoted by Philip Podolsky in 'Communism's poster boy? The truth about Emil Gilels and Stalin', *Guardian*, 19 October 2016.

66 *Time*, 18 December 1964.

67 Harold C. Schonberg, *The Great Pianists: from Mozart to the Present Day* (New York: Simon & Schuster,1963), p. 425.

68 O'Connell, *The Other Side of the Record*, p. 166.

69 Barrie Martyn, *Rachmaninoff: Composer, Pianist, Conductor* (London: Routledge, 1990), p. 397.

70 *Guardian*, 25 November 1929.

71 Martyn, *Rachmaninoff: Composer, Pianist, Conductor*, p. 287.

1939–1943: Gathering In

1 Transcript and audio available online from Miller Center, Fireside Chat No. 14: https://millercenter.org/the-presidency/presidential-speeches/september-3-1939-fireside-chat-14-european-war

2 See Anne Key Simpson, *Follow Me: The Life and Music of R. Nathaniel Dett* – Composers of North America Vol. 10 (Metuchen, NJ: Scarecrow Press, 1993).

3 The three quotes describing the visit of the Ukrainian Chorus come, respectively, from *The Morning Call*, Pennsylvania, 9 March 1923; *Pittsburgh Daily Post*, 30 November 1923; *The Stockton Independent*, California, 5 December 1926. The Ukrainian Chorus made several visits to the US during the 1920s.

4 *The Broad Ax*, Salt Lake City, 4 November 1922.

5 Victor I. Seroff, *Rachmaninoff: A Biography* (London: Cassell, 1951), p. 204.

6 See Christopher H. Gibbs, '"One of the Outstanding Musical Events of All Time": The Philadelphia Orchestra's 1939 Rachmaninoff Cycle', in Philip Ross Bullock (ed.), *Rachmaninoff and His World* (Chicago, IL: University of Chicago Press, 2022), pp. 236–69, for an in-depth discussion of the festival, its background and reception.

7 Pitts Sanborn in the *New York Evening Telegram*, 23 March 1927.

8 Translation by Anthony Phillips.

9 *Oakland Tribune*, 7 January 1940.

10 Sergei Bertensson and Jay Leyda, *Sergei Rachmaninoff: A Lifetime in Music* (New York: New York University Press, 1956; revised edition, Bloomington and Indianapolis, IN: Indiana University Press, 2001), pp. 358–9.

11 Bertensson and Leyda, *Sergei Rachmaninoff: A Lifetime in Music*, p. 357.

12 *New York Times*, 16 September 2011.

13 Reported in *Syracuse Herald*, 21 September 1941.

14 Sergei Rachmaninoff Foundation, Lucerne, Switzerland: https://www.rachmaninoff.org/articles/archive/184-excerpt-from-a-post-card-to-tatiana-conus-rachmaninoff

15 Z. A. Apetian (ed.), *S. Rakhmaninov, Literaturnoe nasledie*, 3 vols (Moscow: Sovetskii kompozitor, 1978–80), Vol. 3, p. 180.

16 Barrie Martyn, *Rachmaninoff: Composer, Pianist, Conductor* (London: Routledge, 1990), pp. 347–8.

17 Apetian (ed.), *S. Rakhmaninov, Literaturnoe nasledie*, Vol. 3, pp. 182–3 and 356; translations by Anthony Phillips.

18 Quoted by Wolfgang Saxon in the *New York Times*, 19 August 1981, in an article reporting Bennett's death, aged 87.

19 Rachmaninoff Archive, Music Division, LOC, ML 30.55., Section B2, Correspondence to SR, A–, File —Bennett, Robert Russell. After Rachmaninoff's death, Bennett made a two-piano arrangement of the Piano Concerto no. 4.

20 See Richard Taruskin, liner notes to *Rachmaninoff Plays Symphonic Dances* (Marston Records, 53022-2).

21 Quoted in Bertensson and Leyda, *Sergei Rachmaninoff: A Lifetime in Music*, p. 363.

22 Letter from M. K. Gandhi to Adolf Hitler, 24 December 1940, quoted in full in *Time* magazine, 25 September 2019.

23 *New York Times*, 8 January 1941.

24 As told by William R. Trotter in *Priest of Music: The Life of Dimitri Mitropoulos* (Portland, OR: Amadeus, 1995), p. 156, pp. 197–8.

25 Trotter, *Priest of Music: The Life of Dimitri Mitropoulos*, pp. 197–8.

26 *Musical Courier*, 5 April 1943.

27 Quoted in Catherine Dale, *Schoenberg's Chamber Symphonies: The Crystallization and Rediscovery of a Style* (Abingdon: Routledge Revival, 2021; first published 2000), p. 159.

28 John Greening, 'Fragments of Life's Song' (review of Daniel M. Grimley's *Jean Sibelius, Life, Music, Silence*), *Times Literary Supplement*, 18 March 2022.

29 Oskar von Riesemann, *Rachmaninoff's Recollections, told to Oskar von Riesemann* (New York: Macmillan, 1934), p. 99.

30 *Etude*, no. 59 (December 1941).

31 Mikhail Bobrov, in *Witness: Camouflaging Leningrad in World War Two*, broadcast on BBC Radio 4, 8 February 2018, accessed by the author via BBC Sounds.

32 Solomon Volkov, trans. Antonina W. Bouis, *Shostakovich and Stalin: the Extraordinary Relationship Between the Great Composer and the Brutal Dictator* (New York: Alfred A. Knopf, 2004), p. 217. This anecdote has also been attributed to Stravinsky. According to the Shostakovich scholar, Gerard McBurney, 'If Sergei Vassilievich did respond in this way – and with his characteristic courtesy of not reacting negatively to music that he can't possibly have liked – then he would most likely have said the standard Russian remark on all occasions: Давайте, попем чай! – literally, 'Come on, let's drink tea!' – as said by millions of Russians every day as the evening draws nigh.'

33 See 'Madame Comrade' by Brigid O'Keefe, Aeon: https://aeon.co/essays/the-peoples-ambassadress-the-forgotten-diplomacy-of-ivy-litvinov

34 Seroff, *Rachmaninoff: A Biography*, p. 201.

35 See discussion in Marina Raku, '"The Case of Rachmaninoff": The Music of a White Emigré in the USSR', translated by Jonathan Walker, in Bullock (ed.), *Rachmaninoff and His World*, p. 273.

36 Bertensson and Leyda, *Sergei Rachmaninoff: A Lifetime in Music*, p. 372.

37 Apetian (ed.), *S. Rakhmaninov, Literaturnoe nasledie*, Vol. 3, pp. 207–8.

38 Robert Craft (ed. and commentary), *Stravinsky: Selected Correspondence*, Vol. 1 (London: Faber, 1982), pp. 10–11.

39 *St Louis Star-Times*, 15 November 1937.

40 Charles Barber, *Lost in the Stars: The Forgotten Musical Life of Alexander Siloti* (Lanham, MD: Scarecrow Press, 2002), p. 123.

41 Igor Stravinsky and Robert Craft, *Memories and Commentaries* (Berkeley and Los Angeles: University of California Press, 1960), pp. 41–2.

42 Quoted in Richard Taruskin, *Stravinsky and the Russian Traditions*, 2 vols (Oxford: Oxford University Press, 1996), Vol. 2, p. 1128. The quote comes from Romain Rolland, *Journal des années de guerre, 1914–1919* (Paris: Éditions Albin Michel, 1952), p. 59.

43 Quoted in Tamara Levitz (ed.), *Stravinsky and His World* (Princeton, NJ: Princeton University Press, 2013), p. 43. The quote comes from Jean Cocteau, 'The Latest Stravinsky', *La Revue Musicale*, Paris, 1 December 1923.

44 Robert Craft, *Stravinsky: Discoveries and Memories* (Potters Bar: Naxos Books, 2013), p. 179.

45 Bertensson and Leyda, *Sergei Rachmaninoff: A Lifetime in Music*, p. 374.

46 Igor Stravinsky and Robert Craft, *Conversations with Igor Stravinsky* (London: Faber, 1959), p. 41. For further discussion on this subject see: 'Rachmaninoff and Stravinsky in Los Angeles to 1943' by Keenan Reesor: https://www.academia.edu/16092712/Rachmaninoff_and_Stravinsky_in_Los_Angeles_to_1943

47 Translation by Anthony Phillips.

48 Charles Chaplin, *My Autobiography* (London: Penguin Books, 2003), quoted by Ariane Todes in a programme note for the pianist Gabriela Montero: https://www.elbowmusic.org/post/chaplin-s-the-immigrant.

49 Craft, *Stravinsky: Discoveries and Memories*, p. 191.

50 Arthur Rubinstein, *My Many Years* (New York: Alfred A. Knopf, 1980), pp. 489–90.

51 Z. A. Apetian, *Vospominaniia o Rakhmaninove*, 2 vols, 5th edition (Moscow: Muzyka, 1988), Vol. 2, p. 320. Translation by Anthony Phillips.

52 Sergei Prokofiev, translated and annotated by Anthony Phillips, *Diaries 1924–1933: Prodigal Son* (London: Faber, 2012), entry for 23 March 1926, p. 279.

53 Stravinsky and Craft, *Memories and Commentaries*, pp. 230–1.

54 Peter Franklin, 'Reading the Popular Pessimist: Thought, Feeling, and Dance in Rachmaninoff's Symphonic Narrative', in Bullock (ed.), *Rachmaninoff and His World*, p. 18.

55 Interview with Jessica Duchen, *Guardian*, Friday 30 April 1999.

56 Obituary of Marina Koshetz, *Los Angeles Times*, 9 January 2001.

57 E-mail to the author via Elger Niels.

58 Letter dated 21 January 1943, New York, reproduced in Apetian (ed.), *S. Rakhmaninov, Literaturnoe nasledie*, Vol. 3, p. 224.

59 Letter dated 28 January 1943, New York, reproduced in Apetian (ed.), *S. Rakhmaninov, Literaturnoe nasledie*, Vol. 3, p. 226.

60 *Capital Times*, 20 December 1942.

61 Apetian (ed.), *S. Rakhmaninov, Literaturnoe nasledie*, Vol. 3, pp. 226–7. New translation by Anthony Phillips.

62 *Daily Collegian*, Penn University, 6 February 1943.

63 *Raleigh Register*, Beckley, Raleigh County, West Virginia, 5 August 1943.

64 All quotes here from Bertensson and Leyda, *Sergei Rachmaninoff: A Lifetime in Music*, pp. 379–80.

65 Details from https://classicaljournal.wordpress.com/2010/08/17/rachmaninoffs-last-performance/

66 Barrie Martyn has made this calculation. See Martyn, *Rachmaninoff: Composer, Pianist, Conductor*, various references throughout the book.

67 Apetian (ed.), *S. Rakhmaninov, Literaturnoe nasledie*, Vol. 3, p. 228.

68 Apetian (ed.), *S. Rakhmaninov, Literaturnoe nasledie*, Vol. 3, pp. 229–30. translation by Bertensson and Leyda, in *Sergei Rachmaninoff: A Lifetime in Music*, p. 381.

69 A. J. and Katherine Swan, 'Rachmaninoff: Personal Reminiscences – Part I', *Musical Quarterly*, Vol. 30 no. 1 (January 1944), p. 3.

70 Apetian (ed.), *S. Rakhmaninov, Literaturnoe nasledie*, Vol. 3, p. 393.

Last Rites

1 *New York Times*, 6 September 2015.
2 Arthur Jacobs, Henry J. Wood, *Maker of the Proms* (London: Methuen, 1994), p. 373.

Image Credits

Illustrations in the Text

1. 1915–1918: Revolution, Departure, Arrival. Album / Alamy Stock Photo
35. Rewind: Life Before Exile. The Tully Potter Collection
49. 1918–1930: America, the Glory Years. GRANGER – Historical Picture Archive / Alamy Stock Photo
145. 1930–1939: France, Switzerland, Second Exile. The Tully Potter Collection
221. 1939–1945: Gathering In. Swiss Tourist Board
285. Last Rites. Eric Schaal/The LIFE Picture Collection/ Shutterstock
303. Wild Strawberries: Remembering Ivanovka. The Tully Potter Collection

Illustrations in the Plates

Page one (top left). Rachmaninoff, aged ten. The Tully Potter Collection

Page one (top right). Rachmaninoff, aged twenty-six, with his dog Levko. Pictured on the Khopyor river, 1899. Matteo Omied / Alamy Stock Photo

Page one (bottom). Rachmaninoff with the Skalon sisters at the Ignatov estate, 1897. Lebrecht Music & Arts / Alamy Stock Photo

Page two (top left). Natalia Satina Rachmaninoff, c.1900.
Lebrecht Music Arts / Bridgeman Images

Page two (top right). First cousins – Rachmaninoff with his wife
Natalia, sister-in-law Sofia Satina and brother-in-law Vladimir
Satin, 1899. Lebrecht Music & Arts / Alamy Stock Photo

Page two (bottom). Rachmaninoff and Natalia, London, 1932.
Sueddeutsche Zeitung Photo / Alamy Stock Photo

Page three (top left). Marietta Shaginian, c. 1920s. The Tully
Potter Collection

Page three (top right). Nina Koshetz, 1916. Richard Bebb
Collection / Bridgeman Images

Page three (bottom). Rachmaninoff and Nina Koshetz, summer
1916. The Tully Potter Collection

Page four (top). Rachmaninoff's daughter Irina, with her husband
Prince Volkonsky, c. 1924. The Tully Potter Collection

Page four (bottom). Rachmaninoff with his granddaughter, Sophie
Volkonsky, in New York, 1927. AP/Shutterstock

Page five (top). Sergei Prokofiev at his desk in New York, 1918.
The Tully Potter Collection

Page five (bottom). Rachmaninoff at his desk in Villa Senar,
Lucerne, Switzerland, early 1930s. The Tully Potter
Collection

Page six (top). Rachmmaninoff and latest automobile. Switzerland,
early 1930s. The Tully Potter Collection

Page six (bottom). (left to right) Baron Solovieff, Sergei
Rachmaninoff and Igor Sikorsky in front of the S-29-A
aircraft, Roosevelt Field, Long Island, NY, in 1924. Igor I.
Sikorsky Historical Archives

Page seven (top). 11 January 1925, Steinway Hall, 109 East
14th Street, New York City: [left to right] Igor Stravinsky,
Nikolai Medtner, Wilhelm Furtwängler, George Engles,

Alexander Siloti, Frederick Steinway, Fritz Kreisler, Sergei Rachmaninoff, Josef Hofmann, Pierre Monteux. Lebrecht Music Arts / Bridgeman Images

Page seven (bottom). Rachmaninoff in rehearsal with Eugene Ormandy at the Academy of Music, Philadelphia, 1939. Lebrecht Music Arts / Bridgeman Images

Page eight (top). Rachmaninoff with his grandchildren, Alexander Conus and Sophie Volkonsky, in 1936. Bettmann Archives/ Getty Images

Page eight (bottom). The extended family at Villa Senar, c. 1936. Rachmaninoff's wife Natalia is on the extreme left. The Tully Potter Collection

Index

Page numbers followed by (fn) indicate footnotes on the same page.
SR = Sergei Rachmaninoff.

Agate, James 131
Aldrich, Richard 90–1
Amis, John 203–4
Ampico recordings 78
Anderson, Marian 217, 240–1
Anschluss 187, 207
Ansermet, Ernest 207
Apetian, Z. A. 113
Armistice Day 51
Ashkenazy, Vladimir 129, 268
Avierino, Nikolai 80–1

Bach, Johann Sebastian: E major Partita
    (trans. SR) 151–2; performed by SR
    123, 201, 202, 277
Bakaleinikoff, Vladimir 257
Balmont, Konstantin xiii, 93–4
Barbirolli, John 212, 275
Barsukov, Sergei 100
Bax, Arnold 164
Beecham, Thomas 190
Beethoven, Ludwig van: 'cancelled' in
    America 118; performed at New York
    World Fair 214; performed by SR
    61, 91, 123, 125, 149, 176, 182, 190,
    202, 205, 207, 226, 275; practised by
    SR 149; recorded by SR and Kreisler
    162–3
    works: piano concertos 182, 190, 207,
        226, 275; piano sonatas 61, 125, 149,
        176, 202; symphonies 214; violin
        sonatas 163
Bennett, Robert Russell 238–40
Berlin, Irving 64, 104, 224, 281
Bertensson, Sergei 257, 262
Black American music 212, 224, 225–6,
    240
Black Sea resort 29–30
Blom, Eric xx

boating (SR's interest in) 197, 233
Bobrov, Mikhail 253
Böcklin, Arnold 19
Bolet, Jorge 219–20
Borisovo estate 40
Bosset, Vera de 258, 261, 264
Boston Symphony Hall: SR performs at
    58–9, 95
Boston Symphony Orchestra: Nikolai
    Avierino in 81; SR conducts 52;
    SR praises 144; SR refuses music
    director role 34, 53, 56; SR refuses to
    assist Nina Koshetz with 87, 88–90;
    Stravinsky dedicates music to 216; at
    World Fair 223
Brahms, Johannes: 'cancelled' in America
    118; performed by SR 149; recorded
    by Marian Anderson 240
Brodsky, Jascha 133, 135
Bunin, Ivan 4, 47
Butakova, Sofia Alexandrovna 39–41

Cannata, David Butler 114
Cannes 117
Cardus, Neville 176, 220
Carnegie Hall, New York: founding 214;
    other concerts 62, 208, 224, 225, 226,
    247; Rachmaninoff Cycle (1939) 227;
    SR performs at 59–61, 62–3, 66, 79–80,
    91, 103, 182, 251–2
Carnera, Primo 133
cars (SR's passion for) 67–72, 81, 143–4,
    177–8, 185, 196, 271
Casals, Pablo 84, 207
Chaliapin, Boris xiii; paints Sophie
    Volkonsky 234; paints SR 142, 234
Chaliapin, Fyodor xiii; autobiography 5;
    children 29; depiction in 'The Assistant
    Producer' 127; dress and appearance

4; exile from Russia 6; friendship with
SR 5, 12, 16, 29–30, 32, 46, 98–9, 107,
161, 191–2; friendships, other 4–5,
80, 140, 259; illness and death 191–2;
personality 4, 5, 16, 99, 140; recordings
29, 74, 98–9, 229; wedding 5
Chaliapin, Fyodor Jr. xiii, 275, 280, 295
Chaplin, Charlie 38, 197, 264, 281
Chasins, Abram 143–4
Chekhov, Anton 4, 19, 29–30, 38
Chekhov, Michael xiii, 160–1, 210, 233
child prodigies, SR's attitude towards 175
Chopin, Frédéric: enjoyed by wartime
workers 245; performed by SR 61,
91, 123, 125, 149, 167, 176, 201,
277; played in memorial to SR 301;
practised by SR 81, 141, 143; recorded
by SR 78, 277
    WORKS: études 143; nocturnes 61;
    piano sonatas 277, 301; polonaises
    61; waltzes 61, 78
cinema (SR's response to) 196–7
Cliburn, Van 119, 323
Coates, Albert 83, 84, 130, 157, 261
Cobb, George L. 65
Cocteau, Jean 260–1
concerts and tours (SR): air travel 177;
America (1909-1910) 37, 56, 136, 214;
America (1918-1925) 34, 58–61, 62–3,
66, 77, 79–80, 82, 91, 95, 114–15;
America (1927-1938) 120, 121, 122–4,
125, 127–9, 130, 155, 158–9, 162, 163,
181–2, 200–1, 317; America (1939-
1943) 226–8, 230–1, 236–7, 241,
251–2, 256–7, 263–4, 270–1, 272–4,
275, 276–7, 280; concert 'habits' 122,
124; Europe (1928-1939) 132, 134,
151, 154, 166–7, 187, 206–7, 258; final
concert 277, 287; ocean travel 131–5,
208; pianos played on tour 120, 121,
122, 125, 132, 273; rail travel 122,
123, 186; Russia (1915-1917) xxi,
10–11, 13, 19, 21–2, 29–30; Russia
(earlier) 37; Scandinavia (1918) 33–4;
total number of appearances 278;
UK (1899) 31, 37; UK (1910) 215;
UK (1922) 96; UK (1929-1939) 125,
130–1, 141–2, 164, 176–7, 182–3, 186,
187–91, 202–5
Conus, Boris 164–5, 208

Conus, Julius 151, 164
Conus, Olga 142
Conus-Rachmaninoff, Alexander (SR's
grandson) 47, 47–8(fn), 199, 208, 314,
315
Cooper, Emil 21
Copenhagen 33
Copland, Aaron 100, 249, 255
Corelli, Arcangelo: Violin Sonata in D
minor and SR's *Variations* 161–2, 318
Cowell, Henry 137–9, 210
Craft, Robert 261, 264
Crociata, Francis 270
Cui, César 45

Dahl, Nikolai 47, 48(fn), 193–5
Damrosch, Walter xiv, 213–14
'Dark Eyes' 98–9, 269
Davis, Jerome 64
Dawson, William Levi: *Negro Folk
Symphony* 226
A Day at the Races (film) 141
Debussy, Claude: *Children's Corner* 81,
176; conducted by SR 37; performed
by SR 125, 176; practised by SR 81
DeMille, Cecil B.: *The Volga Boatman*
(film) 74
Dett, R. Nathaniel 224, 225; 'Listen to
the Lambs' 225; *The Ordering of Moses*
225
Diaghilev, Sergei 4, 19, 133, 166, 259
Diamond, David 248–9
Disney, Walt 131, 201, 238, 242–3, 257,
282
Downes, Olin 55–7, 104–5, 238, 247
Dr Zhivago (film) 268
Dresden 81, 98, 107, 114
Dubensky, Arcady 213
Duke, Vernon (Vladimir Dukelsky)
99–100, 210, 224, 265
Dukes, Paul 83–4

Edison, Thomas 78
Éditions Russes de Musique 32, 259–60
electronic instruments and music 210,
212, 230
Elgar, Alice 9–10
Elgar, Edward: critical reception 55–6;
Dream of Gerontius 244; *Pomp and
Circumstance* 104

INDEX

Ellington, Duke 66
Ellis, Charles 66, 93
émigrés from Russia *see* exiles from Russia
espionage (Paul Dukes) 83–4
Europe, James Reese 65
Eustis, Marie 11
exiles from Russia: American response
  to (Red Scare) 64; European response
  to 81; in Hollywood movies 214, 269;
  at New York World Fair 211, 212–13;
  Russian communities in America 72–3,
  75–6; Russian communities in Europe
  103–4, 106; societal groups 5–6, 64,
  82–3; total number of exiles 6, 64; *see
  also* Russian culture, appropriation by
  Americans; *individual exiles*

famine in Russia (1921-2) 79
Fantasia (film) 242–3
Farrar, Geraldine 52, 66
Finck, Herman 141–2
Finland, Winter War with Soviet Union
  229–30
Firsova, Olga 252
First World War: anti-German backlash
  118; Armistice Day 51; impact on
  workforce 51–2; Spanish flu 53–5, 63
Fitzgerald, F. Scott: *The Great Gatsby* 211,
  232; *The Last Tycoon* 214
Fletcher, Stuart 187–9
Florence 106
Fokine, Mikhail 180, 206, 234, 260, 318
Foley, Charles 93, 115, 162, 181, 183–4,
  228, 295
Frankenstein (film) 197
Franklin, Peter 267

Gandhi, Mahatma 245, 279, 282
Garden of Allah Hotel, Sunset Boulevard
  140–1
Gauk, Alexander 46(fn)
Gershwin, George 100, 209, 223, 238,
  239; *Rhapsody in Blue* 105; SR praises
  105
Gilels, Emil 216–19
Glazunov, Alexander 4, 45, 166, 167–8,
  169–74
Goldenweiser, Alexander 76–7, 112
Golitzin, Alexander 281, 283, 291, 293,
  297, 299; report by 287–90

Golovanov, Nikolai 248
Goodman, Benny 209, 223, 277
Gorky, Maxim 5, 6, 30, 79, 108
Gorman, Ross 105
Goshen (SR's retreat) 81
Graffman, Gary 265
Greiner, Alexander 'Sasha' 119, 120, 135,
  234; SR's letters to 177, 178
Grofé, Ferde 105, 212

Haensel, Fitzhugh 87, 88–9
Hale, Philip 58
Hambourg, Mark 203
Hammerstein, Oscar 238
hands, pianists' 60, 119, 219–20; SR's
  hands 219–20, 290, 292
Harrison, Max 78, 129
health problems (SR): arthritis treatment
  185–6; Dahl's talisman 193–4;
  depression 11, 15–16, 42, 45, 97, 161;
  electrical treatments 95; fatigue/
  exhaustion 95, 122–3, 179, 182, 183,
  192, 202; final illness 265, 270, 278–84,
  287–99; general ailments 12, 106, 184,
  245; hand/wrist problems 12, 162, 169,
  185; hypnotherapy 46–7, 48(fn), 130;
  lumbago 263; neuralgia 97, 130–1,
  194–5, 275; receives 'pine-electrical
  baths' 184; Russian doctors and nurses
  275, 278, 280–1, 282, 290; Spanish flu
  54–5, 62
Hindemith, Paul 248
Hirst, Arthur 142; SR's letters to 227–8
Hitler, Adolf 200, 208, 229, 245; *see also*
  Nazism
Hodges, Eric 125
Hofmann, Josef: concert performances
  59, 212, 301; critical reception 59,
  61; friendship with SR 59, 60, 103,
  128; hands 219; inventions 60, 213;
  Steinway reception for 261
Hollywood movies, Russian exiles in 214,
  269
Holst, Gustav 157, 164; *The Planets* 157
homes and retreats (SR): Black Sea
  resort 29–30; Cannes 117; Catskills
  115; Copenhagen 33; Goshen 81;
  Honeyman Estate 232–5, 237–8, 251;
  Ivanovka estate *see* Ivanovka estate;
  Locust Point 92–3, 98–9; Menlo Park

138; Moscow 19; New York 91, 96, 115–17; North Elm Drive, Beverly Hills 256, 281, 291, 295; Novgorod estate 40, 41, 130; Palo Alto 67; Le Pavillon 147–9; Senar *see* Senar (SR's villa); Sunset Boulevard 140–1; Tower Lane, Beverly Hills 256, 257; Villers-sur-Mers 142; Yessentuki (spa resort) 12, 15, 24
Honeyman Estate, Orchard Point 232–5, 237–8, 251
Honeyman, Marian Stewart 232–3
honeypot, SR delivers to Stravinsky 262
Hoover, Herbert 79, 103
Horowitz, Vladimir: as child prodigy 175; concert performances 17, 207, 263, 276; critical reception 190; friendship with SR 180, 187, 234, 238, 257, 264, 295; marriage 198; meets SR 119; parodies other pianists 152; records SR 234; SR praises 119; other mentions 208, 210
Hotel Montana, Lucerne 153, 154
Hough, Stephen 129
Howard, Leslie 129
Huneker, James Gibbons 60–1
Hupfer, William 120–2, 124
hypnotherapy, SR receives 46–7, 48(fn), 130

Ibbs, Robert Leigh 68–70, 187, 196, 197, 204
Igumnov, Konstantin 20, 76–7
Ipatieff, Vladimir Nikolayevich 279
Ivanova, Maria xvii, 8
Ivanovka estate 7, 22, 23–4, 44–5, 300, 305–9

jazz 65–6, 100, 104–5, 107–8, 208–9, 223

Kislovodsk 16, 25–6, 27
Knipper-Chekhova, Olga 33
Korotneva, Nadezhda 108–9
Koshetz, Alexander 225
Koshetz, Nina Pavlovna xiv; critical reception 90–1, 268–9; donates to church 299; musical training 77; performing career 17, 18, 25, 27, 86–7, 87–91, 100, 210, 225, 268–9; relationship with Sergei Prokofiev 25–6, 85–8, 91;

relationship with SR 13, 16–18, 21, 25, 26, 27, 87, 88–90, 269–70
Kosloff, Theodore 74
Kostelanetz, André 212
Koussevitzky Music Foundation 255
Koussevitzky, Sergei Alexandrovich (Serge) xiv, 21, 163, 223, 231, 254–5, 259–60
Kreisler, Fritz xiv; *Liebesfreud* 134; performed by SR 134; recordings 74, 162–3; SR dedicates work to 162; other mentions 66, 104, 119, 168, 184, 239, 261
Krupskaya, Nadezhda 3
Kshesinskaya, Mathilde 4, 6

Leibowitz, René 137
Lenin Prize 28
Lenin, Vladimir Ilyich 3, 79, 84, 210
Leningrad: Lenin returns to 3–4; name changes xvii, 3; Second World War 251, 252–3
Leningrad Conservatory 158, 166, 251
Leningrad Philharmonic Orchestra 253
letters from SR: to Alexander Glazunov 167; to Alexander Greiner 177, 178; to Alexander Siloti 24–5; to Alfred Swan 148; to Arthur Hirst 227–8; to Dagmar Rybner 117; to Eugene Ormandy 237; to Henry Wood 215; to Marietta Shaginian 28–9; to Mr Tillett 70; to Nadezhda Korotneva 108–9; to *New York Times* 156; to Nikolai Avierino 80; to Nikolai Mandrovsky 257, 263; to Nikolai Rashevsky 278–9; to Nina Koshetz 17, 18, 88–90; to Paul Schmidt 271–2; protest letter about Winter War 229–30; to Robert Ibbs 68–70; to Savage Club friends 204–5; to Sofia Satina 109–11, 177, 183–4, 191–2, 262–3; to Victor Seroff 279; to Vladimir Nabokov 195; to Vladimir Vilshau 77, 95, 107, 122–3; to Yakov Weinberg 235–6; to Yevgeny Somov 70–2, 155, 159, 177–8, 179, 183, 185, 195–6, 200, 206–7, 270, 280–1
Library of Congress, Rachmaninoff archive xvii–xviii, 80, 185, 269–70
Liedloff, Helen 220
List, Eugene 275–6

INDEX

Liszt, Franz: accompanies Wagner 155; performed by SR 21–2, 30, 91, 123, 125, 149, 176, 201, 226; practised by SR 81, 142; recorded by SR 78; teaching 41, 85
  WORKS: Hungarian Rhapsody no. 2 77, 78, 96, 131; in *Mickey Mouse* film 131; *Petrarch Sonnet 123* 176; Piano Concerto no. 1 21–2, 30; *Tarantella* 201; *Totentanz* 226; *Venezia e Napoli* 201
literature, depiction of Russia in 73–4
Llubera, Lina 86
Locust Point 92–3, 98–9
Lodyzhensky, Anna 42–3
Lodyzhensky, Nadezhda 43
Lodyzhensky, Pyotr 42, 43
Lucerne 150, 152–4, 180; *see also* Senar (SR's villa); Tribschen (Wagner's villa)
Lucerne Festival 198, 206–7
Lyle, Watson 31–2, 33, 96–7
Lynn, Vera: 'We'll Meet Again' 212

Mahler, Gustav 79–80
Malcolm, Janet xx–xxi
Malevich, Kazimir 10
Malko, Nikolai 182
Malloy, Dave: *Preludes* (musical) 47
Mandrovsky, Nikolai xiii, 257, 263
Marx, Harpo 140–1
Maugham, Somerset: *Ashenden: or The British Agent* 73–4
Medinsky, Vladimir 300
Medtner, Nikolai: friendship with SR 82, 95, 106–7, 113, 128, 149–50, 151, 187, 230–1; friendships, other 14; leaves Russia 82; performed by SR 82; practised by SR 81; response to modern music 20, 107, 260; SR dedicates work to 128; other mentions 83, 112, 261
  WORKS: *Fairy Tales* 82; *The Muse and the Fashion* 113; *Novellen* 82; Piano Concerto no. 2 128
Mendelssohn, Felix: 'cancelled' in Germany 199, 229; *Midsummer Night's Dream* (arr. SR) 141–2
Menlo Park 138
Menuhin, Yehudi 168–9, 218
Metropolitan Opera (Met) 52, 118

Mickey Mouse film 131, 141, 243
'Mighty Handful' (composers) 45
Miller, Glen: 'Moonlight Serenade' 208, 209; 'Song of the Volga Boatmen' 243
Milstein, Nathan xxi, 150–2, 181
Mitropoulos, Dimitri 226, 248, 271
Moiseiwitsch, Benno 203–4, 253, 301
Mordovskaya, Olga 282; report by 290–9
Möri, Alfred 154–5
Moscow: SR leaves 6–7, 8, 31–3; SR performs in 18, 19, 21–2; SR's life in 7, 19–21, 30
Moscow Conservatory: boycotts SR's work (1931) 158; concerts at 46(fn); other students and teachers 10, 41, 76–7, 112, 119, 157, 257; SR at 10, 37, 42, 43
mushroom hunting 148
Mussorgsky, Modest: conducted by SR 37, 209
  WORKS: *Boris Godunov* 4, 251; *Night on Bald Mountain* 209, 242–3; *Pictures at an Exhibition* 164, 172; songs 90

Nabokov, Nicolas 134
Nabokov, Vladimir 20, 165–6, 214, 231–2; 'The Assistant Producer' 127; *Despair* 19; *The Gift* 166, 195, 232; *Glory* 166
Nazimova, Alla 140
Nazism 187, 200, 229, 230; *see also* Hitler, Adolf
New York: jazz scene 65–6, 104–5; Nina Koshetz's concert appearances 90–1; Russian community 72–3; SR's concert appearances 59–61, 62–3, 66, 79–80, 91, 182; Tin Pan Alley music publishers 64–5, 209; Wall Street Crash 150, 163; World Fair (1939-1940) 210–13, 215, 216, 217–18, 223–4, 238, 240; *see also* Carnegie Hall, New York
New York Philharmonic-Symphony Orchestra 182, 212, 248
New York Symphony Orchestra 79
New York Times, SR's letter to 156
Newman, Ernest 38
Niels, Elger 47–8(fn)
North Elm Drive, Beverly Hills (SR's home) 256, 281, 291, 295
Novachord (instrument) 212, 230
Novgorod estate 40, 41, 130

O'Connell, Charles 20, 219, 247–8

October Revolution 30; *see also* Russian Revolution

The Opry House (*Mickey Mouse* film) 131, 141, 243

Orchard Point, Honeyman Estate 232–5, 237–8, 251

Ormandy archive 243

Ormandy, Eugene xiv; conducts SR/ SR's works 46(fn), 163, 204, 226–7, 237, 241, 242, 243–4, 247, 301, 320; SR dedicates work to 237; SR's letter to 237

Ostromislensky, Ivan 98–9, 156

'Over the Rainbow' 208

Paderewski, Ignacy 66, 230

Paris: Armistice Day 51; Chopin's grave 277; Prince Pierre Volkonsky's grave 114; Russian exiles in 6, 10, 64, 93–5, 166–9, 258; SR in 69, 70, 97, 106–7, 110, 117, 130, 131, 133–4, 147, 151, 166–9, 177, 183, 191, 206, 207, 258; Tair (SR's publishing house) 112–13, 130, 165–6, 181, 195; *see also* Le Pavillon (SR's home)

Parker, H. T. 58–9

Pasternak, Leonid 220

Le Pavillon (SR's home) 147–9

peasant uprisings (Russia) 23–4, 79

Petrograd *see* Leningrad

Philadelphia Orchestra: other performances 226, 243; perform SR's works 46(fn), 127, 143, 226–8, 237, 241, 242, 243–4, 247, 301, 319, 320; 'Philadelphia sound' of 242; recordings 143, 244; SR dedicates work to 237; SR's appreciation of 242

piano practice habits (SR) 140–3, 149, 160, 189, 200, 233–4, 307, 308

piano tuner (William Hupfer) 120–2, 124

pianos, played by SR: at Ivanovka 307; at Senar 313; Steinway 77, 118, 124, 125, 178, 213, 313; on tour 120, 121, 122, 125, 132, 273; *see also* Steinway & Sons

Plevitskaya, Nadezhda 126–7

Porter, Cole 223, 238

Prelude in C sharp minor (SR): arrangements and jazz versions 12, 65–6, 105; as clichéd 38, 202;

'meanings' attributed to 125–6; in *Mickey Mouse* film 131; performed by others 37, 275; performed by SR 80, 125, 159, 183, 190, 201, 202, 272; played by Harpo Marx 140–1; recorded by SR 78; SR declines to play 59, 125; SR's views of 37, 57

Preludes (musical about SR) 47

Pribytkova, Zoya 28–9

Price, Florence 224, 226, 275

Prokofiev, Lina 86

Prokofiev, Sergei: critical reception 55, 91–2; diaries 13, 19, 20, 26, 55, 62, 63, 82–3, 87, 134, 135, 166–7, 265; friendship/rivalry with SR 19, 26, 55, 62–3, 87, 133–5, 166–7; moves to America 55; opinion of Schillinger's music 209; relationship with Nina Koshetz 25–6, 85–8, 91; returns to Soviet Union 230; solo recital 55; telegraph to SR on his 70th birthday 283; visits Alexander Glazunov 166; WORKS: *The Gambler* 19; *Love for Three Oranges* 86–7, 91; *Peter and the Wolf* 243; Piano Concerto no. 1 62; *The Prodigal Son* 133; *Romeo and Juliet* 230; Scherzo for Four Bassoons 62; songs 26, 90

Pushkin, Alexander 10, 14, 42, 232, 282–3, 294

Putin, Vladimir 315

Queen's Hall, London: destroyed in the Blitz 244; SR performs at 31, 37, 96, 162, 176, 182, 190, 205

Rachmaninoff, Arkady 38, 41

Rachmaninoff, Natalia (SR's wife) xi; accompanies SR on tour 122, 123–4, 227, 273; American citizenship 272; bequest to National Library of Congress xvii–xviii; birth of granddaughter 110–12; death 300; early relationship with SR 8, 9, 307; Ivanovka estate *see* Ivanovka estate; leaves Russia 32–3; LETTERS: to Nina Koshetz 17–18; to Tatiana 235; memoir 22, 23–4, 196–7, 265; moves to America 34, 52; musical training and accomplishment 77, 149, 307, 308; with SR in final days 282–3, 289, 290, 291, 295, 296, 297–8; steadfast support of SR 193, 236, 261; wedding 7

Rachmaninoff, Sergei Vasilievich: compositional style: 135–7, 246–7, 267–8; concerts *see* concerts and tours (SR); Conservatory training 10, 37, 39, 41, 42, 43; daily timetable (later years) 236; family 18, 38–41, 44; female admirers 13, 261

FEMALE RELATIONSHIPS AND FRIENDSHIPS: Anna and Nadezhda Lodyzhensky 42–3; Marietta Shaginian 13–14, 15–16, 18, 27, 28–9; Natalia Satina (wife) *see* Rachmaninoff, Natalia (SR's wife); Nina Koshetz 13, 16–18, 21, 25, 26, 27, 87, 88–90, 269–70; Vera Skalon 8–9, 306, 307; financial success 77, 78–9, 95, 154, 182, 190–1; financial worries 183; health *see* health problems (SR); homes and retreats *see* homes and retreats (SR); interests outside music 22, 60, 67–72, 81, 96, 136, 143–4, 148, 177–8, 196, 197, 233, 271, 282, 291; legacy xx, 250; letters from *see* letters from SR

LIFE (KEY TIMES/EVENTS): American citizenship 272; burial 300–1; childhood and youth 22, 38–43, 306; daughters' weddings 107, 164–5; death and funeral 284, 290, 297–8, 299–300, 301; deaths in family 18, 108–9, 130; exile from Russia 6–7, 23–5, 29–33; granddaughter's birth 110–12; move to America 34, 52–5; wedding 7

PERSONAL CHARACTERISTICS: appearance and clothes 20, 58–9, 115, 182, 188, 202, 234, 241, 260, 314; appetite 265; as Buddha (statue)-like 20, 21, 155, 220; drinking 47; enigmatic on stage 155, 200–1, 266; financial benevolence 21, 73, 79–80, 82, 93–5, 96, 102–4, 170–2, 195, 206, 214, 230–1, 251–2, 263, 267, 275; gait 152, 167; hands 219–20, 290, 292;

morbid fears 14; Orthodox faith and influences 40, 41, 98, 106, 136, 216, 246–7, 267, 275, 299; punctiliousness 249; response to criticisms 151–2; self-doubt 11, 15–16, 45, 95, 130, 185, 251; sense of humour xxi, 120, 133, 152, 186, 197, 276; shyness 62, 67, 247; smoking habit 124, 160–1, 202, 245, 257, 263; warmth and kindness 8, 60, 120, 273, 276, 298; youthful laziness 41, 185; piano practice habits 140–3, 149, 160, 189, 200, 233–4, 307, 308; pianos *see* pianos, played by SR; quoted 6–7, 9, 19, 23, 30, 31, 37, 39, 44, 53, 64, 65, 68, 82, 99, 101, 105, 106, 107–8, 119, 125, 131, 135, 136, 144, 147, 155, 158, 159, 188–9, 206, 212, 213, 225–6, 231, 238, 242, 248, 249, 251, 252, 254, 262, 270, 272, 274, 291, 292, 293, 294, 296, 298, 306, 318; recordings 11, 58, 77–8, 126, 130, 134, 162–3, 182, 227, 241, 243–4, 248, 319; Soviet Union attitudes towards 156–9, 174–5, 218, 229, 256, 266–7

WORKS: *Aleko* 42, 98; *All-Night Vigil (Vespers)* 164, 216, 247, 256; Bach transcriptions 151–2; *The Bells* 19, 83, 93, 94, 126, 157, 164, 186, 215, 225, 227, 232, 246; cadenza to Liszt's Hungarian Rhapsody no. 2 78, 96; *Capriccio on Gypsy Themes* 42; chamber works 45; *Études-Tableaux* 21, 91, 125, 163–4, 246, 277; 'Fate' 46; 'Humoreske' 60; 'Before the Icon' 8; *The Isle of the Dead* 12, 19, 56, 63, 94, 97, 250, 301; *Italian Polka* 149, 275; 'Lilacs' 7–8, 275; *Liturgy of St John Chrysostom* 216; 'Lullaby' (arr.) 251; *Midsummer Night's Dream* (arr.) 141–2; *The Miserly Knight* 232, 259; *Monna Vanna* 32; 'The Muse' 14; 'Oh no, I beg you do not leave' 42; *Oriental Sketch* 149; Piano Concerto no. 1 30–1, 32, 62–3, 76, 227, 253; Piano Concerto no. 2 xxi, 17, 22, 45, 47, 63, 76, 79, 163, 204, 215, 230, 246, 253, 275, 314; Piano Concerto no. 3 45, 60, 76, 79, 119–20, 163,

164, 214, 218, 263; Piano Concerto no. 4 115, 117, 128–30, 168, 209, 235, 241, 251, 267, 317; Piano Sonata no. 2 150, 234; Prelude in C sharp minor *see* Prelude in C sharp minor (SR); *Rhapsody on a Theme of Paganini* 47, 179–81, 182–3, 190, 204, 206, 207, 227, 241, 253, 260, 275, 318; *The Rock* 19; 'In the Silence of the Secret Night' 240–1; *Sleeping Beauty* (arr.) 308; *Spring* 126; 'Star-Spangled Banner' (arr.) 58, 78; *Symphonic Dances* 236–8, 239–41, 242, 243–4, 245–8, 257, 269–70, 271, 273, 274, 319–20; Symphony no. 1 in D minor 15, 42–3, 45–6, 92, 130, 246; Symphony no. 2 in E minor 45, 62, 227, 230, 246; Symphony no. 3 in A minor 184, 185, 186, 187, 190, 195–6, 227, 241, 267–8, 319; *Trois Chansons Russes* 126, 127, 175, 317; *Variations on a Theme of Corelli* 161–2, 318; 'Vocalise' 12, 97–8, 100, 210, 213, 225; other solo piano works 31, 43, 55, 59, 60, 108, 176, 218, 265; other songs 7, 18, 43, 45

Rachmaninoff, Vasily Arkadyevich 10, 38–9

Rachmaninoff archive xvii–xviii, 80, 185, 269–70

Rachmaninoff Conus, Tatiana Sergeyevna (SR's daughter) xi; childhood 7; death 300; at Le Pavillon 147; marriage to Boris Conus 164–5; in Paris 151, 164–6, 206, 208, 228; at Riverside Drive 117; on RMS *Berengaria* 134; at Senar 314, 315; and Tair publishing house 113, 165–6; in 'Vichy France' 235, 245, 270

Rachmaninoff Foundation 47(fn), 315

Rachmaninoff Volkonsky, Princess Irina Sergeyevna (SR's daughter) xi; accompanies SR to Nice 117; childhood 7; death 300; death of husband and birth of daughter 108, 110–11; at Le Pavillon 147; marriage to Prince Pyotr Volkonsky 107, 114; in New York 117, 228; with SR in final days 291–2, 297–8; and Tair publishing house 113

radio broadcasts, SR's opinions on 78, 130, 159

Rashevsky, Nikolai 278–9

Ravel, Maurice: *Pictures at an Exhibition* 163–4, 172

RCA Victor 20, 78, 130, 241; *see also* O'Connell, Charles

Red Scare (American response to Russian exiles) 64

Respighi, Ottorino 163–4

Richter, Sviatoslav 219, 323

Riesemann, Oskar von 23, 98, 147, 152–3

Rimsky-Korsakov, Nikolai 19, 45, 172, 259, 300; performed and conducted by SR 37, 256–7
  WORKS: *Ivan the Terrible* 4; *Le Coq d'Or* 32, 246; *Night on Bald Mountain* (arr.) 242–3; *Russian Easter Festival Overture* 251; songs 90

RMS *Aquitania* 208

RMS *Berengaria* 132–5

RMS *Pannonia* 85–6

Rockmore, Clara 210

Rolland, Romain 260

Roosevelt, Franklin 174, 211, 223, 230, 270

Roper, Robert 165

Rosenfeld, Paul 63

Rostropovich, Mstislav 219, 323

Royal Albert Hall, London 130, 253

Royal Philharmonic Society, Gold Medal 164

Rubinstein, Anton 43, 61, 118, 212, 219, 265

Rubinstein, Arthur 217, 264

Rubinstein, Nikolai 41

Russia, depiction in literature and film 73–4

Russian culture, appropriation by Americans 75

Russian culture, SR's adherence to 92–3, 160

Russian Revolution xvii, 3–4, 5–6, 23–4, 30, 79; *see also* exiles from Russia

Russo, Thekla 13

Rybner, Dagmar xii, 67, 93, 106, 117

Sabaneyev, Leonid 91–2

Sachs, Joel 139

St Petersburg Conservatory 39, 83, 84, 209

Sanborn, Pitts 226
Satin, Sophia xii, 29, 113–14, 164–5, 198, 199–200, 207–8
Satin, Vladimir 81
Satina, Natalia (SR's wife) *see* Rachmaninoff, Natalia (SR's wife)
Satina, Sofia xi–xii; chronicles SR's life 8, 92–3, 152; at Ivanovka 307; leaves Russia 46; letter to Nikolai Dahl 193; at Locust Point 92–3; memoir 40, 81; Natalia's letter to 111–12; with SR in final days 282, 293, 294, 295, 297–8; SR's letters to 109–11, 177, 183–4, 191–2, 262–3
Savage Club, London 203–5
saxophone, SR composes for 65, 239–40, 246, 320
Scandinavia 31–3
Schillinger, Joseph 209–10
Schmidt, Paul 271–2
Schoenberg, Arnold 249–50, 264; Chamber Symphony no. 2 250; *Pelleas und Melisande* 85; '*On revient toujours*' (essay) 250; *Verklärte Nacht* 250; Violin Concerto 243
Schonberg, Harold C. xx, 218–19
Scriabin, Alexander xiv, 4, 10–11, 224, 255, 260, 300; performed by others 55, 90, 225; performed by SR 10–11, 15, 134 WORKS: 'Devotion' 26; Piano Concerto 10; preludes 11; Symphony no. 1 10
Second World War: America 270; outbreak of war 208, 217, 223; Poland 282; preceding months 187, 206–8; Soviet Union 251–3, 282, 296; UK 230, 244–5; *see also* Nazism
Senar (SR's villa) 153–5, 159, 163, 177–80, 187, 197–8, 199–200, 206, 207–8; changes hands 315; present day 220, 313–16
Sergei Rachmaninoff Foundation 47(fn), 315
Seroff, Victor 47, 137, 184, 225, 254, 279
Shaginian, Marietta xiv–xv, 13–16, 18, 27–9
Sheffield City Hall 186
Shine (film) 119–20
Shostakovich, Dmitri 184, 209, 251, 255, 283; *Lady Macbeth of the Mtsensk District* 174–5; Symphony no. 7 ('Leningrad') 252–4

Sibelius, Jean 55, 137, 211, 250
Sikorsky, Igor 101–3
Siloti, Alexander xii; concerts 37, 83–4, 220; friendship with SR 7, 252; friendships, other 80, 84–5, 259; hands 220; at Hofmann's reception 261; at Ivanovka 305–6; at Koshetz's concert 100; leaves Russia 83–4; marriage 41; at Moscow Conservatory 41–2; SR's letters to 24–5
Siloti, Kyriena 84, 85
'Silver Age' 4–5
Sirin, Vladimir *see* Nabokov, Vladimir
Skalon, Lyudmila 8–9
Skalon, Vera 8–9; diary 305–9
Slenczynska, Ruth 175–6
Somer, Hilde 275
Somov, Yelena 274
Somov, Yevgeny Ivanovich xii–xiii, 92, 93, 160, 179, 234, 274; SR's letters to 70–2, 155, 159, 177–8, 179, 183, 185, 195–6, 200, 206–7, 270, 280–1
Spanish flu epidemic 53–5, 63
SS *Bergensfjord* 53–4
SS *Champlain* 231–2
SS *Lancastria* 68–9
SS *Mauretania* 69, 70
Stalin, Joseph 159–60, 174, 208, 216–17, 276, 282
Stanislavsky, Konstantin 16–17
'Star-Spangled Banner' 51, 212–13; SR's arrangement 58, 78; Stravinsky's arrangement 58
Steinway, Frederick 77, 261
Steinwey, Heinrich Engelhard 118
Steinway & Sons: 'chief toner' for 121; offers to assist Medtner 82; response to anti-German attitudes 118–19; SR's associations with 55, 77, 124, 213; *see also* Greiner, Alexander 'Sasha'; pianos, played by SR
Stewart, John K. 233
Still, William Grant 224; *Afro-American Symphony* 226; *Rising Tide* 212
Stock, Frederick 163, 248
Stokowski, Leopold xv; conducting style 242; conducts other works 226, 242, 243; conducts SR/SR's works 127, 128, 143, 182, 186, 230, 267, 317, 319; SR dedicates work to 127

Strauss, Richard 37, 107, 137, 207
Stravinsky, Igor 85, 104, 167, 184, 256, 258–9, 260–3, 264–6, 267; *Capriccio* 133; Concerto for Piano and Wind 106–7; *The Firebird* (and suite) 180, 182, 230, 259; *Jane Eyre* film music 255; *Petrushka* 180, 259, 260; *The Rite of Spring* 107, 243; *Serenade* 265; 'Star-Spangled Banner' (arr.) 58; *Symphony of Psalms* 216
Struve, Nikolai von xv, 32, 33, 97–8
Suggia, Guilhermina 84
'Suprematists' (artists) 10
Swan, Alfred xv, 148–50, 162, 197, 283

Tagore, Rabindranath 156
Tair (SR's publishing house) 112–13, 130, 165–6, 181, 195
Taneyev, Sergei xv, 16, 46, 235
Tatum, Art 208–9
Tchaikovsky, Pyotr Ilyich: teaching 37, 41 WORKS: ballets 4, 242, 308; 'Lullaby' (arr. SR) 251; opera 13, 17, 252; Piano Concerto no. 1 22
Tereshchenko, Mikhail 24
theremin (instrument) 210
Theremin, Léon 210
Thomson, Virgil 63, 137
Threlfall, Robert 129, 205
Tillet, Mr 70
Tin Pan Alley music publishers 64–5, 209
Tolstoy, Alexandra 103
Tolstoy, Count Ilya L. 156
Tolstoy Foundation 103–4, 230–1
Tolstoy, Leo 30, 46–7; *Anna Karenina* 43; *War and Peace* 38
Toscanini, Arturo 198, 199, 208, 253
Tower Lane, Beverly Hills (SR's home) 256, 257
Tretyakov, Pavel 83
Tribschen (Wagner's villa) 153, 198–9
Tsar Nicholas II 3
Tureck, Rosalyn 219

Ukrainian Chorus 225
Utgoff, Viktor 101

Vanderbilt II, William K. 232
Vaughan Williams, Ralph 136–7, 164, 215

Verdure, Pasquale 'Joe' 273–4
Victor Talking Machine Company 78; see also RCA Victor
Vienna, New Year's concerts 228–9
Villa Senar (SR's home) see Senar (SR's villa)
Villers-sur-Mers 142
Vilshau, Vladimir Robertovich xvi; SR's letters to 77, 95, 107, 122–3
The Volga Boatman (film) 74
Volkonsky, Prince Pyotr 107, 108, 112, 114
Volkonsky, Sophie Petrovna (SR's granddaughter) 108, 110–12, 113, 180, 201, 228, 234–5, 245, 274–5
Volkov, Solomon 254
Vygodsky, Nikolai 157

Wagner, Richard 7, 17, 153, 155, 229, 237; Tribschen (villa) 153, 198–9
Wall Street Crash 150, 163
Walter, Bruno 182, 207
Wanamaker, Susan Sophia Rachmaninoff Volkonskaya (SR's great-great-granddaughter) 300–1
Weinberg, Yakov 235–6
Whiteman, Paul 104–5, 107–8, 223
Wilson, Woodrow 51, 54
Winter War (Soviet Union and Finland) 229–30
The Wizard of Oz (film) 208, 209
Wood, Henry: bust of 244–5; conducts Shostakovich's 'Leningrad' Symphony 253; conducts SR/ SR's works 12, 31, 164, 186, 190, 195–6, 253; passes SR's compliments to Vaughan Williams 215; sends sympathies to Natalia 301
Woolf, Virginia: *Orlando* 73; *A Room of One's Own* 215
World Fair, New York (1939-1940) 210–13, 215, 216, 217–18, 223–4, 238, 240
World Wars I and II see First World War; Second World War

Yessentuki (spa resort) 12, 15, 24

Zverev, Nikolai xvi, 42, 43–4